THE WORLD OF THE CHILD IN THE HEBREW BIBLE

Hebrew Bible Monographs, 51

Series Editors
David J.A. Clines, J. Cheryl Exum

Editorial Board
A. Graeme Auld, Marc Brettler, David M. Carr, Paul M. Joyce,
Francis Landy, Lena-Sofia Tiemeyer, Stuart D.E. Weeks

The World of the Child in the Hebrew Bible

Naomi Steinberg

Sheffield Phoenix Press
2015

Copyright © 2013, 2015 Sheffield Phoenix Press

First published in hardback, 2013
First published in paperback, 2015

Published by Sheffield Phoenix Press
Biblical Studies, University of Sheffield
45 Victoria Street
Sheffield S3 7QB

www.sheffieldphoenix.com

All rights reserved.
No part of this publication may be reproduced or transmitted in any form or by any means, electronic or mechanical, including photocopying, recording or any information storage or retrieval system, without the publisher's permission in writing.

A CIP catalogue record for this book
is available from the British Library

Typeset by Forthcoming Publications
Printed by Lightning Source Inc.

ISBN 978-1-910928-07-3 (paperback)
ISBN 978-1-907534-76-8 (hardback)

ISSN 1747-9614

CONTENTS

Abbreviations	ix
Introduction: Settings and Interpretations: From Guatemala to Biblical Israel	xi
Acknowledgments	xiii

Part 1
BACKGROUND AND THEORY

Chapter 1
CHILDREN AND CHILDHOOD AS CATEGORIES OF ANALYSIS 3
    The Influence of Philippe Ariès 4
    Post Ariès: A Paradigm Shift 6
    The United Nations Convention on the Rights of the Child 8

Chapter 2
WHAT IS A CHILD? 11
    The Term 'Child': A Chronological Category 11
    The Term 'Child': A Social Category 17
    What Is Childhood? Emic and Etic Perspectives 18

Chapter 3
WORDS FOR CHILDREN IN THE HEBREW BIBLE 26
    Naʿar 28
    Yeled 32
    The Masoretic Text Compared to Greek
        and Later Jewish Texts 39

Part 2
REGARDING CHILDHOOD IN THE HEBREW BIBLE

Chapter 4
THE ISRAELITE FAMILY AS AN ECONOMIC UNIT
    AND CHILDREN'S ROLES 45
    The Social Structure of the Biblical Family 46
    Patrilineal, Patrilocal Endogamy, and Family Economics 50

Socioeconomic Distinctions between Wives and their Children: Monogamy and Polygamy	53
Factors of Infant Mortality, Gender, and Socioeconomic Status in Childhood	57
Other Issues: Illegitimates, Orphans, and Cast-Offs	60

Chapter 5
THE ISRAELITE LIFE CYCLE: ARE THERE ANY CHILDREN HERE?	64
The Cultural Construction of Human Development	65
When Does Childhood Begin?	68
Becoming a Person: How Do Children Develop?	72
Leviticus 27.1-8 and Other Biblical Texts	76
Scholarly Constructions of the Biblical Life Cycle	78

Chapter 6
GENESIS 21: MONOGAMY, POLYGAMY, AND CHILDHOOD EXPERIENCES	83
The Terms *na'ar*, *yeled*, and *bēn* in Genesis 21	86
Ishmael	91
Isaac	95

Chapter 7
1 SAMUEL 1: CHILD ABANDONMENT AND THE BEST INTERESTS OF THE CHILD	98
History of Scholarship	100
Taking Samuel's Rights Seriously: Whose Life Is It, Anyway?	101

Chapter 8
EXODUS 21.22-25: IS THE FETUS A LIFE?	106
Exodus 21.22-25 and the History of Scholarship	107
The Hebrew Phrase ויצאו ילדיה	110
Who Was Hurt? *'āsôn*	113
Conclusions	116

Part 3
FROM THE HEBREW BIBLE TO TODAY:
STASIS AND CHANGE

Chapter 9
SOCIALLY CONSTRUCTED CATEGORIES OF CHILDHOOD	121

Bibliography 131
Index of References 141
Index of Authors 144

ABBREVIATIONS

AB	Anchor Bible
ANET	James B. Pritchard (ed.), *Ancient Near Eastern Texts Relating to the Old Testament* (Princeton: Princeton University Press, 1950)
BASOR	*Bulletin of the American Schools of Oriental Research*
BDB	Francis Brown, S.R. Driver, and Charles A. Briggs, *A Hebrew and English Lexicon of the Old Testament* (Oxford: Clarendon Press, 1907)
BHS	*Biblia hebraica stuttgartensia*
BLit	*Bibel und Liturgie*
BTB	*Biblical Theology Bulletin*
BZAW	Beihefte zur *ZAW*
CASA	Court Appointed Special Advocate
CBQ	*Catholic Biblical Quarterly*
FOTL	The Forms of the Old Testament Literature
HALOT	Ludwig Koehler *et al.* (eds.), *The Hebrew and Aramaic Lexicon of the Old Testament* (trans. and ed. under the supervision of M.E.J. Richardson; 5 vols.; Leiden: Brill, 1994–2000)
HL	Hittite Laws
HSM	Harvard Semitic Monographs
IB	*Interpreter's Bible*
ICC	International Critical Commentary
JAAR	*Journal of the American Academy of Religion*
JBL	*Journal of Biblical Literature*
JNES	*Journal of Near Eastern Studies*
JQR	*Jewish Quarterly Review*
JSOT	*Journal for the Study of the Old Testament*
JSOTSup	Journal for the Study of the Old Testament: Supplement Series
LH	Laws of Hammurabi
LXX	The Septuagint
MAL	Middle Assyrian Laws
MT	Masoretic Text
NCB	New Century Bible
NICOT	New International Commentary on the Old Testament
NIDOTTE	Willem A. VanGemeren (ed.), *New International Dictionary of the Old Testament Theology and Exegesis* (5 vols.; Grand Rapids: Zondervan, 1997)
NRSV	New Revised Standard Version Bible
OTL	Old Testament Library
RB	*Revue biblique*

SBLCP	Society of Biblical Literature Centennial Publications
SBLDS	Society of Biblical Literature Dissertation Series
SJLA	Studies in Judaism in Late Antiquity
TDOT	G.J. Botterweck and H. Ringgren (eds.), *Theological Dictionary of the Old Testament* (trans. J.T. Willis, G.W. Bromiley, and D.E. Green (8 vols.; Grand Rapids: Eerdmand, 1974–)
THAT	Ernest Jenni and Claus Westermann (eds.), *Theologisches Handwörterbuch zum Alten Testament* (Munich: Chr. Kaiser, 1971–76)
TWOT	R. Laird Harris, Gleason L. Archer, Jr and Bruce K. Waltke (eds.), *Theological Wordbook of the Old Testament* (2 vols.; Chicago: Moody Press, 1980)
UF	*Ugarit-Forschungen*
UNCRC	United Nations Convention on the Rights of the Child
VT	*Vetus Testamentum*
VTSup	Vetus Testamentum Supplements
WBC	Word Biblical Commentary
WTJ	*Westminster Theological Journal*

Introduction

SETTINGS AND INTERPRETATIONS:
FROM GUATEMALA TO BIBLICAL ISRAEL

A goal for this study is to increase our scholarly competence to lay bare the culture-bound nature of childhood in ancient Israel. This approach should uncover a deeper understanding of childhood in the Hebrew Bible by revealing some of the narrow conceptions of what is natural and normal as assumed in the values of the child-centered societies of most modern scholarly writers. The theme running through the present volume is that the meaning of childhood is not universal and that all children—past and present—live in culture-bound contexts that shape the understanding of what it means to live a normal and healthy childhood. Just as important, researchers must be conscious of their own culturally constructed ideas about children in order to avoid imposing these ideas onto contexts where they do not belong and do not fit. My approach, then, is to read against the grain of both the biblical writers and redactors, and against contemporary received ideas of the meanings of texts that mention children. Some of my recent experiences are relevant to this goal.

Although it is commonplace to apply the metaphor of a journey to the process of book-writing, my study of the issues raised in this volume is related to a trip to Guatemala City. At the time, however, my trip was not envisioned as field work. From hindsight, the project of writing this book had its inception in summer 2007, when, under the auspices of Cross-Cultural Solutions, an international not-for-profit organization that promotes global understanding through service,[1] I traveled from Chicago to Guatemala City to volunteer at a *hogar*,[2] an orphanage, run by a missionary order of Italian Sisters.[3] For five weeks I worked with about 20 infants who lived in a

---

1. Http://www.crossculturalsolutions.org/ (accessed 29 June 2012).
2. In the interest of authenticity, I prefer to refer to the orphanage by its Spanish term.
3. The following discussion of conditions at the *hogar* is in no way intended to criticize the work being done there but serves as a means to confront ethnocentric views on the raising of children. Given my intention to challenge the universality of contemporary views on childhood in the first world with perspectives from a developing country, rather than as a judgment on the *hogar*, I have chosen to keep the name of the orphanage

large building complex housing approximately 75 children under the age of six. Given the varied circumstances of their arrival at the *hogar*—one child was found at the bottom of a garbage dump—the precise ages of most of its children are unknown; moreover, the physical and emotional circumstances of early neglect for some of the children compounds the problem of determining precise chronological age. Consequently, the children at the *hogar* are grouped according to developmental categories rather than by age; infants are defined as those who have yet to learn to walk.

During my five-week stay, I did whatever was asked of me in caring for these infants: I held them, fed them, changed them, and administered non-technical medical procedures. When there was time, I played with them. The babies at the *hogar* were safe, warm, clean, and fed. The shortage of staff (including volunteers) meant that the babies did not have regular coddling; the first child I picked up—because she was crying hard for the chance to be held by an adult—had a bald spot in her otherwise thick head of black hair. The bald spot was the result of lying in one place for too long.[4] The nuns who ran the orphanage clearly loved the children in their care but there were not enough adults to meet the physical needs of so many infants. Moreover, these babies were unable to receive the intellectual stimulation upheld by the best practices of child development, according to what might be labeled Western or modern values.[5] For example, two and sometimes three babies slept in one crib; they rarely had stuffed animals, mobiles, or other objects and playthings in their cribs to hold their attention. The stuffed animals that were available (usually through donations) were displayed as decorations on wall shelves of the infant room, and the few toys the babies had to play with

---

and the order of Sisters who run it anonymous. Otherwise, no details have been changed in my description of the conditions of the *hogar* or of my experiences working there.

4. The bald spot is a baby equivalent to bedsores in adults; it is caused by not being turned regularly.

5. Although the experiences I recount reflect my middle-class upbringing in the US, at this point in the discussion I introduce the concept of 'the West' as a label to categorize my perspective. I do this fully aware that Guatemala falls within the geographical category of 'the West'. I acknowledge that the distinction between West and East is a product of European history and the Enlightenment and that it is not easy to characterize what specifically constitutes Western culture or values. For that reason, some prefer the term 'Euroamerican' to 'the West', but I will refer to the latter. Terminology aside, the construction of 'Western' is determined by its 'other' or opposite, because without something to oppose, there is no parameter to Western cultural or geographical identity. The construction of Western as an identity/perspective was developed in response to the identity of the 'Orient', or basically anyone who wasn't European, especially those from Asia or the Middle East. Important theorists for further understanding the construction and meaning of 'the West' are Edward W. Said, *Orientalism* (New York: Pantheon, 1978), and Adam Kuper, *The Reinvention of Primitive Society: Transformation of a Myth* (Florence, KY: Taylor & Francis, 2005).

when they were put on the floor outside their cribs were broken and could easily have been swallowed by the babies in the absence of adult supervision. Toys were not washed as they passed from the mouth of one baby to the next.

Certainly, my own culturally constructed ideas based on my experiences of the need to develop the individuality of each and every child had no opportunity to take root in this setting. The circumstances in the *hogar* seemed to be grounded in radically different ideas about childhood than the ones I held, although I was mindful of the integral importance of political and economic factors that shape the lives of children. I was also aware that the quality of life for all children did not necessarily conform to the romantic myth of childhood as a time of innocence and protection that many take for granted. Family violence and abuse, poverty and gang violence, child slavery and child trafficking, wherever it is, hardly guarantee that each child will grow and flourish in a nurturing and loving setting from youth to adulthood. I realized that my ethnocentric perspective about childhood in a developing country had to be reexamined in light of my own American context and what many would regard as the over-sentimentalized ideas about children in the West.

The childrearing practices in the Guatemalan *hogar* stood in sharp contrast to another experience from my past. Beginning about ten years earlier I had worked for over six years as a volunteer one morning a week at the local children's hospital in Chicago. There, too, I spent all my time with infants, in this case a group defined chronologically as those under the age of three. In this hospital setting, the medical problems of the children were, of course, of primary concern, yet staff attempted to attend to the children's happiness in every conceivable fashion, for example through attention to favorite foods and toys. Children were held constantly so as to have physical contact and bonding experiences even while they were in an institutional setting and hooked up to monitors and tubes. All the toys were washed after they were used to avoid the spread of germs between children. However, despite the differences in the plight of the children in the Guatemalan *hogar* and those in the Chicago hospital, as I compared the two experiences in my mind I came to find one commonality: whether or not a child is abandoned or ill, a baby is still a baby, i.e., s/he has no awareness of all the outside forces affecting her/his circumstances. The children in both settings simply wanted someone to hold them, talk to them, and just pay attention to them. They longed for human connection. Viewed from the perspective of the children, rather than from the adults who cared for them, at a very early pre-verbal age children were expressing their needs and asking for attention. I found one way to connect my conceptualization of childhood as a hospital volunteer in Chicago with my experiences as a volunteer in Guatemala—by trying to interpret the needs of children through the eyes of the children themselves.

The dissonance between my values and my experiences, from growing up in a middle-class family in Chicago and my experiences during my five weeks in Guatemala—as short a time as it was—were critical in challenging me to reconsider what is 'natural' and 'normal' about children and family life in different cultures today.[6] The conceptualization and organization of childhood at the *hogar* differed radically from what I was accustomed to in the US and I was challenged to address the distinctions between first world views and practices about child rearing and those in a developing country like Guatemala. The result was the realization that there are multiple understandings of childhood and that these perspectives are often narrowly culture-bound. Ultimately, the differences between my experiences in Guatemala and in the children's hospital in Chicago underscored the cultural construction of childhood and piqued my curiosity about the lives of children in the past.

As a Hebrew Bible scholar, I have been trained to think about life in the past, and I had to acknowledge that childhood in ancient Israel must have elicited different answers to the question 'What is a child?' than the ones I was discovering from my volunteer experiences. But also thinking about current reports in the news of child suicides, child soldiers, children in sex trafficking, etc., I realized that the task of understanding conceptualizations of childhood in the Hebrew Bible as a social construction might offer definitions of children that would further undercut universal ideas of childhood. I began the process of writing this volume with the goal of thinking about categories of childhood today from the perspective of the past and vice versa. What were the conceptualizations of childhood from the context of ancient Israel? Did the command 'Be fruitful and multiply' (Gen. 1.28) mean that children were valued as members of Israelite society, and if so, how were they valued? Is the Bible as 'child-friendly' as some claim? If it is true that childhood in the modern-day US and in Guatemala is culturally constructed, as my direct experience tells me it is, then how much sharper must the contrast be when there is a large gap in both space and time?

From the start, I knew that I should take nothing for granted in my investigations of childhood in ancient Israel. Influenced by the culture-bound differences that I realized were separating my experiences of the treatment of children in Guatemala and in Chicago, two core questions came to mind regarding children in ancient Israel: *How was childhood conceptualized in ancient Israel?* and *Who was a child?* I began to evaluate the nature of childhood in ancient Israel with an awareness that the data on children in the Hebrew Bible was limited, that scholarship on the topic was also limited, and what studies did exist might well be shaped by unexamined ethnocentric

---

6. It was also a challenge to be the oldest volunteer, by probably 25 years, in the Cross-Cultural Solutions home base, and to develop the chicken pox in my mid-50s immediately upon my return from Guatemala.

notions of the universality of childhood. This also seems to be true of the cultures that inhabited ancient Israel. Like Kamp and Whittaker, as well as other scholars who critique the interpretation of ethnographic data from past societies, I suspected that ethnocentric personal concerns and interests in children and childhood reflected 'a stereotypic Western model of the child, living in a small happy nuclear family consisting of parents with one boy, one girl, and perhaps an additional infant, spending considerable amounts of time playing'.[7] This Western model became the lens through which biblical childhood had been evaluated in most past biblical scholarship.

For example, it is assumed in scholarship focused on so-called traditional societies, such as ancient Israel and Guatemala, where social organization reflects patrilineal patrilocal kinship, that social organization favors the birth and survival of sons over infant daughters. This gendered assumption was proven wrong in Guatemala, where many live by the rules of patrilineal patrilocal kinship systems; I witnessed through my experiences at the *hogar* that aside from cases of girls being abandoned because of physical deformity, boys are in fact more likely to be abandoned. I suspect this is true because of a strictly utilitarian perspective; for parents in dire financial straits, girls are more desirable because they are thought to have greater potential to contribute to the economic livelihood of their families once they are old enough to be hired out as servants and nannies to more well-to-do Guatemalans. As the economic aspects of the gendered construction of childhood among certain portions of the Guatemalan population began to unfold during my service there, I began to think about the importance of this insight for reexamining ideas of gender and childhood in the Hebrew Bible.

The circumstances in the Guatemalan orphanage challenged me to confront the ethnocentric assumption that the nuclear family is the ideal setting for raising a child. This caused me to wonder what modern prejudices were being imposed on scholarly analyses of childhood in biblical Israel where it is assumed that the family lived in a multiple-family household. Western values today accept the mobile nuclear family as the normal context for a child to grow and thrive. Thus, I was in no way prepared to hear stories from fellow volunteers of Cross-Cultural Solutions who spoke about the 70 abandoned and abused children who were adopted (with governmental approval) by one Guatemalan couple and how the children felt lucky to live in this setting where they were all members of one family. Given the myriad forms of residential formations, I had to ask myself whether growing up in a family of biologically related individuals is automatically a superior arrangement to life in an orphanage or some other group setting. Is foster care or a group

---

7. Kathryn A. Kamp and John C. Whittaker, 'Prehistoric Puebloan Children in Archaeology and Art', in *Children in Prehistoric Puebloan Southwest* (ed. Kathryn A. Kamp; Salt Lake City: University of Utah Press, 2002), pp. 14-40 (38).

home, with its sense of community, necessarily inferior to life in a nuclear family? In both the present and the past, how does one determine 'the best interest of the child' or think about issues of entitlement in regard to a particular family formation? As I came to recognize the need for a corrective to the unexamined ethnocentric stereotype of the nuclear family as the ideal setting for raising a child, I wondered what other biases were being imposed on scholarly analyses of childhood in biblical Israel. I turned my attention to the task of reconstructing childhood in the Hebrew Bible. As stated above, I was interested in answering the deceptively simple question 'What is a child?' according to the ideologies of ancient Israel.

Back home in Chicago, in spring 2008 I introduced a course at DePaul University entitled 'Religion and Social Engagement: The Problematics of Children in World Religions'. This course continues to the present and is linked with DePaul's Irwin W. Steans Center for Community-based Service Learning and Community Service Studies. In this service-based experiential learning class, students not only engage intellectually with issues regarding children and childhood through traditional book learning and discussion, but they also go out into the larger Chicago community to provide real world service that supplements their classroom learning. Although this class is not solely focused on issues regarding children in the Hebrew Bible, the classroom provided me with a further context for thinking about the lives of children in ancient Israel as I became more aware of the challenges facing children today. Issues regarding children's rights, particularly as expressed in the United Nations Convention on the Rights of the Child (UNCRC), continually brought my thoughts back to the lives of children in biblical Israel as I pondered what rights, if any, ancient Israelite children enjoyed.

I am very grateful to a student who, in that first class in spring 2008, asked if his mother could speak to the class regarding her work with children in the foster care system. Her presentation helped me identify the next phase of my own service with children. That morning was my introduction to an agency in the US that I had never heard of: CASA, Court Appointed Special Advocate. As they are represented on the internet,

> Every year more than half a million abused and neglected children are in need of safe, permanent, nurturing homes. That's where CASA steps in. CASA (Court Appointed Special Advocates) was created in 1977 to make sure the abuse and neglect these children originally suffered at home doesn't continue as abuse and neglect at the hands of the system. As trained advocates, CASA volunteers are appointed by judges to be a voice for these children in court. The result is that a child is placed into a safe, loving home where he/she can thrive. It is the CASA vision to provide a volunteer for each and every abused and neglected child who needs one.[8]

---

8. 'CASA of Cook County', http://www.volunteermatch.org/search/org19953.jsp (accessed 20 March 2012).

Inspired by what I had learned from the student's mother about the work of CASA, it seemed only appropriate for me to begin my own community service in Chicago and to start the training to become a CASA volunteer. In fall 2009 I began my CASA training and by the end of the year I was assigned my first (and still active) case. Before I knew it, I was involved with a young person who had been removed from the home of her biological parents and was in foster care; it became my job to meet with her once a month to get to know her and to make sure that she was receiving appropriate care in her foster setting. Furthermore, I was expected to write reports for the court, to speak as her voice when we went to court, to make recommendations about her situation to the judge, and to verify that the organizations and individuals involved in her case were all doing their assigned jobs. These participants include, among others, the Illinois Department of Children and Family Services (DCFS), the biological mother and father, the foster parent, the social worker, the guardian ad Litum,[9] the psychologist, the school teachers and counselors, the judge, and ever so many lawyers. The system that handles children who are wards of the state is one that requires a great deal of patience in order to advocate for the rights of one's assigned child. This fact was continually stressed to me as I subsequently took on the additional task in the spring of 2012 of becoming a peer volunteer coordinator for CASA. As a seasoned volunteer, I received the extra training needed to mentor new volunteer advocates while I continued with my original CASA case. I learned even more through my experiences as a peer volunteer coordinator about the social organizations that serve children today and all the things that can go both right and wrong in trying to help a child in foster care, through my eyes and through the eyes of the child herself. As I did this work, I had to wonder about what provisions existed in ancient Israel for children who were without parents, beyond the proverbial concern for the orphan as expounded in texts like Deut. 10.18.

The experiences with CASA and its social service agencies and individuals, along with the service in Guatemala and at the Children's Hospital in Chicago mentioned earlier, my teaching at DePaul, and ongoing research on children in ancient Israel, fueled the questions I continued to ask of the biblical texts. Many contemporary questions and issues regarding children may not be reflective of the biblical worldview, and I am not trying to impose a paradigm onto the text where it does not belong. Contemporary awareness of the importance of seeing the world through the many voices and interests of children today in their culture-bound contexts makes it possible to ask new questions about a very old text. The Hebrew Bible is told from the point of view of (probably male) adults; this adult perspective prompts me to ask questions about what ancient authors were trying to convey to their readers

---

9. Http://guardianadlitem.org/ (accessed 16 March 2012).

and hearers when the text was read aloud, and to question the traditional interpretation of this text. My experiences have taught me that the contemporary idealization of childhood as a period of physical and emotional protected well-being and innocence cannot be assumed as universal across the globe today and should not be projected onto the past as we reconstruct the world of the children in ancient Israel.

Overview

In order to address the problem of assuming the universal experience and innocence of children, this book explores the construction of childhood in biblical Israel. As previously mentioned, the central question of this book is: 'What is a child in ancient Israel?' I answer this question through an interdisciplinary methodology informed by a discussion that brings traditional biblical methodology (historical-critical and literary-critical methods) and the sociology of children (social-scientific models and cross-cultural comparisons) into dialogue with each other to recover the biblical perspective in light of contemporary issues regarding children, primarily expressed through the UNCRC, the United Nations Convention on the Rights of the Child, and commentaries on its sections by its signatories.

Part 1 begins to address these issues by drawing on literature that explores children and childhood as categories of analysis. In Chapter 1, I provide a brief overview and theoretical introduction to the study of children as a contemporary category of scholarly investigation. I explore the development of the study of children and explain why such study is worthwhile. Here I look at unexamined assumptions regarding children in both the past and in the present (according to the UNCRC) and argue that what it means to be a child varies across time and place.

Chapter 2 focuses directly on the question: 'What is a child?' First, it addresses issues in defining the term 'child' as it is applied in contemporary discourse. Here we see that 'child' is typically defined as a chronological category and that the terms 'child' or 'children' refer to a part of society bracketed off by considerations of age or biological markers like menstruation, although the boundaries of age used to define who is a child vary from culture to culture. What is clear is that the terms 'child' and 'children' are used in scholarly literature to refer to flesh and blood individuals. These terms are typically juxtaposed against the term 'adult' without consideration of the culturally constructed nature of both of these categories and of the fact that the division is sometimes arbitrary and changing, even in a single culture. Childhood, on the other hand, refers to the socially constructed meaning that a society attaches to the developmental phase when one is a child and to the activities that may be designated by a culture to separate children from adults. As we will see, childhood can be defined as 'a status of person which is comprised through a series of, often heterogeneous, images, representations, codes and constructs'.[10] Second, Chapter 2 looks at the place of a child in family life in ancient Israel with these two points of view in mind: (1) contemporary concerns for the social good of the child today, i.e., the 'etic' point of view; and (2) the perspective of Israelite culture itself, i.e., the 'emic' point of view.[11] Although studies of childhood have come to the forefront recently within the academic study of contemporary world religions, too often they analyze ancient texts only from a contemporary agenda and fail to consider the culture-specific historical frameworks of the documents they study.[12] When these historical texts are mined from an ahistorical perspective, the evidence in the texts becomes distorted. For example, in Hebrew Bible scholarship, the romantic picture of childhood and innocence has been that of 'the little Israelite [who] spent most of his time playing in the streets or squares with boys and girls of his own age. They sang and danced or played with little clay models...'[13] and is probably not accurate.

Linguistic issues come to the forefront in Chapter 3, where Hebrew terminology for children and childhood are explored. Although ultimately our understanding of childhood in the Hebrew Bible will rely on an analysis of the child in the context of the biblical texts themselves, study of the terms *na'ar* (נער) and *yeled* (ילד) will aid in the exegesis of texts. Here the aim is to find, if possible, definitions of childhood based on Hebrew terminology—rather than the definitions used in the contemporary context for discussing children and childhood. I hope to explore contemporary definitions of childhood in contrast to those of ancient Israel in order to grasp ideas specific to

10. Chris Jenks, *Childhood* (London: Routledge, 1996), p. 32.

11. For a history and discussion of issues relevant to 'emic/etic' perspectives, see Thomas N. Headland, Kenneth L. Pike, and Marvin Harris (eds.), *Emics and Etics: The Insider/Outsider Debate* (Frontiers in Anthropology; Newbury Park, CO: Sage Publications, 1990).

12. E.g., Marcia Bunge (ed.), *The Child in Christian Thought* (Grand Rapids, MI: W.B. Eerdmans, 2001); Bonnie J. Miller-McLemore, *Let the Children Come: Reimaging Childhood from a Christian Perspective* (San Francisco: Jossey-Bass, 2003); Danna Nolan Fewell, *The Children of Israel: Reading the Bible for the Sake of our Children* (Nashville, TN: Abingdon Press, 2005); Kristin Herzog, *Children and our Global Future: Theological and Social Challenges* (Cleveland, OH: Pilgrim Press, 2005); David H. Jensen, *Graced Vulnerability: A Theology of Childhood* (Cleveland, OH: Pilgrim Press, 2005); Joyce Ann Mercer, *Welcoming Children: A Practical Theology of Childhood* (St Louis: Chalice Press, 2005); Marcia J. Bunge (ed.), *The Child in the Bible* (Grand Rapids, MI: W.B. Eerdmans, 2008); Mikael Larsson, 'In Search of Children's Agency: Reading Exodus from Sweden', in *Exodus and Deuteronomy* (ed. Athalya Brenner and Gale A. Yee; Texts @ Contexts; Minneapolis: Fortress Press, 2012), pp. 79-94.

13. Roland de Vaux, *Ancient Israel: Its Life and Institutions* (trans. J. McHugh; New York: McGraw–Hill, 1965), p. 48.

the worldview of the ancient Israelite. As semantic patterns become clearer, so will our ability to grasp conceptualizations of the ancient Israelite child. The chapter concludes with the translations of these terms in the LXX and in rabbinic literature with the aim of discovering whether later renderings of these words help us in understanding the nuances of these Hebrew nouns.

Chapter 4 begins Part 2 of this volume. Here the focus of analysis narrows directly on issues pertaining to childhood in the Hebrew Bible in light of topics about childhood addressed in Part 1. Discussions of what is a child assume family relational situations. Chapter 4 explores the relationship between the child and the family in the world of the Hebrew Bible. Here I establish the context of the patrilineal, patrilocal family in the Hebrew Bible by describing the levels of social structure of ancient Israel that contextualized the life of an Israelite child. The place of the child in the family household that relied on intergenerational continuity is the focus here. The discussion will include factors such as gender and whether a child lived in a monogamous or polygamous household—in a society where the preference was for endogamous marriage—as relevant to the conceptualizations of childhood in biblical Israel. What becomes clear from this analysis is that there are multiplicities of childhoods within a single culture that depend on many factors, including gender, socioeconomic status, and age.

Chapter 5 presents data regarding the Israelite life cycle that helps in scholarly understanding of the social construction of childhood in the world of the Hebrew Bible, all the while recognizing the methodological issue of the relationship between the textual sources of the biblical tradition and the lives of ancient Israelites. I argue that the Israelite life cycle was divided by categories of social responsibility rather than chronological age. Questions arise when discussing the life cycle that fall on the dividing line between not yet reaching full membership in the kinship group, and therefore being dependent on the family, and achieving the status of adulthood and independence of the birth family. The chapter considers Lev. 27.1-7, Jer. 6.11 and Jer. 51.22 as part of its construction of the biblical life cycle. Ultimately the question arises regarding what distinguishes a child from an independent adult.

In Chapters 6–8, I analyze specific biblical texts to investigate both narrative and legal traditions. I focus on texts that have been overlooked despite the light they shed on the cultural-construction of childhood in the Hebrew Bible. My approach is to concentrate on the patterns that emerge within these texts that allow the modern researcher to understand the meaning of being a child in ancient Israel from within the biblical tradition. The questions and answers that arise in studying both the contemporary sociology of childhood and the Hebrew terminology for children will shape the perspectives applied to the study of these biblical texts.

Chapter 6 looks at Genesis 21 and takes seriously how the basis of household structure, i.e., a polygamous versus a monogamous household, has an impact on the way childhood was thought about and experienced. I will demonstrate that family structure shaped the social meaning of childhood. The focus on the family of Abraham in Genesis will provide the locus for my analysis. By comparing the lives and experiences of Ishmael and Isaac it will be possible to argue that there are a multiplicity of childhoods within even a single family—a fact that grows exponentially when this insight is applied to a society as a whole. Chapter 7 explores the dynamics of the birth of Samuel to Hannah in 1 Samuel 1 and addresses circumstances of child abandonment that must be acknowledged in order to discuss the construction of childhood in the Hebrew Bible. Chapter 8 turns to the subject of the construction of childhood through an example from the biblical legal corpus, Exod. 21.22-25.

Together, these three chapters serve as examples of childhood both as a social institution created by adults as well as an experience of the children in the texts. They reveal multiple definitions of childhood within biblical Israel that are determined by the place a child occupies in the larger structures of family, religion, and economics.

Finally, in Part 3, I draw conclusions about children in the Hebrew Bible and suggest issues for further study. The topics covered in this final part function as a dialectical exploration of childhood in the Hebrew Bible in light of contemporary issues regarding children (going back again to the issues raised in the UNCRC), as well as a critique of contemporary understandings of childhood in light of the historical record of ancient Israel. It may be unorthodox to state the conclusions of a book before the reader has an opportunity to consider the arguments presented but, in this case, it should be evident that there are no universals when it comes to conceptualizations of children or the experiences of children—either past or present. However, I believe that what we learn about childhood in biblical Israel can have relevance as we think about children today.

Acknowledgments

Interest in the subject of children in the Hebrew Bible is not mine alone. As I look back on the journey that led to writing this book, I remember that I have never been alone in my travels; I am truly grateful for the companionship of those who have accompanied me on my way and been there for me at critical moments. One constant source of support has been James Halstead, the chairperson of the Religious Studies Department at DePaul University. Before I really had a clear sense of how I would refocus my past research agenda on women in the Hebrew Bible to issues relating to children, Jim provided a vote of confidence through financial support for my travels to Guatemala. However, he has moved from fiscal support of my service to enthusiastic endorsement of both my teaching and scholarship on issues relating to children. He has graciously done whatever was asked of him in order to help me move forward in my work and bring this volume to completion.

The CASA (Court Appointed Special Advocate) program is structured in such a way that each volunteer has an Advocate Supervisor to help negotiate the legal system and to help the volunteer work for the best interests of her child. I am fortunate to have been assigned to Annie Higgins, who has been my sounding board, my back-up, and an all around source of support in my CASA case. Annie has given generously of her time not only as my supervisor but also as a guest speaker in my course on the Problematics of Children in World Religions. Her knowledge of the workings of both the Department of Children and Family Services and of the juvenile courts in Illinois has made me better able to be an advocate to my assigned child.

Others have kept me company on this journey as both intellectual conversation partners and as voices to share in my outrage at the many heartbreaking issues facing children present and past. I am particularly grateful to Kay Read for her willingness to spend hours as a conversation partner on issues of how to understand the particularities of childhood in contexts very different from those in contemporary North America and to find English vocabulary that grasps distinctions that express unique ancient Israelite social expressions regarding the conceptualization of childhood. She also shared her expertise by commenting on a draft of the manuscript and making suggestions for its improvement. Others who deserve recognition, each for their own unique contributions to this work, are Frida Furman, Gale Yee, and Thomas Dozeman, all three colleagues and friends. Frida offered enthusiastic and steadfast support throughout the preparation of this book. Gale and Tom both gave of their time and energy to read the manuscript in its penultimate draft and to make suggestions for its improvement. In addition, Christopher Mount helped me better understand the semantic patterns revealed by the LXX translation of the nouns *na'ar* and *yeled*, and Alexei Sivertsev shared his knowledge of rabbinic thoughts on children with me. Special thanks goes to Milton Eng and Laurel Koepf for making available to me prepublication manuscripts of their works *The Days of Our Years: A Lexical Study of the Life Cycle in Biblical Israel* (London: T. & T. Clark, 2011) and 'Inside Out: The Othered Child in the Bible for Children', *Semeia Studies* respectively.

I am indebted to Ali DeChancie, Matthew Fledderjohann, and Arielle Steinberg who read and commented upon this project throughout its preparation. Their questions and feedback helped clarify ideas that might otherwise have been unintelligible to non-specialist readers. Lauri Dietz's role in the editing of the drafts of this manuscript should not go unmentioned. Finally, for abiding editing assistance that always improves the quality of my writing and helps me to clarify and sharpen my ideas, thanks go to Marvin Israel.

Thanks are also due to Nancy Zawayta and Ian Petchenik for valuable technology assistance at numerous points throughout the writing of this work and to Raquel Martinez for careful help in preparing the bibliography at the end of this volume.

I particularly express gratitude to Cheryl Exum, who suggested that I address the topic of children in the Hebrew Bible in a book. This suggestion was made during a serendipitous conversation over coffee on the last morning of meetings at the International Organization for the Study of the Old Testament in Helsinki, Finland, in summer 2010. Her sharing about her study of Genesis 16 and 21 in light of artistic representations led to her suggestion that I write this book. I hope that I am able to do for the study of the meaning of childhood what she has done for the study of the meaning of women's bodies in the Hebrew Bible.

I offer special thanks to my husband, Dave Lerner. Without his enthusiastic support this book could not have happened. He has been a calm presence throughout the writing of this volume and has patiently offered his technological expertise when I have been in a computer crisis. Moreover, his willingness to let me have our house to myself so that I could write in solitude has made the completion of this work possible. He has helped in countless ways.

In working with children, confidentiality must be preserved. Thus, as I write this I am unable to name the many children whose lives have touched mine and who have forced me continually to reexamine my ideas about who is a child, what constitutes childhood, and what is in the best interest of the child. I will never forget my experiences with these young people, and I can only hope that they grow up healthy and safe and have fulfilling lives. I think particularly of the young woman whose case was assigned to me by CASA and who has taught me so much about courage in the face of adversity. It is a privilege to know her; I always look forward to our visits together and to learning about life through her eyes.

As a follow-up to my work in Guatemala, I feel compelled to mention that I have recently seen a photo of a baby from the Guatemalan *hogar* with whom I formed a special bond; she is unmistakable in the photo as the baby with the bald spot whom I held constantly in 2007. Her photo appears on the website of an organization here in the US that traveled to the *hogar* to do volunteer work and has now posted photos from that visit in order to raise money for the orphanage. Although it was a shock to see her, it is a comfort to know that she continues to be surrounded by caring individuals.

Sections of two previously published articles appear here in revised form. I gratefully acknowledge the permission of their publishers to use this material in the present context. They are 'Sociological Approaches: Toward a Sociology of Childhood in the Hebrew Bible', in *Essays on the Interpretation of the Hebrew Bible in Honor of David L. Petersen*, ed. Joel M. LeMon and Kent Harold Richards (Atlanta: Society of Biblical Literature, 2009), pp. 251-69; and '1 Samuel 1, the United Nations Convention on the Rights of the Child, and "The Best Interests of the Child"', *Journal of Childhood and Religion* 1/3 (April 2010), pp. 1-23 (www.childhoodandreligion.com), © Sopher Press.

I am also grateful to the Faculty Summer Research Program of the College of Liberal Arts and Social Sciences at DePaul University for financial support in summer 2011 to do the research that is now included in Chapter 5.

Finally, this book is dedicated to three very precious individuals: Brian, Stephanie, and Jimmy, although they really are no longer children. I am very lucky to have them in my life. 'May you stay forever young'.[1]

---

1. Bob Dylan, 'Forever Young', *Planet Waves* (Asylum Records, 1974).

Part 1

BACKGROUND AND THEORY

Chapter 1

CHILDREN AND CHILDHOOD
AS CATEGORIES OF ANALYSIS

'Child' is itself not an uncomplicated term.[1]

Throughout history, across and even within societies, there is no agreement on what constitutes childhood or when it ends. Nevertheless, every society that depends on procreation for its survival must take into account in its social organization that children initially require a great deal of care.[2]

It seems obvious that interpretations of childhood in different cultures (including biblical Israel) can be skewed by the interpreter's unexamined biases and classifications. A simple example will suffice: the story of the sale of Joseph by his brothers (Gen. 37.27-28) is an example of human trafficking, but we almost never think of it in those terms.[3] If we fail to recognize our interpretive blind spots, how then can we understand the multiple understandings of childhood in another culture? In many areas of the world today, next door neighbors may have very different 'cultures'. Thus, to study children in any culture, we must first be conscious of and understand the categories we have in mind when we talk about value-laden,

---

1. John Boswell, *The Kindness of Strangers* (New York: Pantheon, 1988), p. 26.
2. Sarah H. Matthews, 'A Window on the "New" Sociology of Childhood', *Sociology Compass* 1 (2007), pp. 322-34 (323). For further discussion of this issue, see Jens Quortrup, 'Sociology of Childhood: Conceptual Liberation of Children', in *Childhood and Children's Culture* (ed. Flemming Mouritsen and Jens Quortrup; Denmark: University Press of Southern Denmark, 2002), pp. 43-78 (74).
3. However, Carole R. Fontaine argues this in '"Here comes this Dreamer": Reading Joseph the Slave in Multicultural and Interfaith Contexts', in *Genesis* (ed. Athalya Brenner, Archie Chi-Chung Lee and Gale A. Yee; Texts @ Contexts; Minneapolis: Fortress Press, 2010), pp. 131-45. To be precise on what is meant by human trafficking, we turn now to the following definition: 'Labor trafficking is defined as the recruitment, harboring, transportation, provision, or obtaining of a person for labor services, through the use of force, fraud, or coercion for the purpose of subjection to involuntary servitude, peonage, debt bondage or slavery. Such violations might include domestic services, manufacturing, construction, migrant laboring and other services obtained through subjection to involuntary servitude, peonage, debt bondage or slavery'. http://www.humantrafficking.neu.edu/background/ (accessed 30 March 2012).

culture-bound notions and stereotypes of childhood that have bearing on cross-cultural conceptualizations of childhood. Without self-awareness of these biases, all too often writers are guilty of possessing attitudes of superiority that result in judgments about childhood in other cultures as being inferior to childhood in their own cultures. Are culture-bound ideas and ideals of what one society regards to be normal and healthy for children in any sense universal, and if so, should they be used to judge childhood in other societies?

The Influence of Philippe Ariès

The insight that childhood is a cultural construction—and certainly not a phase of life that can be understood by imposing modern Western viewpoints as though they are universals—goes back at least as far as the anthropological fieldwork and writings of Margaret Mead, whose work exposes the ethnocentric perspective of earlier theories regarding children.[4] All the same, pioneering work in the study of childhood is now associated with the influential writing of French historian Philippe Ariès, who broke new ground in the study of the child in his *Centuries of Childhood: A Social History of Family Life*.[5] In this classic work, he argues,

> in medieval society the idea of childhood did not exist; this is not to suggest that children were neglected, forsaken or despised. This idea of childhood is not to be confused with affection for children: it corresponds to an awareness of the particular nature of childhood, that particular nature which distinguishes the child from the adult, even the young adult. In medieval society this awareness was lacking.[6]

Ariès's argument that the idea of childhood was a distinct and innocent phase of Western European life has now been criticized by historians and social scientists alike for being based on analyses of images of children in art.[7] Even still, no one would deny that credit goes to Ariès for the insight

---

4. *Coming of Age in Samoa* (New York: New American Library, 1928/1961).

5. Philippe Ariès, *Centuries of Childhood: A Social History of Family Life* (trans. Robert Baldrick; New York: Vintage Books, 1962). Of course, between the time of the writings of Mead and Ariès, other scholars turned their attention to 'youth culture'. See, for example, Talbott Parsons, 'Age and Sex in the Social Structure of the United States', *American Sociological Review* 7 (1942), pp. 604-16 and James S. Coleman, *The Adolescent Society: The Social Life of the Teenager and its Impact on Education* (Glencoe, IL: Free Press of Glencoe, 1961).

6. Ariès, *Centuries of Childhood*, p. 128.

7. Classicist Valerie French refers to Ariès's perspective as 'the literalist fallacy'. She writes, '…rendering a young child as a miniature adult does not of necessity mean that adults did not recognize the difference between adults and children. One must consider

that childhood is a social and historical construction. According to Ariès, prior to the later sixteenth or early seventeenth century, and even later in the case of the lower economic classes, children were understood to be 'small-scale adults'.[8] Thus, Ariès maintains that childhood as a distinct phase of life was a relatively recent conception. His thesis that childhood is a social construction resulted in the subsequent study of childhood as a socially constructed category worthy of scholarly inquiry. Although the details of his argument are now refuted by scholars, the tradition of examining the social construction of 'the child' as the subject of historical investigation in recent scholarship builds upon the work of Ariès—even without the Eurocentrism of his analysis, which failed to take into account the social construction of childhood in histories outside of Western cultures.

Ariès's fundamental premise is no longer supportable, as my work here and the research of many others show. However, his thesis has been highly influential in leading the present generation of researchers on childhood to pose the fundamental question 'What is a child?' in culture-bound contexts.[9] The question can only be answered with respect to culture, time, place, and other variables such as gender, socio-economic class, and ethnicity. It is impossible to understand the social construction of childhood in any culture without taking into account more factors simply than the artistic depictions on which Ariès relied when he wrote.

---

here the artistic conventions of the culture. One would not argue that the ancient Egyptians really saw only one eye on a person's face simply because it was their convention to show only one eye in the painting;' see 'Children in Antiquity', in *Children in Historical and Comparative Perspective: An International Handbook and Research Guide* (ed. Joseph M. Hawes and N. Ray Hiner; Westport, CT: Greenwood Press, 1991), pp. 13-29 (24). Two frequently cited critiques of Ariès are Linda Pollack, *Forgotten Children: Parent–Child Relations from 1500–1900* (Cambridge: Cambridge University Press, 1983) and Richard T. Vann, 'The Youth of Centuries of Childhood', *History and Theory* 21 (1982), pp. 279-97.

    8. Ariès, *Centuries of Childhood*, p. 58.

    9. For discussion of childhood as a socially constructed category, with a particular emphasis on the archaeological data, see Joanna Sofaer Derevenski, 'Where Are the Children? Accessing Children in the Past', *Archaeological Review from Cambridge* 13 (1994), pp. 7-20; 'Engendering Children, Engendering Archaeology', in *Invisible People and Processes: Writing Gender and Childhood into European Archaeology* (ed. J. Moore and E. Scott; London: Leicester University Press, 1997), pp. 192-202; and Jane Baxter, *The Archaeology of Childhood: Children, Gender, and Material Culture* (Gender and Archaeology Series, 10; Walnut Creek, CA: AltaMira Press, 2005), pp. 27-37. On how archaeology from the Levant can reflect the construction of childhood see, David Ilan, 'Mortuary Practices at Tel Dan in the Middle Bronze Age: A Reflection of Canaanite Society and Ideology', in *Archaeology of Death in the Ancient Near East* (ed. Stuart Campbell and Anthony Green; Oxford: Oxbow, 1995), pp. 117-37.

Post Ariès: A Paradigm Shift

In response to the intellectual spark ignited by Ariès's work, the topic of childhood began to receive serious scholarly attention in the last quarter of the twentieth century.[10] Recognition of the importance of the sociology of childhood as a topic worthy of study parallels the development of feminist studies in the 1970s.[11] Just as feminist studies critique male-centered scholarship, childhood studies critique adult-centered scholarship. Moreover, just as much recent feminist criticism aims to bring about social changes for the good of women (both in biblical studies and in other areas of feminism), much of the recent scholarship in the sociology of childhood targets the social conditions of children today. This link between the study of women and the study of children has been noted by anthropologists:

> Our neglect of the child as a person, participant, and locus of important events in the process of a culture is probably even greater than our neglect until recently of women.... [A]t present we know surprisingly little of the cultural competence and content of children as constituent participants in culture. The ethnography of childhood remains a genuine frontier.[12]

Furthermore, just as feminist criticism distinguishes sex roles, i.e., biological roles, from gender roles as social constructs, the sociology of childhood distinguishes 'the child' as a human being, albeit a biologically immature being, from 'childhood', as a social construct, i.e., 'a diverse set of cultural ideas'.[13]

New paradigms for feminism and the sociology of childhood move beyond models that attempt to find 'the' essence of the categories of individuals to which they refer. However, the sociology of childhood

---

10. A convenient and thorough review of the history of the development of childhood sociology is found in Suzanne Shanahan, 'Lost and Found: The Sociological Ambivalence toward Childhood', *The Annual Review of Sociology* 33 (2007), pp. 407-28. See also, Alan Prout and Allison James, 'A New Paradigm for the Sociology of Childhood? Provenance, Promise and Problems', in *Constructing and Reconstructing Childhood: Contemporary Issues in the Sociological Study of Childhood* (ed. Allison James and Alan Prout; London: Falmer Press, 1997), pp. 7-33; Robert A. LeVine, 'Ethnographic Studies of Childhood: A Historical Overview', *American Anthropologist* 109 (2007), pp. 247-60, and Matthews, 'A Window on the "New" Sociology of Childhood'. For an historical perspective on the study of childhood, see Anthony Volk, 'The Evolution of Childhood', *Journal of the History of Childhood and Youth* 4 (2011), pp. 470-94.

11. The following discussion comes directly from my arguments in '1 Samuel 1, the United Nations Convention on the Rights of the Child, and "The Best Interests of the Child"', *Journal of Childhood and Religion* 1 (April 2010), pp. 1-23 (3) (http://www.childhoodandreligion.com/JCR/Volume_1_(2010)_files/SteinbergApril2010.pdf).

12. Theodore Schwartz, 'The Acquisition of Culture', *Ethnos* 9 (1981), pp. 4-17 (10, 16).

13. Shanahan, 'Lost and Found', p. 408.

comes late to the scene of critical Western scholarship because of hesitancy with the subject of children as a topic worthy of study.[14] Moreover, the legitimacy of listening to the voices of children in research has been a source of ambivalence between 'top down' research, where adults speak about children, and 'bottom up' theories, which give children a voice in the production of research methodologies and theories on what it means to be a child.[15]

Ambivalence about methods in studying children in American society is reflected in the development of the sociology of childhood. This ambivalence stems partly from the difficulty in separating historical research on the social construction of childhood from studies promoting social policies on the rights of children today. Although both subjects of inquiry have legitimate objectives, these goals have often been blurred due to a failure to separate the study of childhood from the study of children. Topics such as when life begins and babies' rights, as important as they are for contemporary law and morality, are different from questions about the social construction of childhood.

Sociological research continues to grapple with these issues. Attempts to articulate a paradigm for studying childhood cross-culturally have resulted in a consensus on the work to be done. Key concepts for the sociology of childhood according to Prout and James are:

1. Childhood is understood as a social construction. As such it provides an interpretive frame for contextualizing the early years of human life. Childhood, as distinct from biological immaturity, is neither a natural nor universal feature of human groups but appears as a specific structural and cultural component of many societies.
2. Childhood is a variable of social analysis. It can never be entirely divorced from other variables such as class, gender, or ethnicity. Comparative and cross-cultural analysis reveals a variety of childhoods rather than a single and universal phenomenon.
3. Children's social relationships and cultures are worthy of study in their own right, independent of the perspective and concerns of adults.
4. Children are and must be seen as active in the construction and determination of their own social lives, the lives of those around them and of the societies in which they live. Children are not just the passive subjects of social structures and processes.
5. Ethnography is a particularly useful methodology for the study of childhood. It allows children a more direct voice and participation in the

---

14. For more on the problematics of and ambivalence towards the study of children in social scientific research, see Shanahan, 'Lost and Found'.

15. This approach is exemplified in Susan B. Ridgely, *The Study of Children in Religion: A Methods Handbook* (New York: New York University Press, 2011).

production of sociological data than is usually possible through experimental or survey styles of research.[16]

6. Childhood is a phenomenon in relation to which the double hermeneutic of the social sciences is acutely present…That is to say, to proclaim a new paradigm of childhood sociology is also to engage in and respond to the process of reconstructing childhood in society.[17]

Of course, not all aspects of this paradigm can be made relevant when studying the meaning of childhood in an ancient text such as the Hebrew Bible. For example, one cannot go out into the field and do ethnography of an ancient culture, yet the Bible and its contemporary literature function as the ethnohistorical record to be investigated. As such, it is fair to say that the model above provides a solid foundation on which to begin constructing a sociology of childhood in ancient Israel. The consequences of not taking these concepts into consideration are just as unfortunate for the study of ancient Israel as they are for our own society. Research on the culture-bound nature of childhood reveals that:

> Social scientists who study discursive constructions of children and childhoods have analyzed not only the ways in which meanings are made but also their effects in the world. For example, sociologists and anthropologists often puzzle about the gap between the stated goal of public education in industrialized countries—to open equal opportunity for all children—and the reality that schools, by and large, reproduce social class and racial inequalities.[18]

The challenge facing researchers today is how to bring social policy for the good of children into effect in light of the study of culture-bound constructions of childhood, including findings from historical study of the social construction of childhood in antiquity.

The United Nations Convention on the Rights of the Child

Alongside the focus on childhood in academic research and debate, on the international political front, the second half of the twentieth century gave rise to global concerns for children as expressed in the United Nations

---

16. I attempted to lay out a paradigm for sociological study of childhood in ancient Israel in 'Sociological Approaches: Toward a Sociology of Childhood in the Hebrew Bible', in *Essays on the Interpretation of the Hebrew Bible in Honor of David L. Petersen* (ed. Joel M. LeMon and Kent Harold Richards; Atlanta: Society of Biblical Literature, 2009), pp. 251-69 (261-66). Although the principles identified in my earlier work are culture-bound to biblical Israel, they conform to the general concepts for a sociology of childhood specified here in recent social scientific literature.

17. Prout and James, 'A New Paradigm for the Sociology of Childhood?', p. 8.

18. Http://www.faqs.org/childhood/So-Th/Sociology-and-Anthropology-of-Childhood.html (accessed 1 April 2012).

Convention on the Rights of the Child.[19] The UNCRC was adopted by the United Nations General Assembly in 1989 and came into force in 1990 after being ratified by the requisite number of nations. The document focuses on five issues: non-discrimination, devotion to the best interests of the child, the right to life, survival and development, and respect for the views of the child. Children, according to the UNCRC, not only need both physical and emotional protection, but they have rights as individuals. Thus, this document recognizes individual rights for children while simultaneously working to protect them. According to the UNCRC, children are independent beings with rights to autonomy and protection. However, as one analyst of the UNCRC notes, the UNCRC document does 'not provide children with a full citizen's rights to travel, work, choose a place or residence and certainly not to engage in sexual activity. What the children's charters provide is the right to freedom from cruelty, hunger, lack of shelter, lack of "appropriate education", and so forth. It is adults who still decide what is "appropriate".'[20] The question raised in the chapters ahead is whether or not the circumstances for children in ancient Israel were any different than they are for children today.

As we move ahead to answer this question, we must be conscious of the unavoidability of confronting culturally embedded constructions of childhood in the biblical text. Because of this unavoidability we must be simultaneously aware of our own biases and of the cultural constructions that affected life in ancient Israel. The only way to understand the ancient Israelite constructions is by comparing what the biblical data tells us to our own culturally embedded constructions of childhood. In the end, studies of the construction of childhood both in antiquity and in the present are from an emic (insider) point of view: the latter because it is our own era and the former because we are trying understand ancient Israel as the Israelites themselves understood it.

In summary, this chapter briefly surveyed both the scholarly and political emergence of the child as a subject of modern discourse. Universal perceptions of children as innocent and pure cannot be taken for granted. Scholars must address the diverse attitudes and values that particular societies hold about the children in their culture-bound contexts. Theories of childhood also require attention to the reflections of children themselves. For many today, the rights of children have become a focal point of attention in the political arena. Lot's offer of his daughters to the men of Sodom in Gen 19.8 is a biblical example of such a concern.

---

19. Http://www2.ohchr.org/english/law/crc.htm (accessed 29 June 2012).

20. John Alan Lee, 'Three Paradigms of Childhood', *Canadian Review of Sociology and Anthropology* 19 (1982), pp. 591-608 (596).

But what is a child? Definitions of a child are essential in my analysis if I am to grasp the diversities of how 'child' is defined across time and space. To argue that there are no universals in the construction of childhood implies that the term 'child' be used with different interpretations across a variety of cultures. We turn now to this topic.

Chapter 2

WHAT IS A CHILD?

The Term 'Child': A Chronological Category

In the Oxford English Dictionary, the word 'child' is defined both with reference to a state, for example, a newborn child, and to age, to designate a person below the age of legal majority,[1] i.e., when they are deemed an adult according to law. As one recent commentator remarks,

> In English, the word 'child' can refer to anyone between the ages of 0 and 18. Although, at either end of the scale, it may be replaced by more age-specific words, such as baby, infant, toddler, or teenager, generally the word 'child' can be used to denote any young person who has not yet reached social maturity.[2]

Furthermore, the word child can also be used as a relational word. Thus, strictly speaking, the child is defined both by chronological age and in relational terms, typically in relationship to a parent.[3]

Given the definitions above, the question here of what is a child seems rather simple to answer. However, it is not, as the following four differing definitions make clear.

Definition 1: A child is a category of individual from birth to age 18 who has age restrictions not placed on adults.

Thus, we all assume we know what a child is, but do we? For example, in the US an individual legally moves out of childhood into adulthood at the age of 16 for driving, at 18 for voting, and at 21 for drinking. This indicates differing legal definitions of adulthood based on functions. For legal purposes, the boundary between child and adult depends on the set age at

---

1. J.A.H. Murray (ed.), *The Compact Edition of the Oxford English Dictionary* (New York: Oxford University Press, 1971), p. 396.
2. Heather Montgomery, *An Introduction to Childhood: Anthropological Perspectives on Children's Lives* (Oxford: Wiley–Blackwell, 2008), p. 53.
3. A variant on the relational aspect would be the phrase 'a child of the sixties' in which the connection is not to a parent but to a period of time and the ideas associated with it.

which a child is deemed capable and responsible by society to be able to carry out particular behaviors thought to be appropriate for adults.[4]

Definition 2: A child is an individual based on developing psychological maturity and the ability to think rationally.

Apart from legal issues separating childhood from adulthood based on varying age categories, correlated with behaviors that are deemed to be adult activities, another system for categorizing childhood distinguishes the developmental stages of infancy, childhood, adolescence, and adulthood. In this case, there are no hard and fast markers to indicate passage from one phase of life to another, although there may be a general consensus that these phases are age-specific. Yet, they vary with the individual. Thus we should recognize that the dichotomy between child and adult is not always based on rigid boundaries between competence and incompetence.[5]

Definition 3: The UNCRC defines a child as a human being below the age of 18 (Article 1), 'unless under the law applicable to the child, majority [when a child is considered to be an adult] is attained earlier'.

The term 'child' appears to be applied unquestioningly as a chronological category defined by age according to the UNCRC. A primary assumption of the UNCRC, which relies on the Declaration of the Rights of the Child (adopted 1959), is that 'the child, by reason of his [*sic*] physical and mental immaturity, needs special safeguards and care, including appropriate legal protection, before as well as after birth' (Preamble). Through the lens of the UNCRC, childhood is constructed as a phase of life deserving of special protection and limited responsibility for personal actions, i.e., childhood is a specific stage of human development characterized, among other ways, as a

---

4. As will be discussed below, legal definitions are not absolute, however. If a girl below the age of eighteen is married is she a child based on her age or an adult based on her marital status as a social category?

5. According to Jeffrey Jensen Arnett ('Emerging Adulthood: A Theory of the Development from the Late Teens through the Twenties', *American Psychologist* 55 [2000], pp. 469-80), the social construction of childhood in Western industrialized societies now includes a phase of life which he labels 'emerging adulthood' that covers the years between the late teens and the mid-twenties. This is the phase of development, he argues, between adolescence and full adulthood. Full adulthood is characterized as completing school, leaving home, becoming financially independent, getting married, and having a child. Emerging adulthood, by contrast, is the developmental life span when individuals are not fully economically independent of their parents and are focused on self-exploration, with the result that they are postponing marriage and parenthood until their 30s. For further analysis of these issues, see, Jeffrey Jensen Arnett, *Emerging Adulthood: The Winding Road from Late Teens through the Twenties* (New York: Oxford University Press, 2004). On the challenges of life for emerging adults, see Christian Smith, Kari Christoffersen, Hilary Davidson and Patricia Snell Herzog, *Lost in Transition: The Dark Side of Emerging Adulthood* (New York: Oxford University Press, 2011).

period of dependency within the context of family or community. The UNCRC adds to our understanding of the social construction of childhood today by stressing the need for separate space for children to develop both physically and psychologically, through education and identity development and without economic responsibilities. Thus the UNCRC is consistent with the Oxford English Dictionary understanding of a child as defined by a specific chronological age category—typically someone below the age of 18 unless 'under the law applicable to the child, majority is attained earlier'.[6]

Yet the UNCRC is filled with caveats to accommodate the local laws of certain countries. Countries vary on the earliest allowable age for social categories such as marriage. Similarly, according to UNCRC Article 14, a child's 'freedom to manifest one's religion or beliefs may be subject only to such limitations as are prescribed by law and are necessary to protect public safety, order, health or morals, or to fundamental rights and freedoms of others'. The UNCRC emphasizes exactly how to serve 'the best interests of the child' (usually with a caveat as defined by local law, e.g., for many countries the law is to follow the religion of the father). Just as in the US it is difficult to find an answer to the question of what is a child, it is also difficult to answer this question for other times and places based on the UNCRC.

Definition 4: Another view of the child is in emotional terms based on cultural ideas of childhood as a time of innocence, purity, or entitlement that needs to be protected by parents, the surrounding culture, and the law.[7] For example, for some in the US, whom I label as contemporary idealists, the

---

6. For an analysis of the impact of the UNCRC on the global construction of childhood, see William E. Myers, 'The Right Rights? Child Labor in a Globalizing World', *Annals of the American Academy of Political and Social Science* 575 (2001), pp. 38-55.

7. According to sociologist Viviana Zelizer, *Pricing the Priceless Child: The Changing Social Value of Children* (Princeton, NJ: Princeton University Press, 1985), p. 171, the emotional importance of children is in inverse relationship to the economic value of children. In contemporary society, the value of children depends not on their ability to contribute to the family income but on their emotional importance to their parents, i.e., children are valued as cultural capital. She writes, 'While in the nineteenth century a child's capacity for labor had determined its exchange value, the market price of a twentieth century baby was set by smiles, dimples, and curls'. This perspective on children developed in the early twentieth century as children began being separated from the market economy and were equated with social and emotional value instead of economic value. On the other hand, the argument has been made that childhood innocence in the US existed in the post-industrial age but began to erode in the 1950s with the rise of the mass media, which turned children into consumers and exposed them to the horrors of adult life seen through television; for this perspective, see Neil Postman, *The Disappearance of Childhood* (New York: Vintage Books, 1982). Postman argues that these developments blurred the distinction between children and adults in the US with the result that there are three stages of life: infancy, adult-child, senility (p. 99).

properties of childhood include: (1) the fantasy that we in the US are a child-friendly society; and (2) the belief that the child is innocent and in need of protection from the adult world. The result is that childhood has become, for many, an overly sentimentalized and romanticized time of life. Given the broad range of definitions and myths of 'the child' in the contemporary West—legal, developmental, emotional—we have to avoid unjustifiably transposing contemporary sentiments of childhood, particularly romantic, mythical views of innocence, into universal claims. Thus, we must be aware of the myths of childhood that contemporary idealists in the US embrace:

> One is the myth of carefree childhood...[in which] we cling to a fantasy that once upon a time childhood and youth were years of free adventure, despite the fact that for most young people in the past, growing up was anything but easy.... [Another] myth is that childhood is the same for all children, a status transcending class, ethnicity, and gender. In fact, every aspect of childhood is shaped by class—as well as ethnicity, gender, geography, religion and historical era. We may think of childhood as a biological phenomenon, but it is better understood as a life stage whose contours are shaped by a particular place and time...[Another] myth is that the United States is a peculiarly child-friendly society, when in actuality Americans are deeply ambivalent about children. Adults envy young people their youth, vitality, and physical attractiveness. But they also resent children's intrusions on their resources and frequently fear their passions and drives. Many of the reforms that nominally have been designed to protect and assist the young were also instituted to insulate adults from children.[8]

But is it healthy and normal to create a separate sphere for children in order to protect childhood innocence from the realities of the adult world, and at the same time turn children in contemporary American society into active participants in a 'consumer society'? Probably not. To complicate matters, ideas in any society can rapidly change. To verify this, one only needs to reflect on the increased availability of explicit sexual images and changing attitudes on the harm they can cause when children are exposed to them.

However, contemporary views about the appropriateness of sheltering a child from the realities of adult life stand in sharp contrast to the perspectives on childhood expressed in the Hebrew Bible. There the child is not viewed as a protected category, unless one understands Abraham's comment to Isaac before his near sacrifice in Gen. 22.8—'God will provide'—as an expression of the adult assumption that a child will innocently and blindly trust whatever s/he is told by a parent. Is Isaac here innocent and carefree

---

8. Steven Mintz, *Huck's Raft: A History of American Childhood* (Cambridge, MA: Harvard University Press, 2004), pp. 2-3. In my examples of the manifestation of the myths of childhood, I formulate the value-laden issues regarding children from my social location in the US.

and now without concerns because his father has invoked trust in God? Or is he a mini-adult? Here one might also think of the circumstances in Judg. 11.31, the story of the vow of Jephthah to sacrifice whomever comes out of his house to greet him when he victoriously returns from battle against the Ammonites. This vow leads to the death of his virgin daughter. As is evidenced in this example, family interests, dictated by the father, control individual interests.[9] Moreover, there is the example of Abraham casting out Ishmael and leaving him with virtually nothing (Gen 21.14). Only the childhoods of Moses, Samuel, and David are described in any detail, and love of children, a perspective one might expect to find in the texts, is not frequently mentioned.[10]

Until recently, the historical shift in social scientific interest in issues regarding the construction of conceptualizations of children and childhood was not matched in the field of religion. Scholarly interest in children was largely neglected in the study of religion in general until the last ten years[11] and in biblical studies specifically.[12] Now that the spark of interest has been ignited, scholars of early Christianity, for example, have worked to fill the gap in our understanding of childhood in this time frame (c. 100–450 CE). In his monograph *When Children Became People*, historian of early Christianity O.M. Bakke remarks,

---

9. In the absence of a male head of the household, a female household head directs the 'children' as in the case of Naomi and her daughters-in-law, Ruth and Orpah, after the death of Elimelech and his sons (Ruth 1.8-18) and when Naomi and Ruth return to Bethlehem (Ruth 2–3).

10. One example of this love is 2 Sam. 13.21 regarding David's reaction to the rape of his daughter Tamar by his son Amnon, 'When King David heard of all these things, he became very angry, but he did nothing to harm his son Amnon, because he loved him, because he was his firstborn'. The MT lacks 'but he did nothing…because he was his firstborn', but the phrase is added here following the LXX. Of course, David totally disregards his daughter's rape in light of his love for his son.

11. Paula M. Cooey, 'Neither Seen nor Heard: The Absent Child in the Study of Religion', *Journal of Childhood and Religion* 1.1 (2010), pp. 1-31 (http://www.childhoodandreligion.com/JCR/Volume_1_(2010)_files/CooeyMarch2010.pdf). See n. 12 in the Introduction for examples of such recent scholarship.

12. However, the situation is changing. For example, three recent PhD dissertations explore issues regarding the child in biblical Israel and in the ancient Near East: Kristine Sue Henrikesen Garroway, 'The Construction of the 'Child' in the Ancient Near East: Towards an Understanding of the Legal and Social Status of Children in Biblical Israel and Surrounding Cultures' (PhD diss., Hebrew Union College, 2009); Julie Faith Parker, ' "Suffer the Little Children": A Child-Centered Exploration of the Elisha Cycle' (PhD diss., Yale University, 2009); and Laurel Koepf, '"Give me children or I shall die": Children and Communal Survival in Biblical Literature (PhD diss., Union Theological Seminary, 2012).

> It was customary in the classical period to follow Hippocrates, the father of medical science, in his division of the human lifespan into eight chronologically successive phases. The first three of these were (1) *paidion*, the small child (until the age of seven); (2) *pais*, the child (from seven to fourteen); and (3) *meirakion*, the young person (from fourteen to twenty).[13]

Thus, according to the work of Bakke, childhood for early Christians refers specifically to individuals from birth through age twenty. In this example, in answer to the question, 'What is a child in early Christianity?', we learn that the child is a chronological category; it is defined by phases of life with strict age boundaries. This is not the case in the Hebrew Bible because there are few references to a child's age; to cite a few examples, in Gen. 17.25 we learn that Ishmael was thirteen years old when he was circumcised, and in Gen. 21.4 we are informed that Isaac was circumcised when he was eight days old. Moreover, it would seem that in biblical Israel a newborn male is only counted as a member of his patrilineage when he is circumcised eight days after his birth (Gen 17.12; Lev 12.3). For females, the obvious biological marker, menstruation, is a marker of adulthood in some societies, although the onset of menstruation is variable and cannot be used as a strict chronological age for the passage from childhood to adulthood.

Finally, the significance and understanding of age and meaning of biological/physical immaturity as a stage of life vary from culture to culture. The result is that the understanding of the term 'child' is influenced by legal, psychological, and emotional connotations that shape the semantic range of this word in different cultural settings. Thus, a child is not only a distinct physical condition but a social construction. Even in cultures where age may have relevance, one cannot assume that birth marks the beginning of a child's life. Answers to the question of what is a child are contextual and are shaped by a cultural worldview determined by multiple factors such as gender and social class. Isaac and Ishmael have different experiences of childhood due to the relative statuses of their mothers in the household of Abraham. Further, the multiplicities of childhoods cross-culturally provide evidence that childhood is not always a distinct phase of life separate from adulthood across time and place. It is certainly not always a time of protection and innocence, as assumed through the ethnocentric lens of Western culture.[14]

---

13. O.M. Bakke, *When Children Became People: The Birth of Childhood in Early Christianity* (trans. Brian McNeil; Minneapolis: Fortress Press, 2005), p. 1. Although there are other studies of children in early Christianity, I confine the rest of my examples to the scholarly research on biblical Israel, in light of the focus of the present volume.

14. One place in the Hebrew Bible where this is clearly illustrated is Deut. 21.18, the case of the stubborn, rebellious son.

2. What Is a Child?

The Term 'Child': A Social Category

In contrast to the definitions of childhood that are constructed around chronological age, some cultures define childhood by what work or activities a child does. We can consider this 'social age'.[15] A child can be a liability in some cultures until s/he reaches the age of puberty, i.e., reproductive maturity, and is physically competent to perform some type of labor to contribute to the family income, at which time s/he is an economic asset. According to this understanding, a child is defined as someone whose place in the community to which s/he belongs is based on economic contribution. For example, until the late 1800s when child labor laws were first implemented in the US, children under the age of eleven worked in factories alongside adults and had none of the protections assumed for children today. The economic contributions of children shaped notions of childhood in such a way that at a young age individuals were already engaged in the labor force.[16] A child was defined by her/his economic utility.

Although it may offend some contemporary sensibilities to take a utilitarian perspective on childhood, study of foraging societies reveals the attitude that a child is a 'non-person' until s/he is old enough to labor for the family, at which point s/he becomes an economic asset and a 'person'. Regarding the Ache, a Paraguyan foraging society, we discover, 'The Ache are particularly direct in disposing of surplus children (approximately onefifth) because their foraging lifestyle places an enormous burden on the parents'.[17] The construction of childhood in this context is shaped by factors including contributions to the family's economic livelihood.

Let us take another example of the child as a social category. In his study of the Native American Navajo, James Chisholm argues that childhood is grounded in categories determined by social competency and the knowledge associated with it, rather than on age. According to his model, the first stage of childhood occurs when a child begins to exercise self-discipline, behavior

---

15. The term 'social age' was coined by Ann Solberg, a Norwegian sociologist, as a more flexible way to talk about the ideas and images associated with childhood than that of chronological age. Social age was intended as a term that would avoid the absolutes associated with chronological age in the construction of childhood and adulthood. See Ann Solberg, 'Negotiating Childhood: Changing Constructions of Age for Norwegian Children', in James and Prout (eds.), *Constructing and Reconstructing Childhood*, pp. 123-40.

16. For further discussion on this topic, see Stephanie Coontz, *The Way We Never Were* (New York: Basic Books, 1992). Of course, despite child labor laws, child slavery and child prostitution still occur today, but should be labeled as trafficking in children.

17. David F. Lancy, *The Anthropology of Childhood: Cherubs, Chattel, Changelings* (Cambridge: Cambridge University Press, 2008), p. 80.

that he says occurs between the ages of two and four.[18] His work and the other examples cited above make clear that it is problematic to assume that childhood is solely determined by chronological age boundaries. These examples challenge stereotypes of the child as a young dependent who does not contribute to the family's economic income. On the other hand, the work of Chisholm serves as a model for the new paradigm of the sociology of children advanced by Prout and James in the preceding chapter which investigates the unavoidability of culturally embedded constructions of childhood.

What Is Childhood? Emic and Etic Perspectives

> We know nothing of childhood: and with our mistaken notions the further we advance the further we go astray.[19]

As discussed above, conceptualizations of what is a child are culture-bound. My aim now is to explore the conflicting images of the child resulting from the transition from the biblical perspective of the child as a father's private economic asset to current images of the child as an individual with rights of his or her own. However, before using the term 'child' one must first inquire into whether it refers to chronological or social age. To do so takes us beyond the understanding of the child as someone who is simply biologically immature and may tell us more about the stereotypes of the researcher than about the culture under investigation.

Although the terms child and childhood are sometimes merged, I argue that the term child refers to a biologically immature being and that childhood is a culturally determined construction of the meaning assigned to the various developmental stages through which the child passes. Even the idea of an 'age of majority' is culturally dependent. We can imagine cultures where there is no 'age of majority'. According to the UNCRC, category markers can be ethnocentric and have been interpreted differently over time and place. Thus, categories based on age cannot be imposed on ancient Israelite society where we cannot be certain how age was determined. Moreover, the imposition of childhood onto all ages below 18 collapses age-related stages of life that might otherwise be separated (e.g., infant, toddler, adolescence, youth, etc.), and the idea that childhood is a distinct developmental phase of life separate from adulthood does not hold in all cultures. This is exactly what Ariès argues when he identifies children in pre-adult lives as 'small

---

18. James Chisholm, 'Learning "Respect for Everything": Navajo Images of Development', in *Images of Childhood* (ed. C. Philip Hwang, Michael E. Lamb and Irving E. Sigel; Hillsdale, NJ: Lawrence Erlbaum Associates, 1996), pp. 167-83.

19. Jean Jacques Rousseau, *Emile* (1762; trans. B. Foxley; New York: Dent, 1957), p. 1.

incompetent adults'. And yet not all children, i.e., those below a certain culturally determined age, are recognized as human cross-culturally. In some cases, children are 'human becomings'[20] and adulthood becomes an achieved status. In such situations, childhood is not defined universally by chronological age but by economic potential and social responsibility.

Having argued for the importance of understanding 'childhood' apart from number of years lived, my intent now is to provide a dialectical discourse between the past and the present on the construction of childhood in light of contemporary evidence. I will consider ideas and images from the present as a means to raise critical issues regarding childhood in the past. I will first explore contemporary viewpoints on childhood in society today, then I turn in the following chapters to the perspectives of Israelite culture itself.

The evidence for conflicting etic points of view[21] on notions of childhood has occasioned much recent interest in how individual societies construct childhood. The comments of Prout and James exemplify how modern social-scientific research investigates the conceptualization and organization of childhood:

> The immaturity of children is a biological fact of life but the ways in which the immaturity is understood and made meaningful is a fact of culture. It is these 'facts of culture' which may vary and which can be said to make childhood a social institution. It is in this sense, therefore, that one can talk of the social construction of childhood and also…of its re- and deconstruction.[22]

Put in other words, the sociology of childhood centers on both the child and concepts of childhood as central to membership in a society, rather than children as marginal or outsiders to the society maintained by adults. Looking back on past conceptualizations of childhood, anthropologist Heather Montgomery remarks, 'Childhood has been variously claimed as a nonexistent stage in the life-cycle, a time of incompetence and incompleteness, or the period in a person's life when he or she is without fault or flaw'.[23] Or, we can add, as in many traditions, children are not responsible for their promises and transgressions (i.e., their 'sins'). Thus, past analyses have been characterized by the unquestioned understanding of the term 'child' as different from the term 'adult'. In this study I analyze both terms because there is no precise universal boundary that separates children from adults; both categories are social constructions.[24]

    20. Montgomery, *An Introduction to Childhood*, p. 60.
    21. For background on this term, see Harris, Headland and Pike (eds.), *Emics and Etics: The Insider/Outsider Debate*.
    22. Prout and James, 'A New Paradigm for the Sociology of Childhood?', p. 7.
    23. Montgomery, *An Introduction to Childhood*, p. 50.
    24. We should not assume that all cultures have a notion of the child; see Nan A. Rothschild, 'Introduction', in Kamp (ed.), *Children in Prehistoric Puebloan Southwest*,

If we assume that children were important in biblical Israel, how do we understand the fact that they are not offered protection in the laws of the Hebrew Bible? As applied to the study of the child in the Hebrew Bible, this characterization of the history of childhood studies serves as a warning that scholars not mistake contemporary ideas about children for what are, in fact, culture-bound constructions. If one distorts the biblical material by interpreting it in ways that do not adequately address the original setting of ancient Israel, the value of sociological approaches is greatly diminished.

In research focused on children and childhood in antiquity, Sofaer Derevenski argues that childhood is a social category,[25] not a chronological one. Van Gennep,[26] like Ariès, understands childhood as a social construction and argues for culturally determined phases of childhood, e.g., infant, adolescent, etc., which are determined by biological markers of human development and the ability to assume membership in the community through increasing responsibilities. Yet biological markers are unequal to responsibility (capability) markers across individuals. Thus, the multiple meanings of childhood are reflected in the differing approaches and conclusions drawn in the analyses of those who study childhood.

In light of the conflicting issues raised above about children and childhood, it is necessary to raise the question: Is it possible that the contemporary idealization of childhood as a period of protected physical and emotional well-being, coupled with uncritical readings of biblical tradition, combine to and result in the imposition of contemporary stereotypes about childhood onto conceptualizations of children in the Hebrew Bible? Briefly, my answer to this question is yes.

Study of culture-bound concepts of childhood in the present, in comparison with those in antiquity, offers a mechanism for overcoming contemporary Western cultural biases that threaten to dominate and universalize modern scholarly characterization of the construction of childhood in biblical Israel. I highlight this relationship to contrast conceptualizations of childhood in antiquity and in the present in light of issues raised in the UNCRC and its concerns for 'the best interests of the child'.[27] I will demonstrate that

---

pp. 1-13 (40). Thus, Garroway's definition of a child as a NYA, 'not yet an adult', may overemphasize the child/adult dichotomy and the meaning of the progression of social development ('The Construction of the "Child"'). This does not mean that Ariès was correct when he argued that childhood was a medieval invention.

25. Sofaer Derevenski, 'Where are the Children?', p. 2.

26. Arnold van Gennep, *The Rites of Passage* (Chicago: University of Chicago Press, 1960).

27. Given the limitations of space and the social location of the author, it is only possible to address the circumstances of children in the US in what follows. I acknowledge that there are many other social constructs of childhood worldwide and encourage others to explore the application of the UNCRC in other global settings.

in the social construction of childhood in the Hebrew Bible, the biblical point of view of the child as object of parental/economic concerns contrasts with the contemporary point of view in the UNCRC of the child as an individual with personal rights whose well-being is paramount in society. By comparing ancient and contemporary perspectives on childhood with each other, I will make both the past and the present cases more clear.

As of 2013, only the US and Somalia have failed to sign the UNCRC, although many of the signers have added caveats.[28] The failure of the US to sign the document results from (1) fear among some Americans that the UNCRC will undermine parental sovereignty and (2) earlier concern regarding the preservation of individual states' rights. To this point, the UNCRC outlaws juvenile capital punishment (children are defined in Article 1 as those under 18 years of age except in those cases where 'under the law applicable to the child, majority is attained earlier'), which, up until 2005, was allowed in some states for certain 16 and 17 year olds.[29]

Fear that the UNCRC will undermine parental sovereignty in the US has made the document a rallying point for many critics of children's rights to individual independence. These individuals deny the applicability of the UNCRC to the US because it grants children rights to individual freedoms and argue that parental prerogatives take precedence over children's rights. In their own words, the intense controversy and opposition over parental supremacy is justified by the following criticisms:[30]

- Parents would no longer be able to administer reasonable spankings to their children.
- A murderer aged 17 years and 11 months and 29 days at the time of his crime could no longer be sentenced to life in prison.
- Children would have the ability to choose their own religion while parents would only have the authority to give their children advice about religion.
- The best interest of the child principle would give the government the ability to override every decision made by every parent if a government worker disagreed with the parent's decision.

---

28. The UNCRC has been ratified by 193 countries—some with individual reservations or interpretations of the document.

29. The US Supreme Court outlawed juvenile capital punishment in 2005. At that time there were 72 people on death rows who were juveniles when they committed their crimes. The Oyez Project, Roper v. Simmons, 543 U.S. 551 (2005) available at: http://oyez.org/cases/2000-2009/2004/2004_03_633/ (accessed 29 June 2012).

30 Http://www.parentalrights.org/index.asp?Type=B_BASIC&SEC='20 Things You Need to Know About the UN Convention on the Rights of the Child', http://www.parentalrights.org/index.asp?Type=B_BASIC&SEC={B56D7393-E583-4658-85E6-C1974B1A57F8} (accessed 29 June 2012).

- A child's 'right to be heard' would allow him (or her) to seek governmental review of every parental decision with which the child disagreed.
- According to existing interpretation, it would be illegal for a nation to spend more on national defense than it does on children's welfare.
- Children would acquire a legally enforceable right to leisure.
- Christian schools that refuse to teach 'alternative worldviews' and teach that Christianity is the only true religion 'fly in the face of article 29' of the treaty.[31]
- Allowing parents to opt their children out of sex education has been held to be out of compliance with the CRC.
- Children would have the right to reproductive health information and services, including abortions, without parental knowledge or consent.[32]

From the perspective of these UNCRC critics, the issues raised above are parent's prerogatives, rather than children's rights. The final choice in the above matters, argue these opponents, lies in the hands of parents. From the perspective of those who I would label as parental supremacists, children belong to their parents and the rights of parents to control their children are championed by these fierce critics of the UNCRC. For them, children should return to the status of property of their parents. Moreover, according to this argument, children are individuals who need protection from corrupting adult interests that lie outside the perspectives of the parents.[33] Thus,

---

31. Article 29 states, '1. States Parties agree that the education of the child shall be directed to: (a) The development of the child's personality, talents and mental and physical abilities to their fullest potential; (b) The development of respect for human rights and fundamental freedoms, and for the principles enshrined in the Charter of the United Nations; (c) The development of respect for the child's parents, his or her own cultural identity, language and values, for the national values of the country in which the child is living, the country from which he or she may originate, and for civilizations different from his or her own; (d) The preparation of the child for responsible life in a free society, in the spirit of understanding, peace, tolerance, equality of sexes, and friendship among all peoples, ethnic, national and religious groups and persons of indigenous origin; (e) The development of respect for the natural environment. 2. No part of the present article or article 28 shall be construed so as to interfere with the liberty of individuals and bodies to establish and direct educational institutions, subject always to the observance of the principle set forth in paragraph 1 of the present article and to the requirements that the education given in such institutions shall conform to such minimum standards as may be laid down by the State', http://www2.ohchr.org/english/law/crc.htm#art29 (accessed 1 October 2011).

32. Although critics of the UNCRC work to preserve the rights of parents to control their children, in situations of abortion they advocate for the rights of the fetus over the prerogatives of the biological mother.

33. This perspective on childhood as a time of innocence and purity that requires adult protection can be traced back to Rousseau (*Emile*), who characterized childhood as the 'sleep of reason'.

conflicting paradigms of childhood separate the UNCRC goals from those of parental supremacists in the US.

Parental supremacists fear that when the rights of children become a public concern, parents will lose their right to control their children. Such critics argue that children's rights should be determined within the private world of their parents' authority.[34] However, the control of the parent(s) is not absolute. There are norms and laws in the US which can cause children to be removed from the home and be put under the protection of the state.

Ultimately, the objections to the etic perspective of the UNCRC conceptualize contemporary children as objects not in need of further protection from the outside world aside from what their families can provide. They underline the tension between parental rights, and community responsibilities, and the broader world community. I would caution that it is important that adults be aware of whether they project their own desires onto their children and then mistake their own values and needs for the best interest of the child. Should we unilaterally assume that the parent is always the best judge of the interests of the child? My answer is no. The balance between parents' rights and community responsibility towards children is a delicate one. We must keep this in mind when we turn to our analysis of the interactions between parents and adults in the Hebrew Bible and investigate the motives for parental behavior.

Just as adults impose their perceptions of childhood on their understandings of the rights of children, so scholars impose their views of childhood on their study of the past. We must explore both the beginning and end of this phase of life with attention to a specific cultural context in order to investigate how childhood is constructed according to biological and social categories. It requires attention to 'a diverse set of cultural ideas'[35] about how cultures make sense of and organize human development into childhood.

The UNCRC, a consensus worldview with exceptions, adds to scholarly understanding of the social construction of childhood today by stressing the special needs of children. Thus, as noted earlier, according to the UNCRC,

---

34. For a response to these critics, see John Wall, 'Human Rights in Light of Childhood', *International Journal of Children's Rights* 16 (2008), pp. 523-43, and Michael Freeman, 'Why It Remains Important to Take Children's Rights Seriously', *International Journal of Children's Rights* 15 (2007), pp. 5-23. The subject of the child as citizen based on the UNCRC is the focus of a special issue of *Annals of the American Academy of Political and Social Science* 633 (2011) whose stated purpose is: 'Using the CRC as a starting point on the path of achieving functional citizenship for children, the distinguished contributors provide examples of empirical research on children's participation in social and political matters and offer recommendations for conceiving child citizenship in a multigenerational context in which the voice, opinions, and energies of children are included and integrated into society at large'.

35. Shanahan, 'Lost and Found', p. 408.

during childhood the individual is entitled to 'special care and assistance', i.e., 'the child, by reason of his [sic] physical and mental immaturity, needs special safeguards and care, including appropriate legal protection, before as well as after birth'.[36] The UNCRC repeatedly addresses how to serve 'the best interests of the child' given the issues raised about the social construction of childhood in it. However, the UNCRC universalizes childhood and fails to address the distinct culturally bound contexts for the construction of childhood. As Montgomery notes, quoting Esther Goody:

> Nevertheless, the ideal childhood, as conceptualized in much contemporary legislation and set out in the UNCRC, is seen as one where all children are shielded from the workplace and from the necessity to earn money to support a family. In reality, many children do work and are expected to be economically useful, contributing substantially to the household economy from an early age. Outside the West, however, children can still be seen as an economic investment with a specific return, whether this is that they should go to work as soon as they are able to contribute to the family, or whether, in the longer term, they are expected to look after parents in their old age, thereby guaranteeing a safety net for the elderly. The Gonja of West Africa state: 'In infancy your mother and father feed you and clear up your messes; when they grow old, you must feed them and keep them clean'.[37]

The discussion above reveals contested and conflicting constructions of childhood. The UNCRC does have a special category of children above the age of 15 who are allowed to participate in armed conflict, and many countries have raised objections to the caveats other countries have added to their ratifications.[38] All of this warns us of the unavoidability of culturally embedded constructions of childhood. As we address the topic of childhood in biblical Israel we must confront ancient Israelite culture-bound conceptualizations of children and childhood. Ancient Israel valued children as

---

36. UNCRC Preamble.
37. Montgomery, *An Introduction to Childhood*, p. 67. Montgomery is quoting Esther Goody, *Parenthood and Social Reproduction: Fostering and Occupational Roles in West Africa* (Cambridge: Cambridge University Press, 1982), p. 13.
38. E.g., 'The Principality of Andorra deplores the fact that the [said Convention] does not prohibit the use of children in armed conflicts. It also disagrees with the provisions of article 38, paragraphs 2 and 3, concerning the participation and recruitment of children from the age of 15.' Http://treaties.un.org/pages/ViewDetails.aspx? src=TREATY &mtdsg_no=IV-11&chapter=4&lang=en (accessed 27 March 2012). Similarly, there are countries that object to the UNCRC in so far as it conflicts with local religious law: 'The Syrian Arab Republic has reservations on the Convention's provisions which are not in conformity with the Syrian Arab legislations and with the Islamic Shariah's principles, in particular the content of article (14) related to the Right of the Child to the freedom of religion, and articles 20 and 21 concerning the adoption'. Http://treaties.un.org/pages/ViewDetails.aspx?src=TREATY&mtdsg_no=IV-11&chapter=4&lang=en (accessed 27 March 2012).

individuals who continued the lineage systems that made up the community, but it did not regard childhood as a romanticized life stage.

The grand perspectives on the conceptualization of childhood analyzed above are ultimately grounded in the implications of language. At this point I shift from a study of the English terminology for children and its connotations to the Hebrew of the Bible. The most frequently used Hebrew nouns for children are *na'ar* (נער) and *yeled* (ילד). In the next chapter, I will discuss the conceptualizations of childhood revealed by these nouns.

Chapter 3

WORDS FOR CHILDREN IN THE HEBREW BIBLE

As I seek to translate into English the range of semantic meanings expressed by Hebrew terms for children, or any Hebrew terms, I am aware that English may lack the nuances intended by the original Hebrew usage of these words. Moreover, I recognize that the range of meanings intended by a term may have shifted over the course of the approximately one thousand years of literature gathered together in the Hebrew Bible. As cultural anthropologist and linguist Edward Sapir states, 'Distinctions which seem inevitable to us may be utterly ignored in languages which reflect an entirely different culture, while these in turn insist on distinctions which are all but unintelligible to us'.[1]

Thus, it must be stated at the start that the Hebrew terminology for 'the child', either *na'ar* or *yeled*, does not suggest a semantic pattern of meaning that yields information of childhood as an age category, although both terms can be used as independent nouns and in the context of a family relationship. Childhood appears to be a developmental phase that stretches over wide chronological boundaries that seem to end when the child becomes a parent. Whatever else may be said, these Hebrew terms reveal a socially constructed category that defies chronological age limits and refers to social age as defined by an ability to fulfill societal expectations of production and reproduction. However, to argue that a child is 'not-yet-adult'[2] requires clarification of norms of behavior for adults in ancient Israel, i.e., what is required to achieve the social category of adulthood.

There are many Hebrew nouns used to refer to the young.[3] The most common Hebrew terms in order of frequency of occurrence are:

---

1. Edward Sapir, *Selected Writings in Languages, Culture, and Personality* (ed. David G. Mandelbaum; Berkeley: University of California Press, 1985), p. 27.
2. Garroway, 'The Construction of "Child" in the Ancient Near East'.
3. The terms 'son' (*bēn*) and 'daughter' (*bat*) are kinship terms, in addition to (sometimes) indicating the youth. The former occurs in the Hebrew Bible over 4,850 times, and the latter occurs 585 times. In view of the number of times these words occur, I do not study them in this chapter. However, I will explore usages of the noun *bēn* in my analysis

3. Words for Children in the Hebrew Bible

na'ar	'young boy/servant'	239 occurrences
na'arâ	'young girl/maidservant'	62 occurrences
yeled	'child, boy'	90 occurrences
yaldâ	'girl'	3 occurrences
baḥûr	'young man'	45 occurrences
bĕtûlâ	'a pubescent young woman who has not yet borne a child'	51 occurrences
ṭap	'children'	42 occurrences
'ôlāl[4]	'infant'	20 occurrences
yōnēq	'nursing infant'	9 occurrences
'almâ	'girl, young woman'	7 occurrences
'elem	'boy, youth'	2 occurrences
'ăwîl	'nursing child'	2 occurrences
gamûl	'weaned child'	2 occurrences

Several of the words listed above for children will be discussed in Chapter 5 in the context of phases of the Israelite life cycle, where the evidence will suggest that phases of childhood are grouped together around certain Hebrew terms indicating physical dependency and development. However, there is no clear semantic pattern connecting Hebrew terminology for children, particularly when one focuses on the Hebrew terms most often translated as 'child', i.e., *na'ar* (נער) and *yeled* (ילד). Because many of the words listed are primarily confined to limited phases of a child's life, in order to expand our understanding of how biblical Israel conceptualized the child, we will focus this chapter on studying the most prevalent terms *na'ar* and *yeled*. The perspective maintained in this analysis privileges the biblical context for the use of a term over its appearance in cognate ancient Near Eastern languages; philology is not enough to determine the contextual meaning of these terms in ancient Israel. The understanding of 'the child' in the Hebrew Bible derives from the context of the biblical texts themselves; thus, this work will utilize etymological study but will ultimately emphasize context over cognates.[5]

As we examine the terms *na'ar* and *yeled*, we are faced with the problem of how to translate the Israelite experience and understanding of childhood into the terminology of the English language. It is important to recognize

---

of Gen. 21. For more on *bēn*, see *TDOT*, II, pp. 145-59; *HALOT*, I, pp. 137-38; on *bat*, see *TDOT*, II, pp. 332-38; *HALOT*, I, pp. 165-66.

4. *'ōlēl* and *'ûl*, 'to nurse' are associated with this verbal stem.

5. 'The main point is that the etymology of a word is not a statement about its meaning but about its history; it is only as a historical statement that it can be responsibly asserted, and it is quite wrong to suppose that the etymology of a word is necessarily a guide either to its "proper" meaning in a later period or to its actual meaning in that period' (James Barr, *The Semantics of Biblical Language* [Oxford: Oxford University Press, 1961], p. 109).

that the Hebrew terminology for children may be simple but the meaning behind the usage of the terms may be much more complex. We are seeking the patterns through the usage of words that reveal categories from biblical Israelite thought—not modern Western ethnocentric ideas of who or what a child should be. My aim is to discover the patterns behind the two most frequently used Hebrew words translated as the terms for child. Are the nouns *na'ar* and *yeled* words that can be both independent nouns and ones that express the relational aspect communicated through the English usage of the word 'child'? Do they refer to human beings below the age of a legal majority as defined by ancient Israel? In other words, how do we translate the foreign, ancient Israelite terminology for children into the contemporary worldview, or is it appropriate to rely on contemporary definitions of the child when thinking about children in biblical Israel?

Na'ar

The Hebrew term *na'ar* and its feminine equivalent *na'arâ* are the words most frequently translated by the English terms 'boy' and 'girl'.[6] The masculine noun appears 239 times, and there are 61 occurrences of the female noun. Although these words have been the object of much past scholarly investigation, there is no consensus on what the biblical authors actually meant when they used these nouns. For example, the terms have been understood to refer to those who are unmarried and therefore under the authority of the *pater familias*, high-born individuals, servants, and, most recently, to those sent away from their fathers' houses. Thus, the terms are not clearly distinguished by past investigations into their meaning.[7]

However, there is a history of scholarship focused on the meaning of these terms. The first significant full length study of the term *na'ar* was undertaken by Hans-Peter Stähli whose dissertation explored the etymology of the noun in cognate Semitic languages and in its contextualized occurrences in the Hebrew Bible. Stähli argues that the noun *na'ar* is used in two differing

---

6. Scholars agree that the cognates in this case are of little help in getting at the English word that captures the meaning of the Hebrew term. For a discussion of the evidence, see Carolyn S. Leeb, *Away from the Father's House: The Social Location of the na'ar and na'arah in Ancient Israel* (JSOTSup, 301; Sheffield: Sheffield Academic Press, 2000), pp. 13-14.

7. Linguistic analysis with attention to cognates from surrounding cultures has limited function for shedding light on the contested meaning of *na'ar*. The term has too few occurrences in Ugaritic. On the term *na'ar* in Ugaritic, see B. Cutler and John MacDonald, 'Identification of the *Na'ar* in the Ugaritic Texts', *UF* 8 (1976), pp. 27-35. In light of the lack of help from Northwest Semitic languages in understanding the meaning of this term, the focus in this study is on the social location of the individuals identified by the terms *na'ar* and *na'arâ*.

semantic ranges: (1) to refer to dependent individuals; and (2) to refer to a servant. For Stähli, particularly in the case of males, the term *na'ar* refers to those who are unmarried and therefore under the authority of the *pater familias*, i.e., they are not yet the head of a family household. What unites the two definitions offered by Stähli is that both have meanings referring to a position of dependency.[8] The circumstances, and hence the status of being a *na'ar*, for a male, terminate upon marriage. The material surveyed by Stähli leads him to conclude that the noun *na'ar* has more to do with social location than it does with age.

The next significant work on the term *na'ar* was carried out by John MacDonald, whose interpretation of the meaning of the noun coincides with Stähli's interpretation that the word transcended age divisions while providing an alternative definition. MacDonald's assessment of the occurrences of the noun *na'ar* convinced him that the term referred to 'high-born' individuals and he translated the masculine form *na'ar* as 'squire' and the feminine *na'arâ* as 'lady-in-waiting'.[9] Thus, the social position of the *na'ar* as seen by Stähli stands in direct contrast to that of MacDonald; the two scholars locate the *na'ar* at opposite ends of the spectrum of social status. Despite their lack of agreement in understanding the semantic range of the term *na'ar*, the two scholars concur that *na'ar* is a term that reflects economic realities and it is not a noun that specifies age or a phase in the life cycle of an individual.

Lawrence Stager has also addressed the semantic range of the occurrences of the *na'ar* in the Hebrew Bible as he worked to integrate archaeological data with biblical material in order to understand family life in early Israel. Stager's interpretation of the noun *na'ar* relies on the work of Stähli and MacDonald; Stager, like the two scholars before him, assesses the social location of the *na'ar* in economic circumstances. Stager evaluates the position of the *na'ar* as:

> firstborn males waiting for the *pater familias* to 'pass on' or of younger sons who had difficulties establishing themselves as heads of household, with sufficient land and wealth. In ancient Israel, as in medieval Europe and many other countries, this 'safety valve' for young, unmarried males involved careers in the military, government, or priesthood.[10]

---

8. Hans-Peter Stähli, *Knabe-Jüngling-Knecht: Untersuchungen zum Begriff na'ar im Alten Testament* (Beiträge zur biblischen Exegese und Theologie, 7; Frankfurt: Peter Lang, 1978). According to his view, women, even after marriage, remain *na'arôt*, i.e., in a position of dependency upon the male head of the family, because of the hierarchical status of men over women in Israelite society.

9. John MacDonald, 'The Status and Role of the *Na'ar* in Israelite Society', *JNES* 35 (1976), pp. 147-70.

10. Lawrence E. Stager, 'The Archaeology of the Family in Ancient Israel', *BASOR* 260 (1985), pp. 1-35 (25).

Thus, the *na'ar*, according to Stager, is an ascribed status based on circumstances of being forced to seek employment or occupation outside the self-supporting family mode of economic existence; the noun refers to individuals whose professional livelihood is occasioned by limited family resources.[11] Like Stähli and MacDonald before him, Stager rejects assigning chronological age limits to the *na'ar*. The word defines a social status, not an age category. According to Stager, *zāqēn*, which typically is understood to mean 'old person', also does not simply convey an age designation but instead is a status term for a male who has become head of a household. Thus, a *na'ar* can be older than a *zāqēn* if the latter has become head of the household and the former has not. Both word are indicators of social location—not chronological age.[12]

More recently, Carolyn Leeb returns to the theories discussed above regarding the meaning of the nouns *na'ar* and *na'arâ* and offers a fresh new analysis that addresses the problem of scholars understanding the term differently. Her conclusions contradict the arguments of prior scholarship. She writes:

> the common social location that these characters all share is neither age nor marital status nor 'social class' (i.e. 'high-born' or noble). Their function or role is not always as a servant, whether domestic, military, agricultural or governmental. Rather, what these characters share is the situation of being 'away from their father's house', beyond the protection and control of their fathers, while not yet master or mistress of their own households.[13]

Although Leeb's sense of the *na'ar* and *na'arâ* is closer to the meaning of the terms as understood by Stähli, in the end she distinguishes her analysis from his by arguing that the noun should have one singular social connotation. She specifically critiques Stähli because 'he fails to discover the common thread that links these two different uses of the word (servant and unmarried male), nor does he offer any explanation of the fact that some biblical authors use the word with both meanings in close proximity in the texts'.[14]

Recent discussions criticize Leeb's work specifically because it concludes that all individuals identified as *na'ar* and *na'arâ* belong to the same social location.[15] One such scholar is Milton Eng who negatively reviews Leeb's

---

11. Stager, 'The Archaeology of the Family in Ancient Israel', p. 26.
12. Stager, 'The Archaeology of the Family in Ancient Israel', p. 26.
13. Leeb, *Away from the Father's House*, p. 41.
14. Leeb, *Away from the Father's House*, p. 16.
15. See, e.g., Mayer I. Gruber, 'Review of Carolyn S. Leeb, *Away from the Father's House: The Social Location of the na'ar and na'arah in Ancient Israel*', *JQR* 43 (2003), p. 615. Strawn looks at the term *na'ar* in only one text and therefore his interpretation must be generalized through study of more biblical data in order to be useful in

3. Words for Children in the Hebrew Bible   31

conclusions. Eng argues for multiple meanings of the terms *na'ar* and *na'ará*. His study supports the earlier scholarly argument that the noun often refers to a servant or an attendant. However, the primary interest of his research is in the phases of the life cycle intended by the term, so the emphasis in his study leads him to focus on *na'ar* and *na'ará* as nouns that communicate—among other connotations—an age range. For him the semantic pattern of the noun *'na'ar* usually means "a male young person between the ages of weaning and marriage or adulthood"'.[16] As we will see in Chapter 5, the age range of the life cycle phase of childhood, according to him, is three–thirteen: from the time of weaning to the beginning of puberty.[17] Moreover, he maintains, 'נער *does* describe a *Lebensphase* (*pace* Stähli and others) and in particular that stage of life between infancy and full adulthood incorporating the modern categories of childhood, adolescence and early adulthood'.[18] Thus, the term is equivalent to the life cycle phase today identified as that of 'a minor'.

I suggest that each of these attempts to understand the semantic range of the terms *na'ar* and *na'ará* is not without its problems. Each of the scholars discussed above attempts to confine the definition of these terms to a limited setting or social circumstance. Although in some contexts a *na'ar* and *na'ará* may refer to a phase of life, the age range Eng argues for cannot be correct: the noun is used in Judg. 13.5-12 (vv. 5, 7, 8, 12) to refer to the unborn child of the wife of Manoah,[19] and earlier in the Hebrew Bible it is applied to the infant (as yet unnamed) Moses (Exod. 2.6) as well as to both Shechem and Dinah, persons of marriageable age in Genesis 34 (who might also be identified as unmarried individuals of elevated status). Age cannot be the determinative factor in the choice of this term when it appears in the texts.[20] Further study is required to resolve questions of the semantic pattern

---

understanding the occurrence of the term in other texts; see Brent A. Strawn, 'Jeremiah's In/Effective Plea: Another Look at נער in Jeremiah 1:6', *VT* 55 (2005), pp. 366-77.

16. Milton Eng, *The Days of our Years: A Lexical Semantic Study of the Life Cycle in Biblical Israel* (New York: T. & T. Clark, 2011), p. 80.

17. Contrary to Eng's argument, when Joseph is sold into slavery he is described as a *na'ar* and he is 17 years old (Gen. 37.2).

18. Eng, *The Days of our Years*, pp. 80-81.

19. Although in Judg. 13.5-12, the unborn child of the wife of Manoah is called a *na'ar*, in Exod. 21.22 the masculine plural *yĕlādîm* is used for an unborn child. In the later case, the term occurs with a feminine singular possessive suffix, *yĕladêhā*.

20. In Solomon's dream at Gibeon (1 Kgs 3.4-15) he refers to himself as a נער קטן. This statement appears to be a reflection of his humility and submission to the authority of God from the Deuteronomistic historian and does not allow us to know his precise age at the time he ascended to the throne. Although Solomon was coregent with David for several years before becoming the sole monarch, his actual age at this time is unclear from the biblical text, but the evidence suggests he was in his teens at this time,

of the usage of the masculine and feminine forms of these nouns. To say more about these terms, we will study them in later chapters as they appear in their various biblical contexts.

Yeled

The second Hebrew noun most frequently translated as 'child' is the term *yeled*. The root of the noun *yeled* appears frequently in languages cognate to Hebrew, e.g., Akkadian *walādu;* Arabic and Ethiopic *walada*. In all three languages, there is little variation in its basic meaning 'child' in its nominal form and 'to bring forth (children)' in its verbal attestations.[21] The root *yld* also occurs in Ugaritic, where in all of its 40 occurrences it means 'to bear' or 'to beget' in the causative stem.[22] Thus, study of the etymology of *yeled* in cognate languages supports the traditional translation of the term, but does little to help modern scholarship understand the semantic patterns of the use of the noun in its nominal occurrences in the Hebrew Bible.

The noun 'male child' *yeled* (masculine singular) and *yĕlādîm* (masculine plural), occurs 90 times in the Hebrew Bible.[23] The masculine singular appears 43 times: six times it is an indefinite noun, and 37 times it appears with the definite article. Of the 47 occurrences in the masculine plural, *yĕlādîm* appears six times without the definite article, 20 times with the definite article, and the remaining occurrences are either in a construct form or with a pronominal suffix.[24]

---

and not a child. This conclusion is based on the statements that Solomon reigned in Jerusalem for 40 years before he died (this may be a typological biblical number intended to signal a generation and to match the years that his father David reigned; 1 Kgs 11.42; 2 Chron. 9.30) and that his son Rehoboam was 42 years old when he became king (1 Kgs 14.21; 2 Chron. 12.13). The retelling of Solomon's experiences at Gibeon in 2 Chron. 1.1-15 omits the reference to Solomon as a נער קטן. I conclude that this text does not provide evidence that the term נער refers to chronological age. For further discussion on these issues, see John Gray, *I & II Kings: A Commentary* (OTL; Philadelphia: Westminster Press, 1963), pp. 121-22.

21. *TDOT*, VI, p. 76.
22. *TDOT*, VI, p. 78.
23. The number count is based on *BHS* with Westminster Hebrew Morphology (*BHS*-W4) as found in Accordance. According to Eng, there are 89 occurrences of *yeled* (*The Days of our Years*, p. 58). Ellen van Wolde in *Reframing Biblical Studies: When Language and Text Meet Culture, Cognition, and Context* (Winona Lake, IN: Eisenbrauns, 2009), p. 125 reports 88 occurrences. Neither scholar specifies the manuscript tradition that serves as the basis for these number counts.
24. The number count is based on *BHS* with Westminster Hebrew Morphology (*BHS*-W4).

The feminine singular form *yaldâ* occurs twice and the feminine plural *yĕlādôt* appears once. The two occurrences of the feminine singular noun, Gen. 34.4 and Joel 4.3, appear with the definite article; in Gen. 34.4, the noun is used with a demonstrative label. The lone feminine plural occurrence, Zech. 8.5, is without the definite article.

According to BDB, *yeled* refers to a child, son, boy or youth, and *yaldâ* translates as girl or damsel, but in the case of Dinah in Gen. 34.4, it means a girl of marriageable age. For the plural in Exod. 21.22, BDB gives the definition of offspring.[25] In short, the nouns are typically translated as 'boy' and 'girl', but since both of these English words are generally understood to apply to youth, the Hebrew terms *yeled* and *yaldâ* have over time been understood to simply mean 'child'.[26]

The nominal occurrences of *yeled* (in all grammatical categories of number and gender) are widespread throughout the Hebrew Bible and do not cluster in any particular literary genre,[27] although nearly half of the occurrences of the masculine—in either the singular or the plural—are in Genesis (19 occurrences), Exodus (12 occurrences), and 2 Samuel (12 occurrences). Most occurrences of the masculine noun *yeled* appear in narrative texts rather than in poetic material, but two of the three occurrences of the feminine *yaldâ/yĕlādôt* are in prophetic material, in Joel 4.3 and Zech. 8.5. The social locations of the individuals identified by these terms vary widely in the texts.

In accordance with the principles of Hebrew grammar, all the occurrences of the noun types from *yeled* are both number and gender specific. The grammatical gender of the nouns corresponds directly with the biological gender of the child, i.e., *yeled* refers to a boy child (e.g., Gen 21.8). However, in further accordance with Hebrew grammar, the masculine plural form *yĕlādîm* refers not only to a group of exclusively male children (Gen. 32.23) but functions as a generic plural to include children of both sexes (e.g., Exod 21.4). In Exod. 21.22, the form *yĕlādîm* is used to refer to the fetus in a case of miscarriage, and it is impossible to determine whether the number and gender of the Hebrew term carry significance with regards to the biological gender and number of the fetuses.

The masculine forms *yeled/yĕlādîm* represent a wide age spectrum: from an unborn child—whether a fetus or a premature birth (Exod. 21.22)[28]—to newborns (Exod. 1.17, 18), to a child at the age of weaning (Gen. 21.8), to

---

25. BDB, p. 409.
26. See also *TDOT*, VI, pp. 76-81; *THAT*, I, pp. 732-36; and *TWOT*, I, pp. 378-80.
27. The related noun *yaldût*, 'childhood', appears three times: Ps. 110.3 (with a pronominal suffix) and Eccl. 11.9-10.
28. The precise meaning of the term in Exod. 21.22 will be addressed in Chapter 8. The term *'āsôn* in the Hebrew text refers to the woman but in the LXX the text reads *exeikonismenon [paidon]* and refers to 'the fully formed [child]'.

an age appropriate for a member of a body of advisors in the court of Rehoboam (1 Kgs 12.8, 10, 14//2 Chron. 10.8, 10, 14). In the latter example, the term *yĕlādîm* is usually translated as 'young men', although the age category supposedly intended by the use of the term in this context is not immediately evident.[29] Revell writes:

> The use of the term 'child' in 1K 12:8, of those whom the king preferred as advisers, can be seen as suggesting their intimacy with the king as the reason for his preference. They are 'the children (his childhood playmates) who had grown up with him, who were those who stood before him' (הילדים אשר גדלו אתו אשר העמדים לפניו). Since the basic meaning of the word 'child' relates the person designated to his parents, these younger advisers are also pictured as still living with their parents, and so lacking experience of the world, and of decision-making.[30]

Revell argues that the word *yeled* has no age specifications and that in ancient Israel—as today—an individual is still someone else's child no matter how old s/he is.[31]

Furthermore, four additional occurrences of the masculine plural *yĕlādîm* refer to Daniel and his friends who, like the advisers to Rehoboam, also serve in a court context[32] and appear to have the maturity to know the rules of Jewish life and observation. The cumulative evidence therefore suggests that the masculine forms *yeled/yĕlādîm* defy strict chronological age categories. The terms actually appear to mean, both in the examples of Rehoboam and Daniel, 'of his generation'. Thus, caution should be exercised in interpreting the semantic range of the term *yeled*, similar to *na'ar*, solely on the basis of age.

One may contend in addressing the semantic pattern for *yeled* that in some cases nouns derived from the term *yeled* refer not to chronological age but to the status of being unmarried; here one thinks of the feminine *yaldâ* used to refer to Dinah in Gen. 34.4. However, in Ruth 1.5, the noun *yĕlādîm* is applied to Mahlon and Chilion, who are married at the point in the narrative when the term occurs; at least in this example, it cannot be intended as a

---

29. The individuals referred to in this case can hardly be children. Based on Sumerian data, Malamat has argued that the term, in this passage, is a technical one referring to military advisors within the court of King Rehoboam. The example sets up a contrast between the 'young men' and *zĕqēnîm*, 'the elders' (1 Kgs 12.8). For more on understanding *yĕlādîm* as military advisors, see Abraham Malamat, 'Kingship and Council in Israel and Sumer: A Parallel', *JNES* 22 (1963), pp. 247-53. Against this interpretation, see Geoffrey Evans, 'Rehoboam's Advisers at Shechem, and Political Institutions in Israel and Sumer', *JNES* 25 (1966), pp. 273-79.

30. E. J. Revell, *The Designation of the Individual: Expressive Usage in Biblical Narrative* (Kampen: Kok, 1996), p. 30.

31. Revell, *The Designation of the Individual*, p. 30.

32. Dan. 1.4, 10, 15, 17.

noun for unmarried individuals. However, I suggest that we may use certain narratives to examine the idea that in some texts one is a *yeled/yaldâ*, a child, until one has borne or fathered a child of one's own. This appears to be the case in instances when the nouns occur with the definite article or with a pronominal suffix. Thus, the distinction between child and adult as categories of social status comes through childbearing—and not only for women. If this is accurate, Mahlon and Chilion are still children, just as the Hebrew specifies (Ruth 1.5, 'her children'), because they die before fathering sons to carry on their father's name. A man cannot take his place in his patrilineage until he has fathered a child to carry on the patrilineage.[33]

The six occurrences of the masculine singular without the definite article do not include a relational point of reference.[34] The masculine singular is used in construct in Gen. 44.20. In this case, the masculine singular *yeled* is used in reference to Benjamin, who is identified with regards to Jacob as 'a child of old age'. Otherwise, 'whenever reference is made to a child in relation to its parents, the term בן *bēn* with a pronominal suffix is used instead of *yeled*'.[35] Thus, the evidence indicates that masculine singular *yeled* is not a relational term with the semantic range comparable to the relational dimension of the English word 'child'. Rather, it is an independent noun. *Yeled*, in the singular without a definite article, refers to a male child (age unspecified) and, with the exception of Gen. 44.20, does not translate in the masculine singular as 'child of...someone'.

The 37 occurrences of *yeled* preceded by the definite article refer to a specific male child. According to van Wolde, the context in which the term is used reveals that:

> It is...rarely located in contexts of play, joy, or whatever might be deemed cheerful in life, as it might be in English discourses, but quite often in the context of life and death. Thus, the epistemic grounding of this nominal becomes visible: in a time and place where the struggle for life and death is daily fought and of which a child is often the victim, the experience of the death of a child is much more common than in modern Western society. The

---

33. However, adding to the ambiguity regarding the meaning of the term is the use of masculine forms to apply not only to human beings but to animals as well: cow and bear (Isa. 11.7), raven (Job 38.41), and the hind and mountain goat (39.3).

34. The six occurrences are Gen. 4.23; 44.20; 2 Sam. 6.23; Isa. 9.5; Jer. 31.20; Qoh. 4.13.

35. Van Wolde, *Reframing Biblical Studies*, p. 126. See, e.g., 1 Kgs 17.17-24 and the pattern of the usage of 'the child' versus 'her son' or 'your son'. However, in Isa. 9.5, in reference to the royal child, *yeled* is used in synonymous parallelism with *bēn*. Neither term appears with a pronominal suffix although in both the A colon and the B colon of the first line, the pronoun 'to us' is used. However, the pronoun does not signify a biological relationship, 'A child (*yeled*) has been born to us, a son (*bēn*) has been given to us'. Cf. Ps. 2.7.

instances of the nominal *hayyeled* in the Hebrew Bible offer glimpses of these life-threatening circumstances and testify to these epistemic grounds.[36]

On the other hand, Eng argues that for the masculine singular, the term '*yeled* is a more specific kinship term which refers to "an *immediate* (male) offspring"'.[37] Thus, for him it refers to a son but not a grandson. Eng also maintains that the term should be situated at the beginning of the phase of the life cycle; for him *yeled* refers to an infant. He interprets the *yeled* to be the life cycle phase prior to being a *na'ar*[38] and makes these terms relational in terms of a child's age.[39]

One example that supports Eng's theory that *yeled* refers to a male infant is the story of the two prostitutes who come to Solomon (1 Kgs 3.16-28) and ask him to render a decision on the dispute between them. The circumstances of the case are that the two women live in the same house and in relative time proximity to each other, each woman has given birth to a son. However, only one of the sons has survived, and the two women disagree about who is the child's real mother. Solomon's 'wisdom'[40] leads him to the verdict that the surviving child should be cut in half, so that each of the two women can have a share of him. Ultimately this ruse reveals who the mother of the child really is—the woman who would rather give him up than have him killed. In this text, *yeled* undoubtedly means a baby.

The term kinship *bēn* occurs repeatedly in 1 Kgs 3.16-28 to refer to the sons borne by the two women. However, in v. 25, Solomon refers to the child as *hayyeled*, and in v. 26 the mother of the surviving baby refers to her son as *hayyālûd* (a passive participle of *yld*; literally 'the borne one', but probably best translated 'the living child'), and Solomon uses the same passive participle in v. 27. In this example, the terms *yeled* and *hayyālûd* refer to an infant, as Eng argues, possibly even a newborn baby.

In addition to the 43 singular occurrences of *yeled*, there are 47 occurrences of the masculine plural *yĕlādîm* in the Hebrew Bible. These occurrences provide the context for understanding the child in relationship to a

---

36. Van Wolde, *Reframing Biblical Studies*, pp. 126-27.
37. Eng, *The Days of our Years*, p. 88.
38. Eng, *The Days of our Years*, p. 88. This makes sense with the example of Isaac who is identified as a *yeled* at the time that he is weaned (Gen. 21.8); however, after Samuel is weaned he is a *na'ar* (1 Sam. 1.24).
39. He argues that the semantic range of the term may have shifted over the course of time.
40. Only 9 verses earlier (1 Kgs 3.7) Solomon referred to himself as a *na'ar*, i.e., someone too inexperienced to be king and prayed for the wisdom required to carry out the job. The story of how he handled the case of the child contested by the two prostitutes may be intended to illustrate that he has moved beyond being a *na'ar* to become qualified as king.

parental, familial, or group context. The term in the plural can refer to either a group of young males or to a mixed group of males and females. Most occurrences in the masculine plural are either with the definite article or with a pronominal suffix. With the use of the pronominal suffix, the child is placed in a relational status. This relational status is also expressed when the plural noun is in a construct form. In the case of Exod. 2.6, the construct relates the male child *yeled* (later identified as Moses) not to parents but to the children of the Hebrew people. Thus, the masculine plural *yĕlādîm* is both an age category and a relational term. It is the Hebrew term that expresses the inclusion of a child in a parental/familial relationship. On the other hand, the masculine plural *yĕlādîm* in the 'agent-position' can express the possibility of childhood pleasure: Neh. 14.23 (children who rejoice) and Zech. 8.4-5 (children who play).[41] The conclusion from this data is that the plural *yĕlādîm* can be both a relational noun and an independent noun and covers a different semantic range than the singular *yeled* does.

We shift now to the three feminine nouns derived from *yeled*. As noted above, in the singular, *yaldâ* is used to refer to a girl of marriageable age (Gen. 34.4). In Gen. 34.4 the term is also used with the definite article as well as with a demonstrative particle and then again to specify Dinah as 'this (girl) child'. The occurrence of the definite article and the demonstrative particle leads van Wolde to conclude that this is an irregular occurrence of *yaldâ*[42] and to argue that Dinah is referred to by Shechem as an independent individual, i.e., without reference to her as either Jacob's daughter (Gen. 34.3a, 5, 7), as Leah's daughter (Gen. 34.1), or as someone's sister (Gen. 34.13, 14, 17, 27; and 25, 31—referring specifically to Simeon and Levi). The feminine nouns *na'ărâ* (girl, female) and *yaldâ* are paired together in Gen. 34.3-4 in reference to Dinah.[43] As has already been mentioned above, *yaldâ* in this case appears with both the definite article and a demonstrative pronoun, 'this (girl) child'. The former word applied to Dinah comes from the narrator, who clearly understands Dinah in a daughter/parent dependent capacity. In contrast, Shechem conceives of Dinah as an independent young female (indicating age and gender) without relational ties when he calls her a *yaldâ*. He thinks of her as a young woman, independent of family ties. Yet a *na'ar* in the absolute does not indicate the relational dimension inherent in *na'ărâ*.

The other occurrence of the feminine singular *yaldâ* is in Joel 4.3. Here the noun also has the definite article in front of it and occurs parallel to *hayyeled*, suggesting that in this text neither term refers to specific individuals. This example does not refer to a specific individual—unlike the

41. Van Wolde, *Reframing Biblical Studies*, p. 127.
42. Van Wolde, *Reframing Biblical Studies*, p. 129.
43. *Na'ărâ* occurs twice in v. 3, and *yaldâ* occurs once in v. 4.

example of Dinah—and neither occurrence of the feminine singular *yaldâ* expresses a child-parent relationship. Thus, for van Wolde, both *yeled* and *yaldâ* refer to age and gender and are non-relational terms, i.e., they do not make reference to family membership or to the fact that the child is the offspring of a parent.[44]

Of the sole occurrence of *yĕlādôt*, which is related through parallelism to the masculine plural *yĕlādîm* in Zech. 8.4-5, van Wolde writes that it 'does not include…a relation to a family member but is used here as an independent noun'.[45] Together the four occurrences of feminine nouns from the Hebrew word *yeled* are too few to offer much in the way of ancient Israelite understanding of these terms.

From all of the above, we can see that there is no consensus on the semantic patterns in the usage of the Hebrew nouns traditionally translated as 'child', i.e., *na'ar* and *yeled*. I offer one more example to illustrate this conclusion: In Gen. 21.8, when Isaac is weaned, he is called a *yeled*, but in 1 Sam. 1.24, Hannah calls her son Samuel a *na'ar* when he is weaned. The shift in nouns would indicate that they are interchangeable and less than helpful in using Hebrew semantic patterns to determine the meaning of childhood.

To this mix of interpretations, we add the brief comments of Revell who asserts, 'The distinction between the terms used for male infants seems to be, then, that "son" (*bn*) indicates a personal relationship to either parent, "child" (*yld*) views the infant as part of a family, and "lad" (*n'r*) views him without reference to his family'.[46] For Revell, the latter two terms cover the same age range[47] and provide information about familial relationships.

Based on the data above, what semantic pattern emerges from the noun types derived from the terms *na'ar* and *yeled*? We must be cautious when reading the Hebrew terminology not to automatically assume the range of meanings implied through the English translations of these nouns as 'child'. Obvious examples of these verbal differences are found in the way that Hebrew, unlike English, identifies a child by a gendered use of the term; in Hebrew, however, the masculine plural is inclusive of both girls and boys. We see that Hebrew—like English—is not specific about the age of the individual identified by this term and that definitions of the child may shift from one setting to the next (as in the case of the law in the US). In some

---

44. Van Wolde, *Reframing Biblical Studies*, pp. 124-29.
45. Van Wolde, *Reframing Biblical Studies*, p. 128.
46. Revell, *The Designation of the Individual*, pp. 31-32. Thus, he understands *yeled* to refer to an infant, whereas others do not assign age boundaries to the term. The noun ranges to cover a fetus through the married sons of Ruth.
47. Revell, *The Designation of the Individual*, p. 31.

biblical passages the child is an independent being, whereas in others the relational sense of child is implied by the Hebrew.

The difficulty in interpreting the biblical data and coming to an understanding of the semantic range of the nouns *na'ar* and *yeled* possibly results from attempts to impose contemporary norms about life onto ancient Israelite culture where it does not belong. If we are not sure what adulthood comprises, we may have difficulties interpreting the conceptualization of childhood in biblical Israel, and reliance on Hebrew terminology may not be enough to shed new light on the boundaries of separating childhood from adulthood.

The evidence from this study does not support the use of the nouns *na'ar* and *yeled* to mean a fixed beginning and end for a phase of life called childhood. After examining these Hebrew terms, I argue that they refer to both chronological age and social age. Childhood is about both physical and social immaturity, a physiological condition—not an age-specific one—and may extend past puberty and even into marriage (as in the case of Mahlon and Chilion [Ruth 1.5]).[48] If, as will be suggested in Chapter 5, birth is not the significant boundary in ancient Israelite culture that transforms a newborn into a human, we should not be surprised that the boundaries between childhood and adulthood appear blurred to the modern eye.

From the survey above, it is obvious that in isolation from their contexts, it is difficult to arrive at absolute definitions of the nouns traditionally translated as 'child'. Linguistic analysis offers limited insight into the social functions behind the use of this terminology. Since a strictly textual study has not garnered the desired results, it may be possible to gain insight into the conceptualizations of childhood through the understandings in the LXX and early rabbinic commentary on the occurrences of the terms *na'ar* and *yeled*.

The Masoretic Text Compared to Greek and Later Jewish Texts

I now turn to the available evidence from the LXX and the Rabbis. However, these textual traditions offer few clues regarding the semantic pattern of the biblical use of the nouns *na'ar* and *yeled*. Neither the Greek nor the rabbinic texts reveal much difference in understanding between the MT and later conceptualizations and translations of these two terms. There is no evidence of specialized meanings revealed in translations beyond the biblical text or in discussions of the biblical texts from the Rabbis.

---

48. If *yĕlādîm* is a relational term and does not denote age, there is no problem in its referring to fetuses and married sons and everything in-between.

Specifically, problems of meaning associated with the nouns *na'ar* and *yeled* in the MT are not cleared up when one investigates the data from the Rabbis. Their discussions do not appear to acknowledge a semantic distinction that might exist between the terms *na'ar* and *yeled*.[49] It would appear from the commentaries that the two terms are synonymous to each other. Thus, one contemporary scholarly commentator remarks on issues relevant to the question of 'What is a child?': 'We should be aware of the fact that discussions of age are relatively sparse in the ancient sources. Age gradation was not a prominent concern of Josephus or the Rabbis, a phenomenon which may impinge upon an inquiry into the stages beyond puberty as starting the transition from childhood to adulthood, and beyond age twenty in connection with marriage.'[50]

Although the relevant cases will be studied below, the pattern that emerges when one turns to the LXX is that the range of meaning covered by the Hebrew term *yeled* is translated into the Greek abstract term for a living child, *paidon*, e.g., in Exod. 21.22, or *huios* in Ruth 1.5, referring to Mahlon and Chilion (*yĕlādêhâ*). The former Greek term typically is used to refer to a specific child, with no set age, but never to an adult. On the other hand, *huios* is a more general term that has a relational dimension, not emphasizing age, when it is used. Thus, in the case of Ruth 1.5, *huios* conveys that Mahlon and Chilion are Naomi's sons.

A survey of the relevant texts in the LXX reveals that several Greek terms are used to translate Hebrew *na'ar*. These include: *pais, paidiskos, paidiskē, paidarion, neos, neaniskos,* and *parthenos*. In her study of the range of the Greek terms used to translate the Hebrew noun *na'ar*, Leeb concludes: 'These exhibit the same range of meanings as the English words by which the Hebrew is translated. They cover the slave and the free, the child and the young adult. Apparently, by the Hellenistic period, the particular connotations of the Hebrew words *na'ar* and *yeled* had been lost—if there ever was one—and only a general sense remained.'[51] I conclude, based on the study by Leeb, that it is no longer possible to use these ancient texts as resources to tap into the nuances of these terms.

In summary, we see that lexical study alone is insufficient to clarify the understandings of the meaning of childhood in biblical Israel. The social location, or semantic pattern, of the nouns *na'ar* and *yeled* are not evident in

---

49. See, e.g., Jacob Z. Lauterbauch (ed.), *Mekhilta de-Rabbi Yishmael*, I (Philadelphia: Jewish Publication Society of America, 1949), pp. 64-65. This applies in the case of Gen. 21, discussed below.

50. Jonathan Schofer, 'The Different Life Stages: From Childhood to Old Age', in *The Oxford Handbook of Jewish Daily Life in Roman Palestine* (ed. Catherine Hezser; Oxford: Oxford University Press, 2010), pp. 327-43 (330).

51. Leeb, *Away from the Father's House*, pp. 187-88.

the Hebrew Bible nor in later relevant LXX and rabbinic texts devoid of their narratives' contexts. For purposes of the present study, we now move on to an exegetical analysis of texts about children in order to arrive at a clearer understanding of the social location and conceptualizations of childhood in biblical Israel. We turn to narrative analysis in conjunction with culture bound understandings of childhood in biblical Israel in order to reveal the connotations, if any, connected to these nouns. The emphasis lies on context as the locus for the social construction of issues relating to the conceptualizations of childhood in biblical Israel.

Part 2

REGARDING CHILDHOOD IN THE HEBREW BIBLE

Chapter 4

THE ISRAELITE FAMILY AS AN ECONOMIC UNIT AND CHILDREN'S ROLES

> It would appear that progeny are desired, but children are not particularly wanted.[1]

As we have discussed, I use the term 'child' in reference to a biologically immature person and 'childhood' to refer to the meanings a society attaches to the stages through which the child passes as it matures. We also noted that childhood as a social category varies across cultural contexts. In this chapter we see the relevance of these distinctions for understanding childhood in ancient Israel.

From the emic perspective of the case of the Hebrew Bible, I argue that the meaning and conceptualization of childhood lies in the structures of kinship and family life that were the setting of social and economic production and reproduction in agrarian ancient Israel. The family was the site of the intergenerational transmission of property.

We will see that the world of the child in biblical Israel was the world of adults which was first and foremost the world of the family household—a residential and kinship group whose function was the production and reproduction of the family from one generation to the next. Utilizing the textual data of the Hebrew Bible, my concern will be the world of the child in ancient Israel as depicted in literary texts, although I recognize that there is always the question of the connection between ancient reality and the texts that depict it. The problem of how the textual sources reflect the actual life practices of the children and family is not easily solved. Unfortunately, there is not enough demographic information on children in ancient Israel to answer all the questions being raised here.[2]

---

1. Walter Goldschmidt, *Culture and Behavior of the Sebei* (Berkeley: University of California Press, 1976), p. 244.
2. The exception to this statement is the 2009 PhD dissertation by Garroway, 'The Construction of the "Child" in the Ancient Near East'.

The Social Structure of the Biblical Family

I turn now to a discussion of the kinship network that linked individuals to each other within the nuclear family, i.e., the immediate family, the social structure that linked the family to the tribe.[3] The presentation below addresses both social organization and household composition in biblical Israel. It is important to reconstruct the levels of social organization in order to understand better the wider world in which the social meaning of childhood was conceptualized.

Modern studies of the social structure of early pre-state Israel maintain that most Israelites lived in a kinship based village existence in a subsistence economy that can be identified as a pre-modern agrarian lifestyle. Scholars construct this kinship-based family life on three levels: the *bêt 'āb* (בית אב), literally, 'house of the father', a term that is most often translated as the family household; the *mišpāḥâ* (משפחה), sometimes translated as 'clan', the neighborhood or residential kinship group, and is an enlargement of the kinship circle to include lineages related by marriage;[4] and the *šēbĕṭ* (שבט), the so-called tribal level of organization of later Israel which brought together clans related by descent from a common ancestor—whether related by blood or fictitious.[5] These concentric circles of kinship organization structured the society, although an individual's daily life focused on the smallest unit of society, the *bêt 'āb*, the family household. In order to understand the foundation of this society, I will provide an overview of the composition of the *bêt 'āb* (בית אב), the foundational level of social organization, and I will examine the kinship ties that united members of the family household.

---

3. For further discussion of the realities of the family in ancient Israel—as opposed to literary readings of family traditions, basic resources are Stager, 'The Archaeology of the Family in Ancient Israel'; Leo G. Perdue, Joseph Blenkinsopp, John J. Collins, and Carol Meyers (eds.), *Families in Ancient Israel* (The Family, Religion, and Culture; Louisville, KY: Westminster/John Knox Press, 1997); J. David Schloen, *The House of the Father as Fact and Symbol: Patrimonialism in Ugarit and the Ancient Near East* (Studies in the Archaeology and History of the Levant; Winona Lake, IN: Eisenbrauns, 2001).

4. Kinship need not depend upon blood ties but is a socially constructed relationship based upon family relationships that a society considers to be important.

5. Archaeological evidence, too, has changed how we interpret the family and its significance in ancient Israel. As Carol Meyers states, 'We have been concerned with ethnicities and kingdoms, not with individual family groups. The "state" or "city-state" or "tribe" has been reckoned the primary social structure, when in reality the *household*, as the basic unit of production and reproduction, is the primary socio-economic unit of society and should be acknowledged as the social and economic center of any settlement' ('Material Remains and Social Relations: Women's Culture in Agrarian Household of the Iron Age', in *Symbiosis, Symbolism, and the Power of the Past: Canaan, Ancient Israel and their Neighbors from the Late Bronze Age through Roman Palaestina* [ed. William G. Dever and Seymour Gitin; Winona Lake, IN: Eisenbrauns, 2003], pp. 425-44 [427]).

Present day scholarly research understands the *bêt 'āb* as a co-residential group. Generally speaking, the term refers to a group of people who lived together, as well as to individuals who were related to each other. The *bêt 'āb* was comprised of a married couple and any of their unmarried children.⁶ There were, of course, slaves, such as Hagar (Gen. 16; 21), some of whom bore children for the patrilineage. And there were slaves who could inherit, e.g., Eliezer of Damascus (Gen. 15.2-4), but didn't. The term *bêt 'āb* may also apply to a widowed individual living with a child or children. The family household must include, at a minimum, either two spouses and an offspring or a widowed person and an offspring. To take one example, Isaac, Rebekah, and their sons Jacob and Esau form a simple family household (Gen. 25.20–28.5). Other terms used by social scientists for this domestic group include the consanguineal family, the joint family household, and the nuclear family. Individuals less closely connected do not by themselves comprise a family household.

When more individuals, who are relatives, are added to the above grouping, present day terminology refers to the family unit as an 'extended family household'. An upwardly extended-family household occurs when these kin are from a generation prior to the head of the household, such as the father's mother. Conversely, a downwardly extended household refers to the presence of relatives from a generation younger than the head of the household. An extended family household, however, may contain only one conjugal pair. Here one thinks of the grouping consisting of Abram, Sarah, and Lot (Gen. 12.4-9) when they were travelling from Ur of the Chaldeans to Haran on their way to Canaan.

Lastly, the social scientific model of patterns of family organization applies the term 'multiple-family household' to refer to a domestic unit comprised of more than one conjugal pair. The couples must be linked either through marriage or descent.⁷ If Laban's wife was alive when Jacob and his wives Rachel and Leah dwelt with their father Laban, the group would have comprised a multiple-family household (Gen. 29–30) of two conjugal units.

While the definitions above used by social scientists in their discussions of residential units are precise, the same exactness does not always apply when one studies the relevant and corresponding terminology in Hebrew. Problems of interpretation may potentially arise because the same Hebrew

---

6. The discussion of the concentric circles of family life presented here is derived from Naomi Steinberg, *Kinship and Marriage in Genesis: A Household Economics Perspective* (Minneapolis: Fortress Press, 1993), pp. 20-22. For further analysis of these issues, see the studies cited in n. 3 of this chapter.

7. Peter Laslett, 'Introduction: The History of the Family', in *Household and Family Life in Past Time* (ed. P. Laslett and R. Wall; Cambridge: Cambridge University Press, 1972), pp. 1-90 (28-32).

word appears to apply to more than one of the groupings delineated in the social scientific analysis. On the one hand, in the biblical text the term *bêt 'āb* refers to the smallest unit of society, one with a residential character, that was responsible for production and reproduction of the family unit from one generation to the next. However, *bêt 'āb* is used to describe more than one category of family social structure, namely, both simple and extended family households. As a result, the term requires further investigation regarding when it occurs in the biblical text. For example, in the case of Jacob and his sons (Gen. 50.8), the meaning of *bêt 'ābîw* is ambiguous. The phrase may be interpreted to refer to either Jacob's nuclear family or to his extended family. Moreover, '*bêt 'āb* may be used of extended families and of lineages even though as sociological terms these are two distinct levels in societal structure. The extended family was a residential group, while the other, the lineage, was a descent group which was composed of a number of residential groups.'[8] Thus, in Gen. 28.21, when Jacob speaks of returning to *bêt 'ābî*, his meaning is that he is returning to where his father is living, whether it is his father's extended family or his father's lineage group that is living there. In conclusion, the *bêt 'āb* appears to be a comprehensive term referring to the primary unit of biblical family life, as well as to the extended family and to lineages; heirship to the *bêt 'āb* conferred both residential and lineage rights.

Before moving on to a discussion of the next widening concentric circle of family organization, it is important to acknowledge that the term *bêt 'âb* was used in not only the pre-monarchic Iron I period of Israel history through the fall of Jerusalem (1200–586 BCE). It was later adapted to changing political conditions occasioned in the post-exilic period. The terminology shifted from *bêt 'âb* to *bêt 'âbôt* when it adapted to changing political conditions in the post-exilic period. In early Israel the *bêt 'âb* referred to a residential unit composed of related individuals and servants, while in the post-exilic period, the *bêt 'âbôt* was defined as those who could trace their ancestry back to individuals who were part of the Babylonian Diaspora. The primacy of the *bêt 'âb* continued in these changed social and political circumstances and grew in significance, thereby maintaining the importance of the family household throughout Israelite history.[9]

---

8. Niels P. Lemche, *Early Israel: Anthropological and Historical Studies on the Israelite Society before the Monarchy* (VTSup, 37; Leiden: E.J. Brill, 1985), p. 252.

9. For data on 'structural adaptation in exilic society' of the father's house and the descent line, see Daniel L. Smith, *The Religion of the Landless: The Social Context of the Babylonian Exile* (Bloomington, IN: Meyer–Stone Books, 1989), pp. 93-126. See also, Joel Weinberg, *Citizen–Temple Community* (trans. Daniel L.S. Christopher; JSOTSup, 151; Sheffield: Sheffield Academic Press, 1992).

The next level of outwardly expanding social organization was the *mišpāḥâ*. Based upon close scrutiny of the biblical terms, scholars conclude that the *mišpāḥâ*, 'the maximal lineage (or possibly, the clan)',[10] was less significant for understanding social structure in ancient Israel than was the *bêt 'āb*. The *mišpāḥâ* was the enlargement of the kinship circle to include lineages related by marriage. On a daily basis, an individual in ancient Israel would be less directly affected by the *mišpāḥâ* and more acutely aware of his or her position within the *bêt 'āb*. Consequently, the term *mišpāḥâ* typically refers to higher levels of social organization and appears to have been manipulated during times of political or economic conflict, such as the move from a lineage-based social system to the development of a centralized state society in the time of Solomon (961–922 BCE), when the attempt to break down the organizational structures on the local level in favor of organization on the state level was taking place. One mechanism that the Deuteronomist attributes to Solomon in achieving his goal of breaking down local authority and refocusing power toward the national level of government was to emphasize the marital unit at the expense of the extended family in the interest of breaking down larger groups that might unite and foment rebellion against the national level of government.[11] Issues that would formerly have been decided by the father were now decided by officials in the *mišpāḥâ* who answered to authorities in the centralized government, e.g., Deut. 21.18-21; 22.13-21. Because of this shift, children were now subject not only to the authority of the father but also to the jurisdiction of men who operated in the public arena.

Finally, the level of social organization above the *mišpāḥâ* was the *šēbeṭ*, or tribe, a level that appears to be determined by geographical areas and is reflected in biblical texts that are dated later than pre-monarchical Israel and are considered by scholars to have been reworked by later editors of the texts.[12] Thus, the biblical evidence does not support the biblical picture of a twelve-tribe system of organization prior to the establishment of the monarchy.

In light of the importance of the *bêt 'āb* from pre-state Israel onward, this study focuses on the construction of childhood at the level of the father's house/lineage. In a recent study, Douglas Knight discusses the continued importance of the family household in village life from the Iron Age (1200 BCE) on, despite the shifting dimensions of economic and political life over

---

10. Lemche, *Early Israel*, pp. 234, 264.

11. Naomi Steinberg, 'The Deuteronomic Law Code and the Politics of State Centralization', in *The Bible and the Politics of Exegesis* (ed. David Jobling, Peggy L. Day, and Gerald T. Sheppard; Cleveland, OH: The Pilgrim Press, 1991), pp. 161-70.

12. Studies suggest that the tribe was not as important in early Israelite social structure as had been earlier thought; see Lemche, *Early Israel*, pp. 245-90.

the course of ancient Israelite history.[13] He remarks, 'Yet whatever circumstances prevailed at the national level, villages still remained throughout all of Israel's history as the most populous residential option'.[14] He estimates that even with the advent of the monarchy, 80–95 percent of the population retained their traditional pre-modern agrarian existence.[15] These facts suggest that the social conceptualization of childhood remained relatively consistent throughout biblical history and that the cultural ideas and attitudes towards the question of 'What is a child?' were transmitted over the centuries of ancient Israelite history with relative consistency.[16]

Patrilineal, Patrilocal Endogamy, and Family Economics

Sociological models of family organization emphasize the importance of the following issues in regards to family life: marriage choice, heirship, offspring (particularly males), first-born males, and division of inheritance.[17] A pattern of marriage and family life based on patrilineal, patrilocal endogamy[18] whose aim was economic, i.e., intended to guarantee production and reproduction of the family from one generation to the next, emerges from the texts and explains recurring behavior. The focus on patrilineal, patrilocal endogamy means that from the male perspective, a man from the lineage of Abraham, son of Terah, took as his preferred spouse a woman who was also descended from the Terahite line or at least from a male ancestor of Terah. After their marriage, the couple lived with the husband's family in order to live on the land, i.e., the inheritance. The land sustained the family, whose goal was then to produce a primary male heir to move the family forward into the next generation. The family was united along the father/son axis. A child—particularly a male child—was valued and cherished, but not because childhood was viewed as a period of carefree innocence, as it is in the Western mythological idea of childhood today.

---

13. Douglas A. Knight, *Law, Power, and Justice in Ancient Israel* (Library of Ancient Israel; Louisville, KY; Westminster/John Knox Press, 2011), p. 70.

14. Knight, *Law, Power, and Justice in Ancient Israel*, p. 45.

15. Knight, *Law, Power, and Justice in Ancient Israel*, p. 117.

16. For this reason, in this study I will not focus on issues regarding the dating of individual biblical texts and will address questions of the culture-bound conceptualization of childhood in the final form of the Hebrew Bible.

17. Steinberg, *Marriage and Kinship in Genesis*, pp. 137-38.

18. This is also usually true for daughters, as the example of the daughters of Zelophehad in Num. 36 makes clear. Daughters who inherit land are expected to marry within their father's family so that the land will stay within the patrilineage.

Although some have argued that marriage in ancient Israel functioned to establish alliances,[19] I maintain that the data supports the thesis for the interconnection between marriage and patrilineal descent. The preferred marriage pattern for establishing the line of Abraham, son of Terah, was for a man—whose parents were both from this lineage—to marry a women within the patrilineage descended from Terah. Thus, a man married within the lineage (endogamy) continuing the descent line rather than marrying out (exogamy) and forming an alliance. The line of Abraham (entitled to the land of Israel: Gen. 12.1-3) was determined by socially constructed patterns of kinship. A culturally determined emphasis on both blood and marriage[20] was the preferred method for constructing the lineage, rather than on descent, which was an absolute determined solely by blood line.[21] Thus, the biblical text exhibits a pattern of family relationships determined by culturally constructed kinship boundaries for the line of Abraham, and does not rely solely on blood ties to determine who was an insider and who was an outsider to the family.

All of the issues above are relevant for understanding the dynamics of childhood as they are revealed in the biblical text. Childhood was defined on the level of the family household, the *bêt 'āb*, the basic unit in ancient Israel. The meaning of childhood in biblical Israel cannot be separated from an account of the family in ancient Israel; it was on this level of the social structure that childhood took its shape and meaning. Thus, conceptualizations of family life, and similarly childhood, were shaped by definitions of the family household as the locus of production and reproduction—on a daily basis and from one generation to the next. In order for a man to continue his patrilineage, he needed to become the father of a son. The father/son axis provided for the economic survival of the family household. In the biblical tradition of the family household, the economic structure required that the father, the head of the household, have an heir, although as the example of Eliezer of Damascus indicates (Gen. 15.2-4), many of the

---

19. Mara E. Donaldson, 'Kinship Theory in the Patriarchal Narratives: The Case of the Barren Wife', *JAAR* 49 (1981), pp. 77-87; Terry J. Prewitt, 'Kinship Structures and the Genesis Genealogies', *JNES* 40 (1981), pp. 87-98; Robert A. Oden, 'Jacob as Father, Husband, and Nephew: Kinship Studies and the Patriarchal Narratives', *JBL* 102 (1983), pp. 189-205; *idem*, 'The Patriarchal Narratives as Myth: The Case of Jacob', in *The Bible without Theology: The Theological Tradition and Alternatives to It* (San Francisco: Harper & Row, 1987), pp. 106-30.

20. Kinship can be either actual or fictive. Thus, the perspective on marriage in the texts may actually be an idealized view of early history imagined by later writers/redactors, the truth of which is far beyond our reach.

21. Naomi Steinberg, 'Alliance or Descent? The Function of Marriage in Genesis', *JSOT* 51 (1991), pp. 45-55.

biblical stories illustrate how the descent line might be resolved in exceptional cases when no biological heir existed.

The need for child labor in biblical Israel continued over the course of history until the last century. According to sociologist Viviana Zelizer, beginning in the early twentieth century the demand for child labor decreased. Children's necessity as economic producers in the family decreased with the wealth created by capitalism. Capitalism as an economic system reorganized social and economic roles for children (and adults), as the 'worth' of children was separated from the market economy. Towards this end, children were viewed as priceless and sacred; the value of the child was separated from the economic market, and the sentimental value of the American child sky-rocketed.[22] By contrast, we should consider the agrarian society represented in ancient Israel, e.g., in Genesis 16, and the barren Sarah and her need for a child. Sarah's desire to be a mother was based on the child's economic value in the family household, its ability to give her status as a mother, and its potential to take care of her economic needs in her old age. Moreover, the child would provide her husband Abraham with the preferred heir he would need to continue his lineage after his death as well as serve the family economically while the father was still alive. Here we see the reality of the economic value of a child both to his father as his heir and as a protector of his mother in her old age after the death of her husband. Thus, a child in ancient Israel served multiple functions within the family.

Despite a cultural emphasis on the need for children in biblical Israel (particularly sons to continue the patrilineage), a child was the property of her/his parents, typically the father.[23] This perspective on children stemmed from the ancient Israelite emphasis on the family as an economic unit, rather than one grounded in emotional/sentimental ties. The purpose of the Israelite family was found in the production and reproduction of the kinship unit.[24] The more children a man fathered, the more property he owned. In the Israelite family, both wives and children were subservient to the husband. In an effort to preserve the economic returns of the family, protection of family wealth took the form of protecting wives and children. Family dynamics were grounded in economic interests.

22. Zelizer, *Pricing the Priceless Child*.
23. In light our limited knowledge about the world of ancient Israel, consideration should also be given to the data from the ancient Near East on the social value of a child as relates to its economic value. For example, in the Babylonian Code of Hammurabi (dating c. 1792–1750 BCE), law 117 recognizes the right of a father to sell his child to cover a debt or an obligation. The greater the economic ability of a child to meet a parent's debt, the less social value such a child would have. An Israelite son could be taken by a creditor to pay off a debt (2 Kgs 4.1).
24. For an example of an application of this understanding of the sociology of the biblical family to one body of texts, see, Steinberg, *Kinship and Marriage in Genesis*.

Socioeconomic Distinctions between Wives and their Children:
Monogamy and Polygamy

The economic basis of the family household from the perspective of the father as the household head brings us to the topic of the socioeconomic standing, or social status, of the women and their children in the *bêt 'āb*. Since the functions of the family household and the marriage of the head of the household were to produce a child to serve as heir to the father, the relevant questions for understanding family and the construction of childhood include: How would a wife's infertility, or a husband's inability to father male offspring,[25] affect the social status of a married woman in ancient Israel? What alternative options were available for providing her husband with a male heir in order to carry on his patrilineage? How do issues of the hierarchical socioeconomic status of wives relate to the experiences of the children they bear? The links between the economics of family life and the socioeconomic statuses of the women in the family household are highly relevant to this discussion, given that the wives of Abraham, Isaac, and Jacob are barren when they are introduced in the texts, and their fates in their family of marriage would have been in jeopardy had they never borne children. Of course, ultimately their barrenness was reversed: Sarah was cured (Gen. 18.9-15; 21.1-3); Rebecca was cured (Gen. 25.21), and Rachel was cured (Gen. 30.22).

The questions raised above are tied to the diverse marriage arrangements discussed in the following section, whereby women were brought into a marriage for procreative purposes so that there would be a male heir to perpetuate the family line into the future. Moreover, the marriage arrangements expose issues of determining which son is an appropriate heir to the father's descent line in the case of the birth of multiple sons, e.g., Abraham expelled Ishmael, son of Hagar (Gen. 21) and the families of his sons and grandchildren by Keturah (Gen. 25.1-6) in order to secure Isaac, son of Sarah, as his heir. In this example, the primary family line of Abraham through Isaac—rather than through Ishmael—depended on choosing a single heir, i.e., lineal/vertical heirship, rather than multiple heirs, which would be the case with horizontal heirship that included all of the sons fathered by Abraham. The pertinent concept in horizontal heirship is birth order: first son, second son, etc., and first daughter, second daughter, etc., regardless of which woman bore which child.

In the so-called Yahwistic account of creation, the bond between the man and woman in Gen. 2.24[26] suggests a monogamous family in contrast with

25. Num. 27.1-11; 36.1-12.
26. Gen. 2.24-25 (NRSV): 'Therefore a man leaves his father and his mother and clings to his wife, and they become one flesh'.

the polygamous families of Abraham (two wives, Sarah and Keturah; one concubine; a slave, Hagar, belonging to Sarah), Esau (six wives), and Jacob (two wives, and two slaves belonging to his wives) later in Genesis. These polygamous types of family structures appear as legitimate alternatives to monogamy. Indeed, of the major couples, only Adam and Eve, Isaac and Rebekah, and Joseph and Asenath seem to be monogamous. Noah was also in a monogamous marriage (Gen. 6.18), but his wife is not named.

Help in understanding these patterns of marriage in the Hebrew Bible comes from cross-cultural studies of marriage and kinship. The social scientific labels given to the diverse marriage arrangements joining men and women reflect the male point of view regarding the legal status of the women in the marriage. Polycoity, a form of marriage in which a man takes as secondary wives other women who are of lower status than his primary wife, reflects the circumstances of Abraham, married to one legal wife, Sarah, and to one slave/concubine, Hagar. Polygyny, a form of marriage in which a man may have more than one wife at a time but the women are of equal status, occurs in the initial marriages of Jacob to the two sisters Rachel and Leah.[27] However, ultimately Bilhah and Zilpah become secondary wives of Jacob, rendering the household arrangement one of polycoity. The term 'serial monogamy' applies to cases of marriage with only one spouse at a time. Genesis 25.1-6 suggests that Abraham married Keturah after Sarah died. That being the case, the marriage would be categorized as an instance of serial monogamy, although the fact that the children and grandchildren of this marriage are sent away from Isaac with gifts indicates a tension over the division of property. Together these examples—although they are all from Genesis—provide evidence of the competing models of the social structures of marriage and family life[28] and different family organizations that were the setting for childhood experiences.[29]

Kinship structure in biblical Israel was such that the primary wife's offspring functioned as the husband's heir. This means that this son would receive his name, serve as next of kin in the family descent structure, and inherit from him. In the settlement of inheritance claims, these primary heirs displaced any children borne by a secondary wife, a woman of lower socioeconomic status than the primary wife. Understanding the fundamental role of the relationship between the socioeconomic status of mothers and the children they bore in the construction of the Terahite patrilineage is a central way to grasp the diversity of childhoods depicted in the Hebrew Bible.

27. The precise label for this marriage is sororal polygyny.
28. For further discussion of these issues, see Naomi Steinberg, 'Zilpah: Bible', http://jwa.org/encyclopedia/article/zilpah-bible (accessed 27 March 2012).
29. There are also extreme examples of family life that are very far from typical: e.g., Lot and his daughters (Gen. 18.30-38) and Judah and Tamar (Gen. 38.12-30).

The multiplicities of childhoods in the family of biblical Israel were defined by the intersection of gender, socioeconomic status, and age differentials. As discussed above, generational continuity was governed by principles of descent and inheritance from father to son, i.e., the ancient Israelite societal concern for the preservation of the patrilineage-shaped constructions of childhood. However, other factors such as gender, age and birth-order converged with patrilineal interests so that the priority of the first-born son was not an absolute. A number of factors intersected so that two siblings in the same family could have different experiences of childhood. The choice of Isaac over Ishmael as Abraham's primary heir will be discussed in Chapter 6, but for now we acknowledge the differences between the childhoods of Ishmael and Isaac as being defined by the socioeconomic status of their mothers Hagar and Sarah, i.e., the difference between being the son of a secondary or a primary wife.

In this example, Abraham's two sons are objects of his patriarchal control. This control is exhibited in the child abandonment of Ishmael, despite Abraham's distress (Gen. 21.11) regarding Sarah's plan and the near child sacrifice of Isaac. Parental interests took priority over the survival of a child. Abraham's sons were his property. Thus, we should not assume that childhood in ancient Israel was a protected status. Children's lives, in examples such as these, were not separated from the world of adults nor were children granted freedom from adult concerns. Contemporary social institutions and child labor laws currently define children as belonging to a specific and vulnerable class of individuals in need of special protection, but the same construction of childhood is not supported by the biblical data on children. Steven Mintz has already told us that in spite of US ethnocentrism, ours is not in fact a 'peculiarly child-friendly society',[30] and I would argue that the same conclusion applies in biblical Israel.

The situation in ancient Israel was such that the economic focus on heirship made socioeconomic status the most important point of identity. The economic structure required that Abraham have an heir to carry on the lineage. His secondary wife, Hagar, provided him with one, but then Ishmael's childhood was rocked when Abraham's primary wife, Sarah, also provided him with a son. The economics of heirship were the foundation for the influences of social status. For now, I argue that in the biblical tradition, whether a child lived in a polygamous[31] or a monogamous household, shaped the construction of childhood. The constructions of childhood for

30. Mintz, *Huck's Raft*, pp. 2-3.
31. As discussed earlier, technically, the marriage should be labeled polycoity, a form of marriage in which a man takes other women who are of lower status than his primary wife as his secondary wives (concubines). These secondary wives are primarily brought in for the sexual pleasure of the husband.

Isaac and Ishmael were very different from each other due to the different socioeconomic statuses of their mothers in the household of Abraham, who originally required an heir in light of the wider social and political functions of social structure in ancient Israel. However, in the case of Jacob and Esau, sons to the monogamous couple Isaac and Rebekah, other factors—such as parental favoritism—resulted in the two sons having diverse childhoods.

To understand the social construction of childhood is to understand that two children in the same family can have radically different childhoods. Ethnographic studies of pre-modern and modern agrarian societies suggest that the patrilineal family structure was more important than the individual desires of the children. The patrilineal family did not want children for their own sake but primarily for economic purposes and to perpetuate the lineage. The function of marriage and family was to produce an heir for economic purposes of increasing the workforce for the next generation.

The socioeconomic nature of family life, then, had direct bearing on the construction of childhood in biblical Israel. To begin to understand the social and historical conceptualization of childhood, we must take into account further issues that address family life and the role of the family in society as the context for defining the child within the wider social and political world of the biblical text.

Fundamental to the stability of family life was the intergenerational transfer of property, a mechanism for family continuity that highlights the socioeconomics of marriage and family in the Hebrew Bible. Integral to understanding the world of the family and the place of the child within the family is a realization that economic factors were the foundation of marriage and the family in ancient Israel. Family functions included production and reproduction from one generation to the next. These principles established how the patrilineal estate moved from one generation to the next and, as clarified above, delineated which child was entitled to inherit the estate—the family property and rights to be a direct descent in the lineage. In the biblical tradition, heirship entitlement was connected not just to birth order but to socioeconomics, as the case of the half-brothers Ishmael and Isaac illustrates.[32]

The existence of inheritable property and whether or not it is to be passed on to the child are the dependent variables that determine the intersection of socioeconomic class interests and the future of a child. Understanding the socioeconomic interests of the family requires that protection of family wealth—rather than protection of children—was the first priority in family values. A child, whether related by birth or adoption, was someone who would guarantee the survival of family wealth through the patrilineage. The

---

32. Despite the patrilineal system of inheritance, gender is also a factor, as will be discussed below in n. 42 regarding the daughters of Zelophehad (Num. 27.1-11; 36.1-12).

socioeconomic circumstances of the family shaped the contours of a child's life. As stated before, the Israelite family was a socioeconomic unit grounded in production and reproduction and depended on land remaining within the family—being passed from father to son—in order to maintain economic stability. Thus, the child was valued not because he was an individual but because he was a member of the family unit whose continuity depended on the survival of the individual in order to carry the family through to the next generation. On the other hand, daughters seemed to be necessary for other families, not their own. The construction of childhood in ancient Israelite society presumed the family unit was more important than the child, yet the family could not survive without the child. A male child whose survival did nothing to carry forward the patrilineage had little value for the family—as the position of Ishmael in the family household of Abraham, after the birth of Isaac, makes patently clear. Thus, the meaning of childhood must have been defined by the place of children in furthering the economic functions of production and reproduction for the family.

In summary, one should not assume that the relationship between parents and children is uniformly constructed from one family to the next. Classics scholar Valerie French concludes her investigations of children in ancient Greece and Rome with a programmatic statement for future research on the study of ancient childhood. 'One object of such work is reconstructing the kinds of experiences children of different ages, different genders, and different socioeconomic status were likely to have had'.[33] French's categories for interpretation of children in classical antiquity provide a framework for interpreting the data on children in family life in biblical Israel. In the following section, some of the categories that shape the multiplicities of childhoods within the world of biblical family are further addressed.

Factors of Infant Mortality, Gender, and Socioeconomic Status in Childhood

Integral to understanding childhood in biblical Israel is the socioeconomic returns of Israelite children. Archaeologist Lawrence Stager estimates that only two out of every six children in ancient Israel lived to adulthood, based on his study of the highlands of Canaan in the Early Iron Age (c. 1200–1000 BCE).[34] Given the low odds of childhood survival at this time, parents might have been challenged to think hard about their investment in a child. As noted already, a child might have been an investment in the family's generational future, or s/he might have been sold in payment of a debt. We must

---

33. French, 'Children in Antiquity', p. 23.
34. Stager, 'The Archaeology of the Family in Ancient Israel', p. 18.

ask whether or not all children had anticipated economic returns. If a child survived birth, the question of the child's future socioeconomic return required parental consideration. I suggest that the eunuchs of ancient Israel may have been deformed males whose parents thought their sons had nothing to contribute to family production and reproduction later in life because they were unable to bear children and build up the family line. Thus, these sons were given over to institutional settings so that parents would not be burdened with the economic upkeep of these offspring. However, ironically in the case of eunuchs, bodily deformity contributed to their economic survival: it could lead to service to the elites, such as in the harem of a monarch.[35] However, no deformed member of the line of Aaron could offer food at a sanctuary (Lev. 21.16-24). Thus, physical anomalies were relevant for parental decisions of which infants were allowed to survive beyond birth.[36] Not all children were good socioeconomic investments from the biblical perspective.[37] Parents may well have tried to have as many children as possible and selected as best they could from the options available.

Sons were important on all three levels of social organization (the *bêt 'āb*, the *mišpāḥâ*, and the *šēbĕṭ*) for the continuity of the patrilineage and for heirship to land. What do we know of the construction of the meaning of childhood for daughters?[38] We do know that unmarried girls had economic value in their families, e.g., they did chores such as watering their father's animals (Exod. 2.16). A father could sell his daughters (and sons) into slavery to pay off his debt (Exod. 21.7). Moreover, negotiations between families on the economic terms of an impending marriage took place (Gen. 24). Daughters, like sons, belonged to their father's economic property.

Although we know little on how a daughter's childhood was constructed on a daily basis, we do know that she was expected to be a virgin at the time of her marriage (assumed by Deut. 22.13-21). A daughter's virginity[39] was probably her highest economic value, and stoning was the fate of a bride whose new husband did not believe her to be a virgin (Deut. 21.13-21). The

35. See Est. 2 and the figure of Hegai, the king's eunuch assigned to care for the women.
36. Infants in the Guatemalan *hogar* typically manifested some physical deformity which led to their abandonment at birth.
37. According to Deut. 21.18-21, if a son was ill-behaved, his father and his mother could discipline him; if he did not respond to their discipline, he could be stoned to death by the elders in response to a request from his parents. The text specifies in v. 20 that the charges against the son are that he is a glutton and a drunkard. The latter charge suggests that the son in this case is not a small child and more likely in the last stages of childhood.
38. Markers of gendered transitions for daughters in childhood might include skill and menses.
39. Also the captive's virginity was enough to save her from slaughter; see Num. 31.35.

story of Jephthah's daughter (Judg. 11) would suggest that daughters were also socialized into a world where reproduction was the ultimate family value. Stories such as Genesis 34, where Dinah loses her virginity to Shechem (a Hivite to whom she is not married; vv. 5-7) and the hospitality issues that lead Lot (Gen. 19.8) and the householder of Judg. 19.24 to offer their virgin daughters—and thereby lose whatever economic value would later accrue to them through the marriage of a virgin—speak to the importance of virginity in the construction of a daughter's childhood in biblical Israel. Issues of the bride price offered for a virgin daughter are also the subject of Exod. 22.16-17 and Deut. 22.28-29. The economic importance of a daughter's virginity was a defining feature of the construction of childhood for Israelite girls, because only by virtue of a bride's virginity at marriage could the groom be certain that a child born to the couple was a member of his patrilineage (Deut. 22.13-21). Thus, virginity was a gendered feature of Israelite childhood for girls, and it was protected before marriage. However, it does not appear to be essential in the construction of childhood for Israelite boys. Of course, there would be no physical means to track the virginity of a son, which is why it was not essential in Israelite boys' construction of childhood.

Based on the evidence from the sources available to us, it is possible that female infanticide was an example of what was referred to by social scientist Jack Goody as 'a hidden economy of kinship'.[40] In a society that needed sons to continue the patrilineage, the dowry due a daughter for her marriage diminished the wealth of the family and might have resulted in occurrences of abandonment and death of girl babies. Because the evidence does not indicate the men were present at the birth of children, infanticide might have been a matter left in the hands of women. On the basis of this data, the argument has recently been advanced that 'Israelite acceptance of gender-biased infanticide is one of the consequences of these factors',[41] i.e., the economic burden of dowry.[42]

---

40. Jack Goody, *The Development of the Family and Marriage in Europe* (Cambridge: Cambridge University Press, 1983) pp. 183-93.

41. I acknowledge that the biblical texts themselves do not explicitly discuss child abandonment in gendered terms. The evidence for this practice is found in the archaeological record and in discussions of later ancient writers. See, Beth Alpert Nakhai, 'Female Infanticide in Iron II Israel and Judah', in *Sacred History, Sacred Literature: Essays on Ancient Israel, the Bible, and Religion in Honor of R.E. Friedman on his Sixtieth Birthday* (ed. Shawna Dolansky; Winona Lake, IN: Eisenbrauns, 2008), pp. 257-72 (262); Erkki Koskenniemi, *The Exposure of Infants among Jews and Christian in Antiquity* (The Social World of Biblical Antiquity, 2/4: Sheffield: Sheffield Phoenix Press, 2009); Carly L. Crouch, 'Funerary Rites for Infants and Children in the Hebrew Bible in the Lights of Ancient Near Eastern Practices', in *Feasts and Festivals* (ed. C.M.

The book of Proverbs, which serves in large part as an educative tool for how Israelite children should grow into adulthood, clarifies the different values associated with sons and daughters. Proverbs 31, thought to come from the court circles of monarchy, is understood by scholars to address the socio-historical circumstances of an elite population—although Proverbs undoubtedly reflects folk wisdom that predates the final composition of the book. The chapter functions as an instruction manual on how girls should act and what a man should expect from his wife. The emphasis in Proverbs on directing men to remain faithful to the bride of their youth and on avoiding the snares of the loose woman educated young boys on how to maintain the patrilineage and uphold the ideology of heirship from the union of a male and his appropriate wife.

In conclusion, in ancient Israel, the family was the basic social and economic unit of society. Identity for individuals was tied to the family unit, rather than to concerns separate from the family unit. A person's identity was determined by her/his relationships to others, rather than grounded in individual autonomy. The self and the family were integrated as having the same concerns, rather than separate concepts. Thus, children—and particularly sons—were valued for what they contributed to the economic continuity of the family and for their economic support of their parents as they aged. Children were providers for their parents. The issue, in biblical Israel, came down to what a child owed to the family.[43]

Other Issues: Illegitimates, Orphans, and Cast-Offs

Another perspective on understanding the place of children in the family in biblical Israel is through the legislation against adultery. Although laws such as Exod. 20.14, Deut. 5.18, and Lev. 18.20 focus on the fate of the couple who have had sexual intercourse, the understanding of a child as one who continued the patrilineage of his father has direct bearing on understanding childhood as being a life stage only for those who had been born of a 'legitimate' man and woman. A so-called illegitimate child was, by this definition, a non-person. The repeated instructions from father to son that a

---

Tuckett; Leuven/Paris/Walpole, MA: Peeters, 2009), pp. 15-26. I thank Gale Yee for bringing these works to my attention.

42. And yet, the stories of Zelophehad's daughters (Num. 27.1-11; 36.1-12), alert us to the economic value of daughters as recipients of land from their fathers in some circumstances: through inheritance as well as through betrothal and marriage.

43. Of course, a child also owed her/his parents honor and obedience, as laws such as Exod. 20.12; 21.15, 17; Lev. 20.9; Deut. 5.16; 27.16 indicate. As previously mentioned, the rebellious son who is the subject of Deut. 21.18-20 is identified as a drunkard, suggesting that he is probably at a stage of a more advanced childhood.

married man should not go after loose women, e.g., Prov. 5.15-20, draws our attention to the link between adultery and definitions of a child. Thus we must inquire about the fate of a child born outside the protection of the patrilineal family unit. Similarly, texts about prostitution, e.g., Judg. 11.1, suggests that there were children born who did not fall under the family protection of the ancient Israelite patrilineage system. With no links to her/his father's patrilineage because of the indeterminate nature of their parentage, such offspring might be abandoned due to the lack of resources, shame, or insufficient interest of the mother or father in such a child.

Despite the repeated concern in the Hebrew Bible to 'be fruitful and multiply', child abandonment was a reality in ancient Israel. There was the double abandonment of Ishmael, the firstborn son of Abraham: first Abraham abandoned Ishmael and Hagar (Gen. 21.14), and then Hagar abandoned Ishmael (Gen. 21.15).[44] However, despite the fact that the term *yatôm* ('orphan') occurs 42 times in the canon of the Hebrew Bible, critical biblical scholarship has rarely considered the possibility of orphans caused by child abandonment in ancient Israel.[45] The conceptual framework for interpreting the term *yatôm* in Biblical scholarship has focused on whether the term refers to one who was bereft of a father or was parentless, i.e., the literal sense in English of an orphan. But this scholarship has not addressed the evidence for the figurative meaning of an abandoned child—someone lacking the protection of a parent or guardian, either by death or by abandonment.

Another aspect of this topic is the possibility that the abandoned/ orphaned child in ancient Israel was the object of social welfare legislation, e.g., Exod. 22.21-22; Deut. 14.28-29; 24.19-21, because such children were the equivalent of today's 'street children'. Although social policies in many modern countries towards street children appear to be built on social concerns, the reality is that the concept of a street child also builds on the reality that such children are a social problem. They are exceptions to whatever notions a culture may have for how the family should operate. By disrupting such ideas, street children raise the question of what childhood should be. For example, in the US, the 'problem' of street children refers to individuals who fall outside the family norm of children in a family setting cared for by a responsible adult. Child abandonment—as the ancient version of the street child—was a reality in ancient Israel as the example above of Ishmael makes clear (see also Exod. 1.22; Ezek. 16.5).

Yet abandonment was not the only fate for a child who did not inherit family land. The archaeological reconstructions of the closing of the highland

---

44. See also Exod. 1.22 and Ezek. 16.5.
45. It is ironic that Abraham abandons Ishmael in order to protect the inheritance rights of Isaac when earlier—when he had no biological sons of his own—Abraham took in the orphan Lot in order that he might serve as heir to Abraham (Gen. 12.4-6).

frontier at the time of the transition from the pre-monarchic Israel to the monarchical period, and the limits on family land available as a resource for family livelihood, suggest that there were other institutions to which children could turn for economic stability.[46] Sons could be dedicated to the temple or trained for a future profession, according to some scholars, as an alternative to inheriting and farming family land. Sons might also become soldiers (although professional soldering requires a stage of development beyond childhood in most societies) or priests. These professions oriented sons to careers when there was no patrimony for them to inherit.

Although the biblical texts tell us little about the fate of daughters borne into economically deprived families, we have already suggested that either infanticide or abandonment might have been their fates. The high cost of a dowry might have resulted in the family being able to provide for the marriage of only one daughter and other daughters possibly becoming secondary wives (concubines) in polygamous marriages. Without economic goods to bring to the marriage, these daughters had to enter marriages in which they had a lower status, and fewer marriage rights, than a primary wife whose marriage was grounded in economics. Moreover, if a father was unable to provide a dowry for his daughter, she might be forced to marry someone who was undesirable to her (he might be much older than her or physically deformed in some way) but who was able to pay her father for her hand in marriage.[47] A girl might turn to prostitution if the economic survival of her family demanded it; the depiction of Rahab in the first part of Joshua 2 and the latter part of Joshua 6 in no way condemns her for applying this economic strategy on behalf of her family. Finally, a father might sell his daughter as a slave (Exod. 21.7-11).[48]

The foregoing discussion of family life demonstrates the complex variety of influences that weighed upon ancient Israel's perceptions of childhood. I have discussed the importance of the organization of family life within the larger context of ancient Israelite social structure for understanding the issues of childhood in the Hebrew Bible. The system of economics played a key role in defining the place of the child in the family, as did gender.

---

46. Stager, 'The Archaeology of the Family in Ancient Israel', pp. 24-28.

47. Goody, *The Development of the Family and Marriage in Europe*, pp. 83-93.

48. See Joseph Fleishman, *Father–Daughter Relations in Biblical Law* (Bethesda: Capital Decisions, 2011). Lev. 19.29 prohibits a father from selling his daughter into prostitution. These examples reinforce the argument that children (both female and male) served the economic needs of their parents. In Neh. 5.1-6, due to a shortage of food, parents sell their children (both sons and daughters) as slaves in pledge for borrowings. See also, David P. Wright, '"She Shall Not Go Free as Male Slaves Do": Developing Views About Slavery and Gender in the Laws of the Hebrew Bible', in *Beyond Slavery: Overcoming its Religious and Sexual Legacies* (ed. Bernadette J. Brooten and Jacqueline L. Hazelton; New York: Palgrave & Macmillan, 2010), pp. 125-42.

Further, children solidified the kinship bond which defined who is a family. In a lineage-based family society, such as ancient Israel, part of the answer to the question 'What is a child?' is that a child was an economic investment in the future of the family; when there was no economic future for the child in the family household, an alternative fate, such as a life in the military for boys or possibly infanticide for girls, became options. Abandonment for both genders was another way of resolving the problems of futureless children.

In later chapters, we attempt to bring some consistency to the biblical data discussed above and delve deeper into specific texts. We begin this search for coherence by initially returning to the issue raised in the work of Ariès when he explores the question of whether or not childhood was a universal phase of life. Thus, we ask: Was there a concept of childhood as a phase in the Israelite life cycle?

Chapter 5

THE ISRAELITE LIFE CYCLE:
ARE THERE ANY CHILDREN HERE?

> In each life stage, the physical and social parameters of the niche, and the beliefs and values attached to it, will add new elements to the cultural construction of human development.[1]

As discussed in Chapter 2, the Oxford English Dictionary defines a child in two distinct senses: (1) in reference to the life cycle, i.e., a chronological phase between birth and the age of majority; and (2) in relational terms. According to this definition, childhood is universally a distinct life cycle phase. However, the age of majority is not. The Oxford English Dictionary identifies the age of majority as 18 years while the UNCRC sets the age of majority for child soldiers at age 15. The variability in the age of majority supports the theory that each society must be scrutinized individually for its culture-bound understanding of childhood.

Roland de Vaux, who worked to correlate biblical texts with archaeological evidence, suggests that as a stage in the Israelite life cycle, childhood was idyllic and carefree.[2] His research supports the theory that childhood was a distinct phase of life in ancient Israel, although de Vaux does not specify the chronological boundaries of childhood nor does he identify circumstances that might occasion a transition from childhood to adulthood. As reasonable as de Vaux's analysis of the happy Israelite child might appear at first glance, one wonders whether his perspective on the ancient Israelite child reflects contemporary universalizing idealizations of childhood as well as a positivistic reading of the biblical texts.[3]

On the other hand, regarding childhood as a distinct phase in the Israelite life cycle, Joseph Blenkinsopp maintains that '[t]he terminology for periods of the life cycle is…very fluid. It is…consistent with Ariès's thesis that we do not find a clear consciousness of childhood as a distinct life phase; and in fact, no biblical source alludes to childhood or youth in the abstract before

---

1. Sara Harkness and Charles M. Super, 'The Cultural Construction of Human Development', *Ethos* 11 (1983), pp. 221-31 (230).
2. De Vaux, *Ancient Israel*, I, pp. 48-49.
3. I assume that childhood was no less idealized when de Vaux wrote than it is today.

Koheleth [300–200 BCE], who speaks of the days of youth (*yaldût*, Eccl. 11:9-10).'[4] Blenkinsopp's analysis of the standard Hebrew terms for child, *yeled* and *naar* (defined by Blenkinsopp as an unmarried male who has yet to become head of a household) suggests to him a wide ranging semantic pattern such that the results yield a 'vague and ill-focused conception of childhood from the relevant vocabulary'.[5] Other biblical critics are less sure: 'The issue as to whether the Israelites treated their children as children or as 'small-scale adults' remains unresolved'.[6]

These opposing viewpoints on childhood as a distinct phase in the Israelite life cycle necessitate that we determine whether there is evidence in the Hebrew Bible to support the theory of childhood as a distinct phase of life in biblical Israel or whether it was merely 'a period of transition from infancy to adulthood'.[7] Should such evidence emerge, we must search for cultural markers in child development that the biblical texts identify as meaningful in the continuum of stages that comprise childhood. Only if we find coherent data for social behavior that is culturally recognized as critical for human development during the early years of life, i.e., as a meaningful stage behavior, will it be possible to conclude that there was a phase in the life cycle that was understood as 'childhood' separate from adulthood. This conclusion will allow us to arrive at a deeper understanding of the meaning of the transitional stages that comprise the continuum of childhood. To that end, in this chapter I explore life cycle data and some of the relevant Hebrew terminology assigned to this phase of life. Consideration of these issues will help us answer this guiding question 'What is a child in the Hebrew Bible?'

The Cultural Construction of Human Development

The Hebrew Bible does not contain explicit data that allows the interpreters direct access to the ancient perspective on the human life cycle and issues related to the experience of childhood. Thus, the ability to move beyond contemporary Western ethnocentric understandings of childhood requires that we search for meaningful patterns underlying the observable behavior in the biblical texts. On the one hand, the definition of developmental stages of life is based on observable human growth; on the other hand, the meanings, and indeed the perception of them, assigned to these developmental stages were, in ancient Israel as everywhere else, culturally variable. In order to begin to search for evidence of childhood as a stage of life that an individual

---

4. Joseph Blenkinsopp, 'The Family in First Temple Israel', in Perdue *et al.* (eds.), *Families in Ancient Israel*, pp. 48-103 (67).
5. Blenkinsopp, 'The Family in First Temple Israel', p. 67.
6. Philip J. King and Lawrence E. Stager, *Life in Biblical Israel* (Louisville, KY: Westminster/John Knox Press, 2001), p. 41.
7. King and Stager, *Life in Biblical Israel*, p. 40.

passes through, we can mine the texts for ritualized markings of significant events in the life cycle, or what van Gennep calls *rites de passage*.[8]

In a 1942 study, anthropologist Ralph Linton remarks that *rites de passage* are highly ritualized for those transitions where 'the transfer from one category to another entails the greatest changes in the individual's culture participation'.[9] For example, in the Hebrew Bible, circumcision and weaning are ritualized occasions. These events represent socially constructed points of significance that move an individual from one phase of physical and social identity to the next. In the example of circumcision, this ritual performed eight days after birth (Gen. 17.12; Lev. 12.3) incorporates a newborn male into the covenant community that connects Yahweh and Israel (Gen. 17.10-14) and the infant is understood to assume membership in the patrilineal descent line that constitutes the kinship groups of ancient Israel.[10] In the case of the ritual associated with weaning, clearly identified as an occasion for celebration (Gen. 21.80),[11] the child moves from nutritional biological dependency on another human being (whether the child's biological mother or a wet nurse, e.g., Num. 11.12) to a stage of nutritional autonomy that results in a stage of semi-independence and separation.[12] Cross-cultural data reveals that the age of weaning depends not only on cultural variation concerning ideas of the mother-child bond but also on the timing of the birth of a new sibling who displaces the first child as the one being nursed by the mother.[13] Thus, the continuum of the phases of childhood depends on the

---

8. Van Gennep, *The Rites of Passage*. See further, Victor Turner, 'Liminality and Communitas', in *A Reader in the Anthropology of Religion* (ed. M. Lambeck; Oxford: Blackwell, 2002), pp. 358-74.

9. Ralph Linton, 'Age and Sex Categories', *American Sociological Review* 7 (1942), pp. 599-603 (600).

10. For the most recent work on this topic, see David A. Bernat, *Sign of the Covenant: Circumcision in the Priestly Tradition* (Atlanta: Society of Biblical Literature, 2009).

11. Blenkinsopp, 'The Family in First Temple Israel', p. 68. Based on his interpretation of 1 Sam. 1.23-28, van der Toorn argues that Samuel was three years old when he was weaned by Hannah and dedicated to Yahweh at Shiloh; see Karel van der Toorn, *From her Cradle to her Grave: The Role of Religion in the Life of the Israelite and the Babylonian Woman* (trans. Sara J. Denning-Bolle; Sheffield: Sheffield Academic Press, 1994), p. 24. Wolff also believes a child was weaned at age three. To support his argument, he cites 2 Chron. 31.16; 2 Macc. 7.27; 1 Sam. 1.21-22. He also brings in Isa. 28.9; Lam. 4.3-4. (Hans Walter Wolff, *Anthropology of the Old Testament* [trans. Margaret Kohl; Philadelphia: Fortress Press, 1974], p. 121.) Mayer I. Gruber, 'Breast-Feeding Practices in Biblical Israel and in Babylonian Mesopotamia', *JANES* 19 (1989), pp. 61-83 maintains that weaning took place between ages two and three.

12. Gale A. Yee, '"Take this child and suckle it for me": Wet Nurses and Resistance in Ancient Israel', *BTB* 39 (2009), pp. 180-89. This study addresses the variability of weaning durations in ancient legal contracts.

13. Harkness and Super, 'The Cultural Construction of Child Development', p. 221.

physical development of the child accounted for in chronological age and on family growth that moves an individual from infancy to early childhood in terms of social position and capabilities. If adulthood was the ultimate goal in the human life cycle in ancient Israel, each stage marked by *rites de passage* moved a child further along on the continuum connecting childhood and adulthood. These phases of life may not have been age specific (chronological age) but were activity specific (social age). As the discussion of adulthood from the perspective of law in the US earlier indicates, phases of life may involve assuming more responsibility for one's personal behavior, although the legal definitions in the US combine chronological age with specific responsibility for behavior, e.g., being legally deemed an adult at 21-years old for purposes of the consumption of alcohol. Although the assumption of these responsibilities imposes a sharp separation between adults and children, the dividing line need not be as rigid as it is in the case of these contemporary examples.[14]

The significance attached to both circumcision and weaning suggest the complex process of understanding the meaning of childhood in ancient Israel and of locating childhood as a phase within the life cycle of an ancient Israelite. The discussion reminds us also of the importance of focusing on the cultural construction of the stages of human development. In other words, a key characteristic in the study of boundaries and meaning of childhood is recognizing the cross-cultural variation on the timing of life-cycle phases. However, as those familiar with the biblical text are already aware, the literature provides precious little data on other life-cycle rituals, with the exception of Jephthah's daughter's gender-segregated ritual bewailing her virginity before her death[15] and, of course, circumcision.

Divisions between these phases reflect culturally constructed understandings of the meaning of human existence. From a cross-cultural perspective, the boundaries of life-cycle phases are dependent variables interpreted in terms of culturally determined ideas about the place of the individual within the nuclear family or the larger social group. What it means to be a child, and the boundaries of the developmental phase called childhood, are tied to the roles and understandings of what it means to be an adult in a particular culture.

14. '…a rigid dichotomy between adult and child is not always apparent, nor is the sense that adulthood is the end product of socialization'; see Montgomery, *An Introduction to Childhood*, p. 50.

15. There are many studies of this ritual and its meaning; see, e.g., Phyllis Trible, 'The Daughter of Jephthah: An Inhuman Sacrifice', in *Texts of Terror: Literary-Feminist Readings of Biblical Narratives* (Overtures to Biblical Theology; Philadelphia: Fortress Press, 1984), pp. 93-116; and Peggy L. Day, 'From the Child Is Born the Woman: The Story of Jephthah's Daughter', in *Gender and Difference* (Minneapolis: Fortress Press, 1989), pp. 58-74.

When Does Childhood Begin?

One of the challenges in deciding whether or not childhood was a phase of the Israelite life cycle involves answering the question of when does life begin.[16] Modern legal issues about when life begins aside, in some cultures a child may physically emerge from its mother's body and yet not be considered a person based on these cultures' definitions of personhood. Beth Conklin and Lynn Morgan comment on the concept of determining personhood and the boundaries between a person and a nonperson:

> Every society must determine how its youngest will come to achieve the status of persons, how they will be recognized and granted a place within a human community... In all societies, the complexities and contradictions in normative ideologies of personhood are heightened during the transitional moments of gestation, birth and infancy, when personhood is imminent but not assured.[17]

For example, in the US legal personhood is conferred at birth: a birth certificate is issued at this time that bestows personhood on the newly born infant and grants the newborn legal standing. Similarly, the UNCRC is grounded on the premise that all human beings at birth are individuals who are entitled to certain rights as specified in this document. However, in biblical Israel, the act of circumcision for infant males at eight days of age (Lev. 12.3, which seems to allude to the wording of Gen. 17.11-12a) appears to be the *rite de passage* that signifies that social identity, i.e., membership in the kinship group, was conferred on the infant as a member of the covenant community. Circumcision was the ritual that not only signified the birth of a son but also recognized him as a social person.[18] In other words, a newborn boy may have been alive but he did not become a person, i.e., a socially gendered human being until circumcision, which functioned to incorporate him into the patrilineage of his father.[19] The analysis here distinguishes between a newborn as a physical body and as a full human being who

---

16. Although I raise this question, I have no intention of entering into the contemporary debate on abortion. My concern is strictly with the biblical data.

17. Beth A. Conklin and Lynn M. Morgan, 'Babies, Bodies, and the Production of Personhood in North America and a Native Amazonian Society', *Ethos* 24 (1996), pp. 657-94 (657-58).

18. This analysis sidesteps questions regarding whether or not in biblical Israel the fetus was a person or a nonperson. This issue will be addressed in Chapter 8 where the focus will turn to Exod. 21.22-25.

19. For a gendered analysis of the connection between sacrifice and the establishment of male descent, i.e., membership in the patrilineal descent group, see Nancy Jay, *Throughout your Generations Forever: Sacrifice, Religion, and Paternity* (Chicago: University of Chicago Press, 1992).

5. The Israelite Life Cycle

assumes membership in the community. To be more precise, it was the ritual of circumcision that conferred gender on the male infant and started him on the continuum of the Israelite life cycle that ultimately assigned him the social category of adult male social person.[20]

Circumcision then seems to mark the start of community identity for a male infant. This perspective is remarked upon in the later rabbinic texts where the earlier Hebrew Bible perspective is made explicit. Rabbinic scholar David Kraemer remarks:

> One who is uncircumcised is not only not fully *Jewish* but also not *fully male*. Circumcision and Jewish maleness are so much tied to one another in the rabbinic consciousness that it is possible for these rabbinic authors to argue that the presence of a foreskin obscures the male identity of the one who has it. In the end, the uncircumcised Jewish male is not only barely a Jew—he is also, from the Jewish perspective, barely a male.[21]

To sum up: I have argued above that at birth an infant was neither a member of the community nor assigned a gender, at least for a male. If a boy achieved the status of a gendered social person through circumcision at eight days of life,[22] he was still only at the very initial stage of the continuum through which he needed to pass before becoming fully integrated into the community through his contributions to the group at large. Leviticus 12.3 stipulates that a newborn male be circumcised only at the end of the impurity associated with childbirth; the statement was based on the logic of the purity laws of the Priestly source. Leviticus 12.3 suggests that at least in the case of birth and circumcision, the passage of time, i.e., chronological age, had

---

20. Howard Eilberg-Schwartz argues that the priestly community stressed infant circumcision as a means to establish descent lines early in life in order to compete with the Deuteronomist, for whom membership in the covenant community was a matter of choice (Deut. 30.20); see *The Savage in Judaism: An Anthropology of Israelite Religion and Ancient Judaism* (Bloomington: Indiana University Press, 1990), p. 176. Given the distinction between D and P that Eilberg-Schwartz argues for, D would have a different construction of childhood stages than P. From a different vantage point, there may also have been a practical reason for waiting eight days before circumcising a male baby if the intention was to get past a period of early death and to allow for the infanticide of malformed baby boys.

21. David Kraemer, *Reading the Rabbis: The Talmud as Literature* (New York: Oxford University Press, 1996), p. 123. Italics in original.

22. Rabbinic thought would appear to support this perspective. Commenting on the topic in his study of *Yeb.* 70a-72a, David Kraemer remarks further, 'If I understand it correctly, the gemara's claim is that the uncircumcised male, like the *tumtum,* is a person of ambiguous sexual identity. Or, to frame it from the opposite perspective, the Jewish male is the one with the circumcised penis' (*Reading the Rabbis*, p. 123). I thank Alexei Sivertsev for pointing out that my interpretation of the biblical tradition had continuity into the rabbinic period.

bearing on this gendered life cycle ritual. Thus, a newborn male was not considered a gendered social person until he was circumcised. The ritual of circumcision recognized him as a full human being.[23] After this ritual point he was more than just a physical body; he was a full human with potential to contribute to the economics of the family and to be a member of the family lineage. Yet only through marriage and fatherhood did a boy pass from childhood into full adulthood.

The question obviously arises of when a newly born female was assigned a gender and community membership. To answer this question we turn to Lev. 12.5[24] and conclude that a baby girl was considered a gendered person after 15 days of life, i.e., one week later than a boy, although no ritual comparable to circumcision is identified that incorporated the baby girl into her descent line. It would seem that at the start of life a male infant was gendered sooner than a female, and considered a social person and member of the group earlier than a baby girl, because gender is formally ritualized for boys and not for girls. Possibly this differentiation between the designation of boys and girls as social members of the kinship group was a function of the father/son axis on which the family household turned. 'So in terms of gender construction, it [Lev. 12.5] certainly implies that that the birth of males is less threatening for society than the birth of girls, but this hierarchy is itself justified by reference to the rite of circumcision. Without this rite, there is no reason to think that the birth of males would be regarded as less threatening than the birth of females; so the male/ female dichotomy is a very "ritualized" one here, as in Genesis 17 already'.[25]

To repeat, there is no specific ritual identified in Leviticus to initiate a newborn female into full personhood. Based on the data, Israelite ideas about the personhood of infant girls are oblique. Was she was recognized as a person or a nonperson in the early years of life?

---

23. In a personal communication, Christophe Nihan writes: 'Although the rite of Lev. 12 builds upon the ritual prescription of Gen. 17, it shows two significant differences. The rite of Gen. 17 seems to be strictly confined to the sphere of the household, and is entirely under the authority of the paterfamilias (see Gen. 17.23); it is really a ritual that includes only males, and implies transmission of what is construed as a masculine privilege within the household. The ritual of Lev. 12, however, connects the sphere of the household to the sphere of the temple, where the mother must offer a sacrifice at the end of her period of impurity (interestingly, the same sacrifice whether it is a girl or a boy). So the mother now plays a much more active role than in Gen. 17; she really is the "ritual subject" of the entire legislation.'

24. I suggest this interpretation of the data although I am aware that the biblical text is only addressed to the circumstances of the mother and does not say anything directly about the female child.

25. Christophe Nihan, personal communication.

Based on cross-cultural data, for an Israelite girl, social personhood may have been signified through the blood of menstruation, just as the blood of circumcision incorporated a male at eight days of age into the patrilineage of his father. Possibly it was the blood of menstruation that marked the stage when social personhood was attributed to a girl because the girl was now ready for childbearing. Menstruation would be an obvious biological marker, although the onset of menstruation would be at a variable age, possibly around age twelve,[26] what today would be labeled as puberty. For a girl, the blood of menstruation may have marked the nexus between gender and personhood, and signaled passage to the next phase in the life cycle when a girl's childhood began to come to an end. With the onset of menstruation, a girl entered the next stage of social age as she moved to adolescence and prepared for marriage and childbearing.[27] I suggest that only through childbearing was a girl considered to have completely moved out of childhood and into adulthood; menstruation was the antepenult division for girls separating childhood from adulthood, marriage the penultimate stage, and childbearing the ultimate stage of female adulthood.[28] As anthropologist Heather Montgomery remarks, 'It is often children who cement marriage and transform their parents into full, adult persons'.[29]

It would seem that the beginning of community membership was different for boys and girls as they had to pass through different transitional phases in the movement from childhood into the social world of adulthood.[30] Similarly, the meaning of marriage was different for males and females. Through marriage and fathering a son, a male took his place in the father/son hierarchy and may have inherited the family name and property depending on his place in the hierarchy; a female was in a position to fulfill the destiny

26. Van der Toorn, *From her Cradle to her Grave*, p. 18.
27. Of course, one thinks here of the story of Jephthah's daughter (Judg. 11) who bewails not just her virginity but the fact that she has not yet borne a child, i.e., she dies before becoming a fully gendered Israelite woman. I argue that *bĕtûlâ* (v. 37) refers not only to virginity but to someone who has yet to bear a child; see Naomi Steinberg, 'The Problem of Human Sacrifice in War: An Analysis of Judges 11', in *On the Way to Nineveh: Studies in Honor of George M. Landes* (ed. Stephen L. Cook and S.C. Winter; Atlanta: Scholars Press, 1999), pp. 114-35.
28. The barren married woman never became a full adult. She remained in a liminal stage between childhood and adulthood.
29. Montgomery, *An Introduction to Childhood*, p. 64.
30. We should keep in mind that in some cultures circumcision occurs only with the onset of puberty and is a coming of age ritual. In such cases, circumcision would be comparable to menstruation as a transitional point in moving out of childhood towards adulthood. Possibly the biblical tradition's emphasis on the virginity of the bride accounts for the fact that only when she is of childbearing ability is she thought to make a social contribution to the family.

of all girls in ancient Israel, to become mothers to sons who would continue the patrilineage of their fathers or to become mothers to daughters who would provide sons to males in another branch of the hierarchy.

The interconnections between the phases of the life cycle in ancient Israel are not absolute. Harkness and Super address these associations in their sociological analysis of the human life cycle:

> We suggest that a primary function of culture in shaping human experience is the division of the continuum of human development into meaningful segments, or 'stages'.... The result, we hypothesize, is that cultures vary not only in the timing of roughly comparable development stages, but also in the developmental issues which are seen as primary to each stage.[31]

The focus of the following section shifts to a discussion of the subsequent phases in child development/personhood that appear to be based on physical development and that made possible an individual's contribution to the economic survival of the family. We add new data in answering the question of 'What is a child?' in ancient Israel.

Becoming a Person: How Do Children Develop?

The boundaries separating the stages of child development are culturally constructed. For example, one may think of some labels applied to children in the US. According to the semantics of contemporary Western culture, 'child' accounts for the following phases: infancy (0–18 months), early childhood (18 months–3 years), childhood (3–5 years), middle childhood (6–11 years), puberty/adolescence (12–18 years), and young adult (18 years–?).[32] Yet when we use these different terms, we intuitively understand the distinctions between them—which are usually grounded in chronological age. We unthinkingly lump some of these ages together into the category of 'youth'. Moreover, we further distinguish some of these ages by the life stage that in the contemporary West is called being a 'teenager', a stage that I suggest had no correlation with the life cycle of an ancient Israelite and should not be applied to analyses of the social construction of childhood in biblical Israel.[33]

---

31. Harkness and Super, 'The Cultural Construction of Child Development', p. 223.
32. These phases derive from Erik H. Erikson's theory of psychosocial development; see *Childhood and Society* (New York: W.W. Norton, 1950).
33. The cultural construction of the category 'teenager' can be traced back to the economic and cultural conditions of the 1940s when the conditions of the Great Depression and the end of World War II combined to push 14–17 year-olds out of the workforce and into high school in order to free up jobs for returning veterans and other adults in need of employment. Schooling was no longer the privilege of the upper classes. As a result 'teenagers' came to signify an age group with the common experience of

5. *The Israelite Life Cycle*

Although terminology such as that listed above is ingrained in our minds and we typically assume a normative and universal application of these labels in assessing child development, the goal of adulthood towards which these categories lead is also a socially constructed category. In the following section, I aim to provide a more comprehensive picture of the biblical life cycle with special attention given to the stages of childhood that appear (and don't appear) in the Hebrew Bible.

My thesis in this chapter is that the biblical texts provide evidence of certain life cycle divisions in ancient Israel. Analysis of these divisions will reveal that childhood in ancient Israel was a transitional stage in an individual's social journey toward full incorporation into the family household and the patrilineage. In contrast to the construction of childhood in the contemporary West, childhood in biblical Israel was not about developing one's individuality and learning to speak one's mind; instead it was about learning to think like the group and to put group interests before individual ones.

According to the biblical data, the construction of the phases of childhood should be nuanced into small events. As noted above, for a male child in ancient Israel, the initial stage was circumcision eight days after birth (Isaac [Gen. 21.4]). Whether or not a newborn was considered a person through the physical act of birth or only through circumcision is not clear in the texts, although in the case of boys, I am in favor of the latter interpretation.[34] Next, the Hebrew text speaks of two initial phases of developmental physical independence. The first was independence from the body of the mother who bore the child. Thus, we read of infancy in terms of the nursing child (e.g., Moses; Exod. 2.9), followed by what we might call early childhood which is demarcated by the weaning of the child (Isaac [Gen. 21.8] and Samuel

---

extended adolescence spent in high school classrooms. The cultural construction of this distinct period of life has evolved over the twentieth century to have different ideas about growing up associated with it. It continues to be a shifting multi-faceted socially constructed category in American culture as changing economies affect the role of children/teenagers in the family. Youth roles continue to change with new social contexts—industrialization and development also (typically) means more education, higher literacy rates, more stable population due to better living standards, less need for large families, and children having more freedom to play. In addition, women are not confined to domestic roles. For more on these issues, see Grace Palladino, *Teenagers: An American History* (New York: Basic Books, 1996).

34. In some cultures, one can be considered a child and yet not be thought of as a person. 'Questions about the nature of childhood have profound effects on the ways children are treated. In the case of older children, if they are classified as nonhuman and have the recognition of personhood withdrawn from them, they are immensely vulnerable. In the case of newborn children, this is even more apparent; not only are they most physically vulnerable when in their infancy, but this is also the time when personhood is negotiated and contested most explicitly' (Montgomery, *An Introduction to Childhood*, p. 101).

[1 Sam. 1.23-24]). The second phase for which we find evidence is toddling (*ṭap*, 'toddling but not capable of walking', e.g., Ezek. 9.6), but we do not find mention of what is an important hallmark for child development in Western societies of when a child takes her/his first steps.³⁵ Other benchmarks of a child's physical development that are marked today as important in the US seem to have also gone unnoticed, at least based on our understanding of biblical Hebrew. These include turning over, sitting up, crawling, walking, teething, developing first teeth, and acquiring first words. Perhaps these stages of development may have been deemed culturally unimportant from the perspective of childhood in biblical Israel. In modern Western societies, these behaviors are culturally constructed markers in the transition from birth and infancy to what today is identified as early childhood (from birth to approximately three years of age). As stated, biblical sources do not remark on the occasion of these stages of development, yet one might assume that they were aspects of childhood with social import because they marked early transitions into the ability to contribute to the economic life of the family.³⁶

As noted earlier, Blenkinsopp argues against the notion of childhood as a recognized and distinctive phase of the cycle of Israelite life. He notes the vocabulary identifying the early developmental stages of existence:

> For the period from birth to weaning, generally about three years, there are three terms (*'ôlēl*, *'ôlāl*, *yônēq*), all derived from two verbal stems with the meaning 'suck' or 'suckle'. Once past this stage (a passage that many, perhaps most, would not have survived), the child is a *gāmûl* (fem. *gĕmûlâ*), 'a weaned child' (Isa. 11:8) or simply a *yeled* or *na'ar*.³⁷

---

35. Cross-cultural data suggests that a developmental phase of childhood occurs when a young child is superseded by the birth of a sibling and dynamics with the mother shift for this child. This appears to be the case when Ishmael is superseded by the birth of Isaac—although issues of age are unclear here. It is a phenomenon that continues into the present. For an ethnographic example of the dynamics described here, see Sara Harkness and Charles M. Super, 'Why African Children Are So Hard to Test', in *Cross-Cultural Research at Issue* (ed. L.L. Adler; New York: Academic Press, 1982), pp. 145-52.

36. One might speculate that there was less emphasis placed on an infant's developmental stages because as pointed out earlier by Stager, the infant mortality rate was much higher in ancient Israel than its is today in the US or other developed states. Furthermore, wealthier states with higher standards of living tend to sentimentalize children more than states/societies with poorer economies. The same developmental connection in the separation of children into different rooms in the orphanage can even be seen in the Guatelmalan *hogar* discussed in the introduction to this volume.

37. Blenkinsopp, 'The Family in First Temple Israel', p. 68. The term *yônēq*, from the root *ynq* 'to suck' is used consistently to refer to infants who are nursing. The word clearly indicates a phase of life characterized by a particular action. This phase of life ends at the time a child is weaned, *gāmûl*, as Isa. 11.8 specifies. Six times the word *yônēq* is paired with the word *'ôlēl*, child (1 Sam. 15.3; 22.19; Ps. 8.2 [3]; Jer. 44.7; Lam. 2.11;

On the basis of the terms cited by Blenkinsopp, suckling and weaning are the two phases of nurturing in childhood for which we have direct information.

Childhood as a culturally defined life cycle phase appears to be shaped by attitudes regarding the necessary preparation for adulthood. In regards to ancient Israelite perceptions of the social construction of family life, adulthood was about intergenerational continuity and family interdependence in fulfillment of the larger societal emphasis on production and reproduction. Family members depended on other family members to sublimate individual desires and goals to larger group goals.

As will be discussed in greater detail in Chapter 6, in no small measure the timing of the expulsion of Ishmael in Genesis 21 was occasioned by Isaac's movement along the continuum of childhood. Ishmael was rejected at the point when Isaac was weaned. The text recounts these events in terms of Sarah's reaction to Ishmael's behavior at a celebration honoring Isaac having been weaned. As noted above, scholars suggest that a child was weaned at age three. In constructing the stages of childhood by linking chronological age with the stage of weaning, Isaac is an example of a younger child whose weaning brings about major changes in the structure of Abraham's family as he displaces Ishmael as primary heir to the Terahite lineage.

Childhood can also be correlated with a young person's growing ability to tend animals, carry firewood, and participate in other relatively simple chores that contributed to the ongoing life of the family. If we set aside the legendary and exaggerated issues reflected in the narrative of David's battle and defeat of Goliath and focus instead on the details of 1 Sam. 17.12-18 from the life of David, we learn more about the responsibilities of a child. Without assigning a precise age to David in these events, we note that he was at a life stage too young to fight in battle but old enough to be expected to carry out certain activities, i.e., tending sheep (1 Sam. 16.11), bringing food to his brothers in the battle camp (1 Sam. 17.17-18),[38] and conveying information. These activities move him along a life cycle continuum of human development and increasing contribution to societal goals. David, as a child in these events, possibly in middle childhood, participated in the family economy. When Saul inquires of the identity of the young person responsible for the death of Goliath, he refers to David by the unspecified age term *'elem* (1 Sam. 17.56; cf. 1 Sam. 20.22).[39] Earlier in the story,

---

Joel 1.16). Once it precedes the plural *'ôlālîm* (Lam. 4.4). Thus, a phase of biological development is expressed by *yônēq*.

38. For another task that children do, see Gen. 27.5-14 where Esau hunts for game for his mother Rebekah.

39. The term only appears in the masculine singular twice in the Hebrew Bible.

1 Sam. 17.14, David is identified as a *na'ar qāṭān*, literally 'a young child', but used in such a way that the term is not intended as an age designation but to convey that David was the youngest son of his father Jesse. Blenkinsopp translates the phrase as 'little boy',[40] but in his new volume on the Israelite life cycle, Milton Eng simply translates it as 'boy' and argues that the term refers to someone within the age range of three to thirteen years.[41] Regardless of the exact translation of the phrase, this story exemplifies the social responsibilities and work roles relating to someone older than three and probably closer to age thirteen. David is an example of a middle-aged child.

For an example of an almost-adult, we turn to Genesis 24. Rebekah's willingness to travel with Abraham's servant to Canaan to marry Isaac is witness to her socialization into the values of the Israelite family and her ability to function as a member of a larger group—independent of personal interests. Each stage in the process of development along the continuum of childhood manifests socialization into larger cultural norms of adulthood. When Isaac and Rebekah marry we find the penultimate transition between childhood—as preparation for life in the social group characterized by patrilineal patrilocal endogamy—and adulthood. Childhood was a time to acquire the skills to assume social responsibility for production and reproduction of the family structure. Thus, the construction of childhood was a movement towards group identity, not individuality. However, it appears that for both a bride and a groom, marriage alone did not make them adults in ancient Israel; they needed to also produce a (male) child to continue the intergenerational patrilineal growth in order to be Israelite adults. With the births of Jacob and Esau, Rebekah and Isaac attained full adulthood.

Most biblical scholars assume that ancient Israelite life was structured by phases of a life cycle that included childhood. I agree with these other researchers. However, while there is support for the theory that there were stages of childhood that were part of the life cycle continuum, the biblical texts are not specific about these stages. In light of this conclusion, I now clarify why certain biblical passages that break down age categories actually do not shed light on the life phase of 'childhood'.

Leviticus 27.1-8 and Other Biblical Texts

The texts of the Hebrew Bible offer only limited help in understanding the cultural construction of the stages of childhood. The emphasis in the biblical texts falls on chronological age without a direct indication of the work responsibilities that are associated with development.

40. Blenkinsopp, 'The Family in First Temple Israel', p. 67.
41. Eng, *The Days of our Year*, p. 127.

First we turn to Lev. 27.1-8.[42] The apparent purpose of the text is to address the redemption values by chronological age divisions in the event that a vow for the consecration of an individual could not be fulfilled; under such circumstances, an individual could offer money instead of a person as a gift to Yahweh's sanctuary. The text specifies redemption values as follows:

AGE	FEMALE/shekels	MALE/shekels
0–5 years	5	3
5–20 years	20	10
20–60 years	50	30
60–	15	10

According to Carol Meyers, the text specifies age, sex, and monetary value that appear to 'preserve an authentic ancient assessment of human worth according to age and sex in a relative sense. Further, the notion of human worth is clearly in terms of value in the "labor pool".'[43] However, in the Leviticus passage the references are to age in terms of years lived (chronological age) as opposed to possible social contributions (social age). For example, in Lev. 27.5, the text lists 'ages 5–20' but does not specify activities that either a female or a male can do during those fifteen years. One might imagine individuals between the ages of 5 and 20 'being able to run around and help in the family economy, in addition to being about to bear children (if a woman)'.[44] If the text does represent social age and

42. The text is part of the Holiness Code and therefore reflects cultic perspectives that may not have applied in other settings.

43. For full discussion of these issues in light of both age and gender, see Carol Meyers, 'Procreation, Production, and Protection: Male–Female Balance in Early Israel', *JAAR* 51 (1983), pp. 569-93 (582-86). Block labels these age breakdowns with life cycle phases: 1 month–5 years, infancy; 5–20 years, youth; 20–60 years, adulthood; and sixty years and upward, old age; see Daniel I. Block, 'Marriage and Family in Ancient Israel', in *Marriage and Family in the Biblical World* (ed. Ken M. Campbell; Downers Grove, IL: InterVarsity Press, 2003), pp. 33-102 (79).

44. Wolff refers to the list as one of 'working capacity' (Wolff, *Anthropology of the Old Testament*, p. 121). As to why 5–20 year olds are in the same category, given that a child's ability to economically benefit the family increased as they aged and become more capable, Meyers writes: 'Obviously, children below the age of five can contribute very little in terms of actual work to the activities of a community and the absolute values set upon them are low, whether for males or females. Moreover, as a potential source of productivity, the high mortality rate of youngsters up to the age of five—35% being a suggested figure—would keep the valuation low. Thereafter, the absolute level for both sexes rises, with the highest levels being reached for the adult population over the age of twenty.' She suggests that the absolute value for females in this group is only half the value of males because the span between the ages of 5–20 includes childbearing years and 'her potential during that period for contribution to subsistence would thus decrease because of her greater productive responsibilities and the concomitant increase in her own

societal responsibilities, one might expect that there would be a breakdown between ages 5–12 and 12–20 as representative of the increased work contributions connected with puberty and the increased economic capabilities that accompany the physical maturity associated with puberty. I conclude that the list does not represent social age and social responsibilities.

Second, Jer. 6.11 addresses the life of an Israelite but does so in terms of broad life phases. This text divides life into five stages of the life-cycle: (1) children (*ʿôlāl*), (2) the young man (*bāḥûr*), (3) man and woman (*ʾîš* and *ʾiššâ*), (4) the elderly (*zāqēn*), and (5) the very aged (*mĕlē ʾyāmîm*). Neither the age ranges nor the work/activities associated with these different stages of life are listed.

Third, Jer. 51.22 also provides data on the construction of the Israelite phases of life. Here the final two stages of life found in Jer. 6.11 are collapsed together. In Jer. 51.22 the life cycle is divided into four divisions: (1) children (*naʿar*), (2) youth (*baḥûr* and *bĕtûlâ*), (3) man and woman (*ʾîš* and *ʾiššâ*), and (4) the elderly (*zāqēn*). One notes that these life cycle stages sometimes make gendered distinctions, but at other times the masculine form alone is listed. Specifically, for the first and the final phases of life, the terms used are inclusive of both men and women. However, neither text from Jeremiah explicitly sets out to list the Israelite life cycle; the poetic nature of the texts may account for the format of these lists. Furthermore, we note the contrasting terms used for the first stage of life (*ʿôlāl* versus *naʿar*) in these two texts from Jeremiah and wonder about the absence of the term *yeled*, which is so often used for children at other places in the Hebrew Bible. Thus, as interesting as the texts of Leviticus and Jeremiah may be, they contribute little to our understanding of the social construction of childhood as a phase of the Israelite life cycle due to their reliance on chronological age as absolutes in the biblical life cycle.[45]

Scholarly Constructions of the Biblical Life Cycle

In order to understand what a child is in biblical Israel, we must also address the question of when a child stops being a child. These questions together ground us in the topic of the biblical life cycle as the focus of scholarly reconstruction.

Hans Wolff assesses the stages of the life cycle that can be recovered through the biblical data, and argues for three basic phases based on

mortality risks'; Meyers, 'Procreation, Production, and Protection', pp. 585-86. Meyers maintains that a female would likely bear most of her children between ages 15–20.

45. I would be remiss if I did not include Eccl. 3.1-8 in this discussion. However, the composition of the text suggests that it is a literary device expressing opposite human conditions rather than an expression of the totality of the life cycle.

categories of physical maturity: children, young but fully grown men and women, and the mature or elderly. Wolff writes:

> at least three phases of life are distinguished from one another: children (*yōnēq*, the sucking child, Deut. 32.25; *na'ar*, the boy, Ps. 148.12; *tap*, pattering, not capable of walking, Ezek. 9.6); young but fully grown men and grown-up girls (*bāḥūr* and *bĕtūlā*, Deut. 32.25; Ezek. 9.6 and Ps. 148.12); and mature, elderly men and women (*zāqēn*, who wear a beard, Ezek. 9.6; Ps. 148.12; *'îš śēbā*, the grey-haired man, Deut. 32.25; *'iššā*, Ezek. 9.6).[46]

Thus, for Wolff, the phases of the life cycle are primarily based on visible physical characteristics. The central problem of his analysis is that the divisions of the life cycle he discerns rely solely on physical characteristics. His interpretation provides no indication of the connection between physical maturity and social age and life responsibilities.

Another contribution to the study of the social construction of Israelite childhood is found in Karel Van der Toorn's study of the gendered life cycle of an Israelite (and a Babylonian) woman.[47] His reconstruction draws on data from the social sciences in order to analyze the religious roles of women based on their social location. Van der Toorn clearly differentiates between chronological age and social age by delineating the societal functions that correlate with chronological age and contribute to the full personhood of an Israelite woman. In brief, he separates five life stages for an Israelite woman characterized by social age and social functions, which he then correlates in general terms with chronological age:

1. The *nursing* period[48]   0–3 years
2. *Youth*   4–11 years
3. *Puberty*   12–16 years
4. *Married Life*   16–40 years
5. *Widowhood*   40-60 years

---

46. Wolff, *Anthropology of the Old Testament*, p. 120; see pp. 119-27 for his discussion of 'To be Young and to Grow Old'. For further discussion of the Hebrew terminology relevant for this categorization and the roles and responsibilities associated with each of these phases of life, see Block, 'Marriage and Family in Ancient Israel', pp. 33-102; on the status and roles of children in the Hebrew Bible, see pp. 78-94.

47. Van der Toorn, *From her Cradle to her Grave*, p. 18. Van der Toorn assumes that a woman's husband preceded her in death. Of course, the exact age at which the husband's death would have occurred is difficult to determine. For the sake of argument, he rounds the husband's death to when a woman would be approximately age 40 and he argues 'the woman has finished raising her children'. His estimation of the age at death of the woman is also an approximation.

48. Van der Toorn here refers to the years when the woman is still an infant and she is the one being nursed—not the age when she is the one nursing a child.

Van der Toorn's methodology explicitly aims to connect social function with chronological age and contributes to understanding the construction of childhood within the Israelite life cycle based on social contributions to the family.

Finally, the life cycle is the subject of the work of Milton Eng.[49] Unlike Van der Toorn who relates social functions to chronological age, Eng's analysis is based primarily on linguistic analysis. In his word study, Eng aims to establish the rhythms and continuum of the Israelite life cycle for 'the young' based not on chronological age alone, like Wolff, but on physical maturity and on the roles the individual assumes within society, i.e., social age, like Van der Toorn. A similar argument to the one made by Eng has already been advanced in anthropological study[50] and finds support in ancient Near Eastern scholarship. Martha Roth comments,

> In many societies, especially non-Western preindustrial societies, these life stages are not tied to strict chronological age, but rather are signaled by observable outward signs or behavior. Thus, for example, weaning might mark the transition from infancy to childhood, menarche that from childhood to adolescence, physical prowess or intellectual achievement that from adolescence to adulthood.[51]

Eng's research relies on a linguistic methodology of comparison focusing not only on Hebrew terminology but on the contextualization of relevant words in light of age categories and evidence of the life cycle in the ancient Near East. His study emphasizes the cultural construction of the life cycle, i.e., that culture bound 'facts' shape the age and sex specifications for determining both the number of stages in the life cycle and the transition points between these stages.

Eng avoids assigning absolute chronological age limits to the phases of the Israelite life cycle (for both men and women) such as Van der Toorn offers. Eng provides a *preliminary*[52] breakdown of the phases of Israelite life:

infancy	to weaning	עול, יונק
childhood	weaning to puberty	טף, עולל
youth/young adulthood	puberty to marriage	בתולה, בחור
mature adulthood	marriage/work	איש, אשה
old age	menopause/retirement	זקן
extreme old age		מלא ימים

---

49. Eng, *The Days of our Years*.
50. Linton, 'Age and Sex Categories', pp. 589-603.
51. Martha Roth, 'Age at Marriage and the Household: A Study of Neo-Babylonia and Neo-Assyrian Forms', *Comparative Studies in Society and History* 29 (1987), pp. 715-47 (716).
52. Italics inserted by Eng, *The Days of our Years*, p. 57.

Thus, for him the Israelite life cycle breaks down into phases marked by physical maturity that make possible roles and responsibilities that mark an individual's increasing contribution to the ongoing life of the family and the larger community/society.

For both Van der Toorn and Eng, marriage marks a major transition in the life cycle of an individual and could be considered the end of childhood. The two scholars differ in the labels they assign to the phases of life prior to this event, and, of course, Van der Toorn does not address the male gendered life-cycle phase. Since marriage may have conferred adulthood in biblical Israel and it is impossible for modern scholars to assign an absolute age for marriage, it continues to be difficult to answer the question 'What is a child?'

Before marriage, while still residing in the home of her parents, a daughter, like a son, might tend the sheep as Rachel did in Gen. 29.9. A daughter would also draw water for the animals (Gen. 24.11; Exod. 2.16), cook (2 Sam. 13.8), and perform other household-related chores. Boys probably were involved in domestic activities but also learned farming and shepherding from their fathers.

Studies suggest that girls married in their (early) teens but boys waited until their twenties or early thirties before being married.[53] This discrepancy should be related to the fact that a young man typically did not marry until his father had died and he assumed the role of heir to the patrimony. Only then would he be able to support a family economically.

We turn again to the work of Martha Roth, whose arguments on the connections between a boy's age at marriage and the time of his father's death have important implications for understanding the construction of the life-cycle phases. Roth's study of Neo-Babylonian and Neo-Assyrian marriage contracts reveals that while diverging life expectations influenced the age at which marriage first takes place, the relative difference between the spouses' ages was typically over a decade. This being the case, a girl was married approximately ten years earlier than a boy.[54] Although we cannot automatically assume the same ancient Near Eastern marriage dynamics apply to biblical Israel, and we certainly cannot consider the inflated ages of individuals in the Bible as reliable indicators of life expectancy in ancient Israel, the age difference in Genesis between Sarah and Abraham is in basic conformity with the data in Roth's study: Abraham is ten years older than Sarah, according to Gen. 17.17.

In summary, our study thus far suggests that childhood was a distinct phase of Israelite life. Its contours were reflections of the cultural construction of family life that emphasized the production and reproduction of the

---

53. King and Stager, *Life in Biblical Israel*, p. 37.
54. Roth, 'Age at Marriage and the Household', pp. 715-47.

family household from one generation to the next. Life cycle distinctions were constructed on the basis of a child's increasing capacity to contribute to the subsistence and survival of the family. My analysis of the construction of the biblical life cycle has been grounded in economically based stages of life.

However, none of the biblical texts discussed above match up with the scholarly reconstructions of the Israelite life cycle, and none of the biblical texts contribute to understanding childhood as both a biological and culturally constructed category. I turn now to specific biblical texts that shed light on the meaning of childhood in biblical Israel as both a biological and a culture-bound construction.

Chapter 6

GENESIS 21:
MONOGAMY, POLYGAMY, AND CHILDHOOD EXPERIENCES

As this study purports, the construction of childhood is defined in ancient Israelite society by the place of the child in the family and a range of factors determined the structure of the family in biblical Israel. One dynamic that had an impact on the shape of the family and the experience of childhood within the family was whether the family household was a polygamous or a monogamous household. The position of a child in a monogamous versus a polygamous household can be explored through a study of Genesis 21 that focuses on the relative statuses of Ishmael and Isaac who are, respectively, the sons of Hagar and Sarah, wives of Abraham.

In Genesis 21, the son promised to Abraham through Sarah (Gen. 17.15-22) who has been barren up to this point in Genesis, is born at last. This son, Isaac, will cement the patrilineal marriage bond between Abraham and Sarah. Genesis 21 covers many events: it announces the birth of a son, Isaac, to Abraham by Sarah (vv. 1-3) in fulfillment of God's earlier promise (Gen. 18.10) and gives notice of the circumcision of Isaac (v. 4). The occasion of Isaac's circumcision leads up to Sarah's demand for the expulsion of Ishmael, Abraham's firstborn son, and his surrogate slave mother Hagar, on the occasion of the weaning of Isaac (v. 8). The performance of the rituals of circumcision (at the age of eight days; v. 4) and weaning of Isaac (no age is specified; v. 8) exemplify the earlier argument that *rites of passage* move an infant along the continuum of non-person to personhood and contribute to understanding the social construction of personhood in the phases of the life of a child. The significance of these rituals may explain why the subsequent events in Genesis 21 occur precisely at this point in the childhood of Isaac and Ishmael. Isaac is moving along from the category of non-person to social personhood and his social membership in the patrilineage of Terah through Abraham. Isaac's status in the patrilineage is threatened by the presence of Ishmael who, as a son of Abraham, has reached the social age—regardless of chronological age—allowing him to be a member of Abraham's family.

In order to fully understand the family dynamics of Gen. 21.1-21 that are factors in shaping the childhoods of Ishmael and Isaac, the reader must recall the details of Genesis 16 and issues regarding the fertility—or the infertility—of Sarah going back to Gen. 11.30. Genesis 16 focuses on fertility and recounts the circumstances that lead to the birth of Ishmael, who is borne to Abraham by Hagar, through a plan devised by Sarah. According to Gen. 20.12, Sarah is related to Abraham through his father's lineage, i.e., theirs is a marriage categorized as patrilineal endogamy. Their kinship relationship establishes Sarah as Abraham's primary wife and Hagar, being an Egyptian slave with no economic standing in the family, is a secondary wife (concubine) due to her lower status in a culture that treats marriage to a woman from one's kinship line as the preferred marriage pattern. Thus, with her status as Abraham's primary wife grounded in their patrilineal endogamous marriage, Sarah has priority over Hagar in her marriage to Abraham, and she works to establish her son Isaac's rights (and his affective ties to her) after his birth as a means to secure his position as Abraham's primary patrilineal heir.

In Genesis 21 the emphasis of family dynamics shifts from fertility to inheritance when Isaac is borne by Sarah to Abraham.[1] Now, with the existence of two sons borne to a man who formerly had none, Genesis 21 becomes an important source for understanding the factors surrounding the social construction of childhood in a polygamous rather than a monogamous household. In other words, when Ishmael was Abraham's only son, he could expect certain rights based on his status as Abraham's sole heir. However, the birth of a second son to Abraham in a household where Ishmael's mother, Hagar, is a surrogate mother and Isaac's mother is Abraham's primary wife, have bearing on the acceptance that Ishmael can expect in the home of his father Abraham. The status of his mother Hagar vis-à-vis the status of Sarah affects Ishmael's position and his future. When Ishmael was Abraham's only son, he was reckoned as the child of Sarah (Gen. 16.2)—despite the fact that he was borne by Hagar. It is as if, at that time, he lived in a monogamous household whereas the birth of Isaac shifts the family into a polygamous one and demotes the status of Ishmael. Thus, the social location of Ishmael and Isaac and the dynamics of their childhoods in a setting where heirship is vertical through only one son determine how each child will be treated in this polygamous household. As we will demonstrate in the following analysis, the answer to the fundamental question 'What is a child?' is different for different offspring based on the type of marriage that holds the household together. As anthropologist Montgomery states, 'Whether children live in a polygamous or monogamous household, the relative status of their

---

1. In his source critical analysis, Thomas B. Dozeman argues that the theme of family conflict belongs to a pre-Priestly history focused on Hagar but the expulsion of Ishmael interrelates the narrative into the Priestly history and its concern with life in the wilderness; see Thomas B. Dozeman, 'The Wilderness and Salvation History in the Hagar Story', *JBL* 117 (1998), pp. 23-43.

6. *Monogamy, Polygamy, and Childhood Experiences*

mother, whether they have kin around or whether they are legitimate all affect their status and the subsequent way that they are treated'.[2] Thus, the conceptualization and experience of childhood can be affected by who the parents of the child are. In the example of the family of Abraham, it is ultimately the status of the children's mother that shapes the construction of the childhoods of Ishmael and Isaac respectively and how each son is treated after the birth of Isaac.

In order to designate and legitimate Isaac—rather than Ishmael—as the primary heir to his father, the pattern of behavior exhibited by Sarah is shaped by dynamics that have cross-cultural analogues.[3] Sarah becomes the agent of change by which Isaac replaces Ishmael as primary heir to Abraham. Isaac's childhood is shaped by factors that are initiated by Sarah and obligate him to his mother; and by events that disenfranchise Ishmael from the patrilineage of Abraham and disrupt the shape of Ishmael's earlier childhood experiences as Abraham's only son.

While the two half-brothers, Ishmael and Isaac, are both sons of Abraham, what it means to be a child in this family leads to the conclusion that there is no uniform, generic conceptualization of childhood even within a single family. Rather, childhood is defined for each son by specific factors that shape the dynamics of Genesis 21, and these factors lead to the expulsion of Ishmael and the choice of Isaac as primary heir to their father Abraham.

As stated above, the social construction of the childhoods of Ishmael and Isaac are tied to the social location of the mothers of the two sons. This is the primary factor shaping their treatments as sons of Abraham. Furthermore, their childhood experiences are the reversal of what readers might expect in the narratives of the Hebrew Bible, where it is commonplace for the firstborn son to be the primary heir to his father. In the case of Ishmael and Isaac, the order of birth of the sons to two different mothers, who have different statuses vis-à-vis Abraham, does not hold the key to how their childhoods are defined. In other words, as stated in the law of Deut. 21.15-17, Ishmael as Abraham's firstborn son would expect to enjoy certain rights and privileges and have a higher family status than his younger half-brother, Isaac. However, in Gen. 21.1-21, we are presented with clear data that childhood is a social construction, and its meaning derives from a multiplicity of circumstances that extend beyond birth order and can vary from one family to the next. In Genesis 21, the status of Hagar as a slave who functions as a secondary wife in a polygamous household[4] has significant impact on the

---

2. Montgomery, *An Introduction to Childhood*, p. 54.
3. Montgomery, *An Introduction to Childhood*, pp. 63-67. Many cross-cultural examples are cited within these pages.
4. Another example of these dynamics will be discussed in the next chapter where the focus will be on 1 Sam. 1. Here we will see how polygamy shapes the lives of Peninnah, Hannah, and ultimately, Samuel.

differences between the social construction of childhood for her son Ishmael and the social construction of childhood of Sarah's son Isaac.

Thus, behind the dynamics of Genesis 21 and the different childhoods of Ishmael and Isaac lay the antagonistic social status competitions over fertility that come together in the polygamous household of Abraham back in Genesis 16. In Genesis 21, the sons Isaac and Ishmael never speak and are not even emphasized as individuals because the conceptualizations of their childhoods hang on the differences in the relative status of wives in a polygamous marriage and the discrepancy in the care given to the higher ranking wife's child over that of the secondary wife. In fact, Ishmael is not identified in this passage by name, only by pronouns.

In the example of Genesis 21, the life of the child is shaped by issues of competition between women for social status occasioned by the differing forms of marriage that tie Sarah and Hagar to Abraham.[5] Yet, the distinction between being the son of a monogamous or a polygamous marriage is a highly important factor that past research has failed to address when analyzing factors that shape the construction of childhoods in ancient Israel. However, this factor demonstrates how the social construction of childhood in Genesis 21 is conditioned by issues relating to a child's place in the wider social structure of ancient Israelite marriage, kinship, and lineage.[6]

One sees, then, that Genesis 21 exposes the status discrepancy between children in a polygamous household based on the statuses of their mothers. We continue to analyze these issues by examining the distribution of nouns used to describe Ishmael and Isaac in Genesis 21.

The Terms na'ar, yeled, and bēn in Genesis 21

The difficulties in establishing the semantic pattern for the terms for childhood that were discussed in Chapter 3 abound in the expulsion of Ishmael in

---

5. In the US, one might argue, the competition is not so much within families—although sibling rivalry cannot be discounted—but between families. For example, in the US, parents compete over who can produce the 'best' child, whether the issue is who walks first, who gets into a better school, etc.

6. Read in its canonical context, regardless of Isaac's age in Gen. 21, he was old enough to carry wood in Gen. 22.6 and to help his father as Abraham prepared to sacrifice him. The text assumes a boy who is able to walk on his own for some distance, to talk and question his father, to carry wood, and someone old enough to be in the process of socialization to accept parental authority as would reflect the behaviour of a child learning that his place in the family structure is one of obedience towards his father (parents). Isaac is not one to think for himself and to exercise intellectual autonomy and challenge—as one might expect of a young person today with questions (doubts?) about what is happening to him. Isaac is one who obeys and does what he is told, just as his father Abraham does.

Genesis 21. Here, Ishmael is never referred to by name, but he is identified as a *yeled*[7] (vv. 14, 15, 16) by the narrator in speaking about the relationship between Ishmael and his biological parents, although neither Abraham nor Hagar use the term specifically. The term appears only after Ishmael has been expelled from Abraham's household. Meanwhile, God calls Ishmael a *na'ar* (vv. 12, 17 [2 times], 18, 20), and Sarah—who has instigated the plan for Ishmael's expulsion—refers to Ishmael as *bēn*, 'son' (vv. 9, 10 [2 times]). In v. 9 the narrator calls Ishmael 'the son (*bēn*) of Hagar'; but in v. 10 Sarah speaks directly of 'this slave woman and her son (*bēn*)' and 'the son (*bēn*) of this slave woman' in contrast to 'my son (*bēn*) Isaac'. Thus, three different Hebrew terms are applied in close proximity to each other as a means to identify Ishmael as the narrative comes to focus on the inheritance issues that bring the two sons into conflict with each other.

A first step in moving towards a deeper understanding of the construction of Ishmael and Isaac's childhoods is to give attention to the semantic pattern of the Hebrew terminology as it is applied to Ishmael and Isaac in Genesis 21. My aim now is to explore the application of the nouns *na'ar*, *yeled*, and *bēn* to Abraham's two sons and to return to issues discussed in the previous chapter concerning the semantic pattern of this terminology. We will see if this contextual study of linguistics reveals information on the social construction of childhood for sons in a polygamous household. Perhaps further insight into the social construction of the childhood experiences of a surrogate mother's son in a polygamous marriage will come through linguistic analysis.

Through the linguistic study of the Hebrew terms for 'child' in Chapter 3, we have already acknowledged the difficulty of limiting the semantic range intended by the Hebrew nouns *na'ar* and *yeled*. Added to this problem is the frequent occurrence of the term *bēn* in this chapter. Although the latter noun is typically understood to have a self-evident meaning, a question arises regarding the distributive significance of these three words in Genesis 21 and whether that distribution contributes to an understanding of the culture-bound nature of childhood in biblical Israel. By tracing the distribution of

---

7. In the LXX the term *paidion* is used to translate both *na'ar* and *yeled* throughout Gen. 21. It is used to refer to the weaning of Isaac (Gen. 21.8) and the expulsion of Ishmael. The Greek term is understood to apply to a specific/independent child but neither implies a chronological age nor is a relational noun type. Based on these findings, we conclude that the LXX of Gen. 21 is of little help in understanding the semantic pattern in the earlier use of the Hebrew terms *na'ar* and *yeled*. As we will see, the other Greek word for child, *huios*, a term used to establish a relationship but without an age reference, is rarely used in the LXX to translate *yeled*. Furthermore, as discussed previously, for the Rabbis the two Hebrew terms appear to be synonymous with each other. The Rabbis make no mention of the shift in terminology in Gen. 21.

these three terms, I hope to determine whether or not these nouns provide evidence for the social location of the childhoods of Ishmael and Isaac.

On the one hand, Ishmael is central to the dynamics of the events that unfold in this chapter, but on the other hand, he is never presented as a child/person in his own right or referred to directly by name. Leeb offers the following comment on this fact:

> During the early years of his life, Ishmael is described as Abraham's 'son' (Gen. 16:15; 17:23, 25, 26; 21:11). The narrator is recounting this detail in all of these cases. As Ishmael's disenfranchisement approaches, he begins to be known as Hagar's son (21:9, 10). In Gen. 21:9 the narrator uses the term but Sarah is the speaker in 21:10 who speaks of the 'son of this slave woman'. Neither uses Ishmael's name but the narrator does refer to Hagar by name— even if Sarah does not. God refers to Ishmael as 'the son of a slave woman' (21:13) but throughout the discussion of his fate, Ishmael is never referred to specifically by name. Yet, in Gen. 21:12, God refers to Ishmael as נער for the first time.[8]

The way the narrative is related, there is a disparity between the viewpoints of God and the narrator. Sometimes Ishmael is seen as an independent being and other times he is labeled through his relationship with one of his parents. From Sarah's perspective, one intended to distance Ishmael from herself and the rest of the biological family of Terah through Abraham and his son Isaac, Ishmael is 'the son (*bēn*) of Hagar the Egyptian' (v. 9). To Abraham, Ishmael is 'his son' (v. 11). To Hagar, Ishmael is 'the child' (*yeled*, vv. 14, 15), and to God Ishmael is 'the youth' (*hanna'ar*, vv. 12, 17 [two times], 18, 20). There is a negative distinction between the social locations of Ishmael and Isaac as expressed starkly by Sarah in Gen. 21.10 when she asks Abraham to 'cast out *this slave woman* and *her son*, for *the son of that slave* shall not share in the inheritance *with my son Isaac*' (italics added).

The text also introduces the term *bēn*, 'son', used as a gendered relational term in this context. Genesis 21.10 applies the term twice to Ishmael (who is identified only through his relationship with a slave, and once toward Isaac, who is identified both by his name and as the son of Abraham's primary wife. The conflict is clear: the social status of the unnamed son of a slave versus the named son of the primary wife.

Bēn occurs 12 times in the first 13 verses of Genesis 21. It occurs seven times regarding Isaac and five times regarding Ishmael. In the larger context of the stories of Sarah, Abraham, and Hagar, Ishmael is Abraham's son (Gen. 16.15; 17.23, 25, 26; 21.11). He is Hagar's son in Gen. 21.9, 10 or the son of the slave woman (Gen. 21.13). *Bēn* is a term that can be used to indicate a male relationship specifically, or it can be used in a more generic sense, e.g.,

---

8. Leeb, *Away from the Father's House*, p. 95.

a nation (Isa. 23.10) or, e.g., a people (Isa. 22.4).⁹ It is a word used with great frequency throughout the Hebrew Bible (4,850 times) and has cognates in a wide range of related languages; thus, I have not devoted a separate discussion section to this noun in the prior chapter. All the same, the commonality of the use of this word in Genesis 21 underscores the importance of kinship for this chapter because kinship establishes inheritance.

In his analysis of the terms under investigation here, Revell argues that *bēn* is used to indicate a relationship between the offspring and the parent, that *yeled* indicates family membership, and finally that *na'ar* need not refer to family relationship.¹⁰ Using this perspective to analyze the distribution of terminology for Ishmael in Genesis 21, God's use of the term *na'ar* seems to point to a different perspective on the place of Ishmael in the family than does the perspective of either Abraham or Hagar. The narrative points to different perspectives on childhood, as well as the viewpoint of God, as reported by the narrator. The semantic pattern indicates an attempt to disenfranchise Ishmael from the biological family through the use of *na'ar* in Gen. 21.12, 17 (twice), 18, 20. The term appears first in this chapter (v. 12) when God instructs Abraham to do as Sarah demands, i.e., expel Ishmael and Hagar, but not be distressed by this action. The introduction of the term *na'ar* may be intended to inspire confidence in Abraham that despite the boy's young age at the time of this hardship, Ishmael will survive. In this case, *na'ar* is used to express assurance that Ishmael will be under God's protection. And, if childhood is constructed by social age, rather than by chronological age, the text expresses the vulnerability of a child who is unable to fend for himself when the water runs out in the skin of water on his mother's back (vv. 14-15).

Another perspective on the semantic significance of the terminology applied to Ishmael is provided by Hamilton. He writes,

> It is interesting that every time God refers to Ishmael, he calls him a *lad* (*na'ar*; cf. vv. 12, 17 [2 times], 18, 20). But when Abraham or Hagar refer to him they call him a *child* (*yeled*; cf. vv. 14, 15, 16). The latter word denotes a biological relationship. The use of the former word by God minimizes Ishmael's relationship to Abraham as son. Thus Ishmael is a *yeled* to Abraham and Hagar, but he is a *na'ar* to God. It is almost as if God is siding with Sarah in calling Ishmael Abraham's *na'ar* rather than his *yeled*.¹¹

---

9. See *TDOT*, II, pp. 145-59; *HALOT*, I, pp. 137-38.
10. Revell, *The Designation of the Individual*, p. 31. As noted in Chapter 3, scholars have challenged Leeb's thesis in *Away from the Father's House* that *na'ar* refers solely to one social location and does not reference age.
11. Victor P. Hamilton, *The Book of Genesis: Chapters 18–50* (NICOT; Grand Rapids: Eerdmans, 1995), p. 81.

However, Hamilton has not read the text accurately. It is the narrator who uses the term *yeled* in vv. 14, 15, and 16 and not Abraham or Hagar. Nonetheless, Hamilton is correct that Ishmael is a *na'ar* to God. According to the *NIDOTTE*, 'From this passage one could conclude that *yeled* and *na'ar* are semantically distinct: *yeled* describes a biological relationship—Ishmael is the biological son of Abraham and Hagar—while *na'ar* suggests care and concern'.[12] This understanding of the semantic range of *na'ar* finds support in the work of Van Wolde who posits that the masculine singular absolute *na'ar* signifies only age and gender but not relationship, i.e., God views Ishmael from outside the family context of his parents Abraham and Hagar— possibly because Ishmael's fate lies elsewhere (as stated in Gen. 16.12; 25.12-18). Viewed from this perspective, when God refers to Ishmael as a *na'ar* the biological relationship that ties Ishmael to his parents is being loosened, although in God's eyes Ishmael is still deserving of the care and support that will guarantee the fate promised him in Genesis 17.

Just as the narrator in Genesis 21 understands *yeled* as a kinship term when applied to Ishmael, Eng points out that it is a noun that can in some cases be connected to the noun *bēn* and emphasizes the offspring relationship rather than indicating age.[13] If this is correct, the Hebrew terminology in Genesis 21 conveys that Ishmael is no longer of the primary Terahite kinship line of Abraham, but he does continue as a kin of Hagar. Thus, he is a *yeled* to Hagar but not to Abraham. In fact, Ishmael is referred to as a *yeled* by the narrator only after he is travelling in the desert with Hagar.

This being so, in the instances where Ishmael is a *yeled* (vv. 14, 15, 16— again from the narrator's viewpoint) the noun occurs because it conveys a biological relationship, and at the point in the story where the word appears, Ishmael is in the sole parental care of his mother Hagar. Due to the circumstances that have unfolded, Ishmael is now the *yeled* of Hagar but not of Abraham. Finally, after his expulsion, Ishmael is never referred to as *bēn* by either Hagar or Abraham. In his evaluation of the distribution of the three Hebrew nouns as applied to Ishmael in Genesis 21, Bar-Efrat notes, 'Thus, for Sarah Ishmael is merely the son of Hagar, the Egyptian woman, for Abraham he is his son, for Hagar he is the child, her child, while for God he is what he is, namely, the lad. The narrator refers to him by different terms in accordance with the various attitudes to Ishmael.'[14]

Another term that appears in Genesis 21 that has yet to be addressed is the noun זרע, *zera'*, 'seed'.[15] It appears in Gen. 21.12, 13 where it is used to

---

12. *NIDOTTE*, II, p. 457.
13. Eng, *The Days of our Years*, pp. 87-88.
14. Shimon Bar-Efrat, *Narrative Art in the Bible* (Sheffield: Sheffield Academic Press, 1997), p. 37.
15. See *NIDOTTE*, I, pp. 1151-52; *TDOT*, IV, pp. 143-62.

underscore the fact that Isaac and Ishmael will be Abraham's heirs, i.e., the line of Abraham will be traced through Isaac and through Ishmael. The term is used earlier in Abraham's life: first, in Gen. 15.3 where it refers to Eliezer of Damascus (v. 2), whom Abraham believes will be the one to carry on his lineage, and second, in Gen. 15.5, when God tells Abraham that his descendants will be as many as the (uncountable number of) stars in the heavens above.

I suggest that the bearing of offspring is the dividing line separating childhood from adulthood, and the use of the term זרע at the point when Isaac and Ishmael are designated heirs to Abraham is a means of clarifying that Abraham's full adult status in the vertical descent line is now secured. The term indicates both a long term patrilineal kinship connection as well as Abraham's immediate successor—Isaac, although Ishmael will also be a זרע. It is a term that creates generational continuity for Abraham now that his descent line is established. With Isaac's circumcision and weaning and the expulsion of Ishmael and Hagar, Abraham and Sarah transition to the social age category of full adulthood. Their advanced chronological ages are less significant than the fact that upon Isaac's birth they have become socially recognized as full adults.

In order to understand further the differing perspectives on Ishmael and Isaac held by the Abraham, Sarah, and Hagar as conveyed through the Hebrew nouns discussed above, I now examine how the boys' childhoods are further defined by their social locations in Abraham's family.

Ishmael

In recounting details of Ishmael's life before the birth of Isaac, the narrative stresses a strong bond between Ishmael and his father Abraham. For example, in Gen. 17.15, after God promises Abraham that Sarah will bear him a son, Abraham asks 'that Ishmael might live in your sight' (v. 18). God responds to Abraham's request in 17.20, stating that, 'I will bless him and make him fruitful and exceedingly numerous; he shall be the father of twelve princes, and I will make him a great nation' (v. 20). Furthermore, Ishmael is included in the covenant of circumcision (Gen. 17.25-26) initiated by God with Abraham and his offspring. All the same, God tells Abraham that the everlasting covenant between the deity and Abraham's offspring will come through a child (unborn at this point) borne by Sarah, Abraham's primary wife. Thus, Ishmael is integral to Abraham's family history and continuity until Isaac is born.

The narrative tradition of Ishmael has presented problems of interpretation that take us beyond the facts of the construction of childhood discussed above. Scholars have long noted that in Gen. 21.14, Ishmael appears to be a young child but according to Gen. 17.25, he would be about 16 years old when the events of Genesis 21 occur. The contrast between Gen. 17.25 and Gen. 21.14 concerning Ishmael's age at the time he is expelled from Abraham's house suggests two independent traditions regarding Hagar. In other words, Genesis 16 and 21, are doublets of each other from different literary sources recounting Hagar in the wilderness. These traditions now co-exist in the context of the narratives of Abraham's family and the telling of details of Ishmael's life.

The discrepancy in Genesis about Ishmael's age takes us back into the family conflict between Sarah and Hagar, and Isaac and Ishmael, and brings in a discussion of literary critical arguments concerning the relationship between Genesis 16 and 21 and whether or not these chapters are doublets of each other. Scholars cite various details in support of the doublet theory. Traditional source criticism assigns Gen. 21.8-12 to the Elohistic account of the expulsion of Hagar and Ishmael that parallels the Yahwistic story of Gen. 16.1-16, which is said to include some material from P. The separation between E and J hangs on the shift in the use of divine names, the shift in the characterization of Abraham from passive in response to Sarah's plan for him to impregnate Hagar in 16 to angry in 21 when Sarah demands that he expel Hagar and Ishmael, and the shift from a haughty Hagar in Genesis 16 to a passive slave woman in Genesis 21.[16]

Source-critical analyses of the relationship between Genesis 16 and 21 provide an entry point into debates in the scholarly literature on the redactional issues surrounding Genesis 21. Here, with a focus on the discrepancy between Genesis 17 and Genesis 21 over the age of Ishmael at the time of the events described, commentators address the redactional design that holds the stories of Abraham's family together. According to Gen. 17.25, Ishmael was 13 years old when he was circumcised, and Abraham was 99 (Gen. 17.24). However, in Gen. 21.5, Abraham was 100 years old at the time of the birth of Isaac. Then several years had undoubtedly passed before Isaac was weaned and Ishmael was expelled, with most scholars contending that weaning took place around the age of three.[17] Taken together, these details add up to the conclusion that Ishmael was approximately 16 years old at the

---

16. Thomas B. Dozeman rejects the argument that Gen. 16 and 21 are doublets. He argues that the stories concern the wilderness setting, and he notes, 'there is no parallel etiology of place in Genesis 21' ('The Wilderness and Salvation History', p. 27). The theory of 16 and 21 as doublets is also called into question in Hamilton, *The Book of Genesis*, p. 77.

17. E.g., Claus Westermann, *Genesis 12–36: A Commentary* (trans. John J. Scullion S.J.; Minneapolis: Augsburg, 1985), p. 338. He remarks, 'A child was usually weaned in its third year; the feast celebrates the close of life's first stage: one could describe it as a "rite of passage" (cf. 1 Sam. 1; 1 Kings 11:20)'.

6. *Monogamy, Polygamy, and Childhood Experiences*   93

time of the events recounted in Gen. 21.1-21 when he and his mother were driven out from Abraham's household.[18] Ishmael's age would not be an issue were it not for the fact that according to Gen. 21.14, when he was expelled from Abraham's household, Ishmael is young enough, i.e., small enough, to be carried on Hagar's shoulders, or in her arms; later she puts him under a bush (v. 15) and then she gives him something to drink (v. 19).[19] Of course, the experience of expulsion from one's father's house would be traumatic at any age, but the impact would presumably be different if one were approximately 16 years old, and possibly able to fend for oneself, than if one were a youngster.

Westermann addresses the inconsistency in the timeline of Ishmael's life between the two narrative traditions and convincingly explains the textual discrepancy regarding Ishmael's age at the time of his expulsion. 'Ishmael is a child in Gen. 21 whereas according to 17:25 he was about sixteen years old. A transmitter has made a rather clumsy attempt at harmonization by changing the object to הילד so as to gloss over Abraham lifting Hagar's child on to her shoulders.'[20] In the text we are told of Abraham, 'he took bread and a skin of water and gave (them) to Hagar, putting (them) upon her shoulder, and the child' (v. 14). Thus, the MT has harmonized its perspective on Ishmael as a young child with the P text (Gen. 17) of him being about 16 years old by saying that Abraham gave Ishmael to Hagar and not that he put Ishmael on her shoulders.

Genesis 16 and 21 are not doublets. The latter text addresses the competition over inheritance between Abraham's two sons—who face very different futures depending on which one is chosen as his father's heir. As he prepares to send off Ishmael and Ishmael's surrogate mother, Abraham's distress at Sarah's request is grounded in his affection for his son—although the text does not speak of his emotional ties with Hagar.

---

18. Speiser assigns all but vv. 1-5 to the Elohist (E.A. Speiser, *Genesis* [AB, 1; Garden City, NY: Doubleday, 1964], p. 56); see also, John Skinner, *A Critical Commentary and Exegetical Commentary on Genesis* (ICC; New York: Charles Scribner's Sons, rev. edn, 1910), p. 320.

19. Von Rad argues that the discrepancy in age stems from the combination of JE and P. For the latter, Ishmael was about 17, but not for the narrator of the text in its final canonical form; Gerhard von Rad, *Genesis: A Commentary* (trans. John H. Marks; OTL; Philadelphia: Westminster Press, rev. edn, 1972), p. 235. In his source analysis, George W. Coats argues, 'With the exception of the P element in vv. 1b-5, these scenes belong to J, or better, to JE'; *Genesis with an Introduction to Narrative Literature* (FOTL, 1; Grand Rapids, MI: W.B. Eerdmans, 1983), p. 154.

20. Westermann, *Genesis 12–36*, 341. This line of thinking is followed by Gordon Wenham, *Genesis 16–50* (WBC, 2: Waco, TX: Word Books, 1994), p. 14, who argues that the delay in inserting the term *yeled* adds to the drama of the separation between Abraham and his son Ishmael.

Despite the putative points of contact between the two stories, for purposes of this discussion I am concerned with the details regarding the expulsion of Ishmael and Hagar and what these reveal about the distinctive features of childhood in a polygamous family based on the relative statuses of the two mothers of Abraham's two sons. The displacement of Ishmael by Isaac from the family household and the family patrilineal inheritance comes in Genesis 21 when family conflict surfaces and pits the two sons against each other. This demand and the ultimate expulsion of the young child Ishmael and Hagar from the household of Abraham lead Ishmael to a childhood and life in the wilderness. As stated in Gen. 16.12; 25.12-18, Ishmael's fate is to live as a 'wild ass'; he will live at odds with his kinsmen. As an offspring of Abraham, however, God protects him. As Genesis traces the fate of Ishmael after he survives the expulsion from his father's home, the promise made by God in Gen. 17.20 continues. This point is brought home in the narrative through God's intervention in Ishmael's life as he lies near death in Gen. 21.17-19. Despite all that has happened to him, Ishmael never speaks in Genesis 21, signifying that he lacks assigned agency in the family of his father Abraham.

Thus, we have seen that the childhood experience of Ishmael before and after the birth of Isaac is characterized by a significant decline from favoritism to expulsion from the perspective of Sarah, Abraham, God, and the narrator. Ishmael's declining social location is corroborated by data of cross-cultural studies of childhood in a polygamous versus a monogamous marriage.[21] The result is that two aspects of the social construction of childhood for Ishmael consist of rejection and exile from his father Abraham.[22] Hagar and Ishmael wander hopelessly in the wilderness (Gen. 21.14) until their bread and skin of water are depleted, at which time Hagar expects her young son to die—a sight she cannot bear to watch (vv. 15-16). Despite the future promised for Ishmael by God, at this point Ishmael's death appears imminent.

Ishmael's expulsion limits the vertical lineage of Abraham to descendants through Isaac. Of course, ultimately God rescues Ishmael, and later he is present with his half-brother Isaac to bury Abraham (Gen. 25.9-10). Ultimately, Ishmael becomes the father of twelve tribes (Gen. 25.12-17)—as God had promised in Gen. 17.20. The ending for Ishmael takes the narrative from the realm of family and childhood to larger concerns regarding connections between nations.

In summary, the text reveals that Ishmael has very few rights after the birth of Isaac. Childhood is not synonymous with innocence for Ishmael. Children in the Hebrew Bible did not have rights as we think of them today;

---

21. Montgomery, *An Introduction to Childhood*, p. 54.
22. And more so for the children of Keturah (Gen. 25.1-6).

they were at their father's mercy.[23] From the 'emic' or insider point of view of Israelite culture itself, the treatment of Ishmael and Keturah's children (Gen. 25.1-6) conforms with dynamics associated with the child's place in the wider sphere of the family and the will of the father, but from the 'etic' perspective of the UNCRC, Ishmael's rights as a child are violated and the behavior he endures constitutes child abandonment. In writing on children's rights today, one scholar remarks, 'The most fundamental of rights is the right to possess rights'.[24] It would appear, thus far, that Ishmael is denied his rights in the story of his treatment in the household of Abraham after the birth of Isaac.

In Genesis 21, Isaac and Ishmael are central to the events that unfold but their voices are never heard. Rather, like the case of 1 Samuel 1 with Hannah and her son explored in Chapter 7, the conceptualization and experiences of childhood are determined by parental desires. We see that children are not valued as individuals but for what they contribute to their parents' social status. The story of Genesis 21 ultimately focuses on inheritance and the social construction of childhood and the accompanying experiences of a son borne to a surrogate wife (and slave) in contrast to the son borne to a primary wife.

The contrasts between the social constructions of Ishmael's life and Isaac's life have already been emphasized in multiple ways above. The focus of study in the following section will now shift to Isaac alone and bring to the forefront the dynamics regarding the construction of childhood for him. Before Isaac was born, the environment in which Ishmael was raised was defined by the fact that he was the sole biological son of Abraham; after the expulsion of Ishmael, the fact that Isaac is the sole biological son of Abraham greatly affects the environment in which he will be raised and the nature of his childhood. I hope to demonstrate that Isaac's childhood after the expulsion of Ishmael is shaped by factors that have turned a polygamous household into a monogamous one, although it was a childhood that faced its own challenges.

Isaac

The birth of Isaac in Gen. 21.2 ends the years of Sarah's barrenness that are first recounted in Gen. 11.30. In Gen. 21.1-7, which reports his birth and circumcision, Isaac is a *bēn* (6 times), and his name is explicitly mentioned; but once he is weaned in v. 8 he is identified as a *yeled*, and his name is

---

23. The example of Jacob and Esau vis-à-vis their father Isaac makes this clear, as well; see Gen. 27.
24. Freeman, 'Why It Remains Important to Take Children's Rights Seriously', pp. 5-23 (8).

mentioned at the end of the verse. However, Abraham never refers to Isaac by any of these terms. Abraham's feelings about Isaac come through the narrator. The shift in terminology at the time of the *rites of passage* suggests to us that Isaac is now on his way to becoming a social person, based not on age but on categories of ritual which transform him into a member of the kinship group. The expulsion of Ishmael is one of the many factors that establish Isaac as a member of his father's group. Thus, the details of Isaac's early years concern matters of social age and not chronological age.

Genesis 21.12 makes clear that Isaac will be the sole vertical heir of Abraham in the patrilineage going back to Terah (Gen. 11.27). Although the term זרע can be used as a collective, in Gen. 21.12 it refers to an individual, Isaac. Yet despite the expulsion of Ishmael, Isaac is forced to face his own ordeal in the wilderness due to God's command to Abraham. No sooner is Isaac singled out as Abraham's heir than his life is threatened in Gen. 22.1-19 through God's test of Abraham.[25] The sacrificial ordeal that Isaac faces in Gen. 22.1-19 can be interpreted as a *rite of passage* that moves him further along the continuum towards adulthood. He is leaving childhood and moving along through the stages preparing him for adolescence and then marriage (Gen. 24). Although he stands up to the test that his father faces from God, the so-called 'binding of Isaac' in Gen. 22.1-19 helps us to recognize that what happens to a child—even the primary heir—is controlled by the will of the child's parents and the assumed will of God. Of course, the reality is that in Gen. 22.1-19, Sarah is never mentioned. We are never informed if she is aware of what God is asking Abraham nor do we have any idea of what her reactions were if she had such knowledge. Ironically, Sarah assured the fate of her son Isaac when she arranged for the expulsion of Ishmael, but she has no voice when the fate of her son has him on the brink of death due to the actions of her husband in his response to God's command.

Although commentators focus on the anguish of Abraham, who has just lost one son and is about to lose another,[26] such an approach looks at the text from the point of view of the adults—typically the male adults—who wrote the Hebrew Bible and whose interests control the view point of the narratives. Such a perspective fails to grasp the construction and experience of childhood for the children whose lives are woven throughout the biblical texts. My agenda is to uncover the child culture of Isaac in this text.

The social location of Isaac becomes a bit clearer if we return to the Hebrew nouns relevant for childhood. In Gen. 22.2-3, the emphasis on Isaac as the *bēn* of Abraham ('your son, your only son, whom you love', v. 2) conveys the pathos from the perspective of the father regarding the sacrifice

---

25. One cannot help but notice that Abraham objects to the expulsion of Ishmael in Gen. 21, but raises no objections in Gen. 22 when he is told to sacrifice Isaac.

26. For example, see the discussion in Westermann, *Genesis 12–36*, pp. 364-65.

of his heir. In Gen. 22.5 the noun *na'ar* is applied both to the servants of Abraham who accompany him on his journey and to Isaac. In Gen. 22.12, as Abraham raises the axe to kill Isaac, the angel of the Lord intervenes with a message telling him not to kill the *na'ar*. In Genesis 22, Isaac is identified both as a *bēn* and a *na'ar*, but not as a *yeled*. *Bēn* here emphasizes kinship, or family closeness. However, when the language shifts later to the use of *na'ar*, the emphasis is on the social location of Isaac as someone who is being distanced from his father at this crucial point in the story.

If we take the text of Genesis 22 to reflect the mindset of a child in biblical Israel who finds himself in the circumstances described in this narrative, there is no doubt that Isaac's near death in Genesis 22 raises questions about his childhood experiences. Isaac speaks in this chapter only in v. 7 to inquire about the whereabouts of the sacrifice that will be offered, possibly suggesting his youth and naiveté regarding what is about to occur. The reader can only imagine that the experiences of both Ishmael and Isaac at the hands of their father Abraham were psychological and physical nightmares. Both sons are totally dependent on their father for their well-being, but in both cases their lives are put in jeopardy due to his decisions. One of the concepts in the paradigm of childhood studies explored earlier in the discussion of the new paradigm for the sociology of children is: 'Children are and must be seen as active in the construction and determination of their own social lives, the lives of those around them and of the societies in which they live. Children are not just the passive subjects of social structures and processes.'[27] This is clearly not the case in the lives of either Ishmael or Isaac.

Thus, despite the variation in the childhoods of sons whose mothers are of different statuses and despite the different constructions of childhoods in relationship to polygamous or monogamous households, neither Ishmael nor Isaac are members of a child-centered household. And, although Isaac is the heir to the endogamous marriage between Abraham and Sarah, his welfare and survival are at times precarious. However, as the chosen heir, the culture-bound nature of his childhood was conceptualized in the wider kinship sphere of biblical Israel and thus, as in Genesis 24, every effort is made to find a wife for him who is a kinswoman through the patrilineage of Terah (Gen. 22.20-24; 24.24).

I conclude this analysis by noting that in Genesis 21, Ishmael and Isaac are central to the events that unfold but their voices are never heard. Rather, like the case of 1 Samuel 1 with Hannah and her son, to be discussed in the next chapter, the conceptualization and experiences of childhood are determined by parental interests. Children are not valued as unique individuals, but they are valued for what they can contribute to the social status of their parents.

27. Prout and James, 'A New Paradigm for the Sociology of Childhood?', p. 8.

Chapter 7

1 SAMUEL 1: CHILD ABANDONMENT AND THE BEST
INTERESTS OF THE CHILD

From the perspective of the good of the child according to contemporary understanding in the UNCRC, i.e., the 'etic' point of view, 1 Samuel 1 is a troubling text.[1] As a result of Hannah's religious vows, made to reverse her infertility, Samuel is consecrated to a life of service to God at the sanctuary of Shiloh. Hannah's request to God for a child, who if born will be given over for cultic service, enhances her social status through childbearing. The child will legitimize Hannah as a mother in a society where a woman's worth, and her very status as an adult, was determined by her ability to produce a son for her husband. Further, Hannah gains personal prestige by offering her child for service to God. Not only does a child offer Hannah an increased social status but it also provides economic advantages. As argued above, it was not marriage but parenthood that marked the dividing line between childhood and adulthood.

1 Samuel 1.2 lists Hannah before Peninnah as wives of Elkanah, but then quickly notes that Peninnah had borne children to Elkanah and Hannah had not. This verse is reminiscent of Gen. 11.30 which recounts Sarah's childlessness as the dynamic that shapes family events in the generation of Abraham and Sarah (and Hagar); it underscores the jealousy between a fertile wife and a barren one discussed in the previous chapter. Despite the translation difficulties with 1 Sam. 1.5 regarding the portions given to Hannah and Peninnah by Elkanah[2] when the family goes to Shiloh to

---

1. Scholars consider 1 Sam. 2 a secondary insertion into the text; hence I will not consider it in this study. For further discussion of the Deuteronomistic purposes for the insertion of the Song of Hannah (1 Sam. 2.1-10) into the narrative at this point, see Robert Polzin, *Samuel and the Deuteronomist: A Literary Study of the Deuteronomic History*. II. *1 Samuel* (Bloomington: Indiana University Press, 1993), pp. 30-36.

2. The MT reads *mānâ 'aḥat 'appāyim*, but the exact meaning of the last word, which normally translates as either 'nose' or 'face' in the context of sacrificial offerings is uncertain here. Literally the text translates, 'portion of the face'. Suggests one commentator, 'Perhaps 'portion of the face' signifies a particularly large piece, a portion of honour: earlier exegetes suggested a portion for two people' (Hans Wilhelm Hertzberg, *I & II Samuel* [trans. J.S. Bowden; OTL; Philadelphia: Westminster Press, 1974], p. 24).

worship and offer sacrifices, the text bears witness to Peninnah's taunting Hannah because 'the Lord had closed her womb'.

Against those who might view delivering a child into cultic service as a privilege, I argue in this chapter that the child in 1 Samuel is a victim of what *today* would be labeled child abandonment. I will demonstrate that Samuel is exploited at the hands of his mother Hannah, based on his vulnerability as someone who cannot speak for himself, precisely because the social construction of childhood as represented in 1 Samuel 1 renders him the property of his parents. Samuel is made an object of his mother's wishes.

My thesis concerning 1 Samuel reacts against patriarchal, hegemonic dynamics in ancient Israel and against some earlier critical biblical scholarship. My intent is to analyze the fate of the child Samuel in light of his parents' interests. I will focus on the character of Hannah and the social dynamics that prompt her actions and also raise questions regarding the fate of her child—from the child's point of view. As has previously been established, not only has the topic of children been absent from most investigations of life in ancient Israel, but, as this book purports, the fact that there are many constructions of childhood in any society has not been brought to the forefront in most past biblical investigations of 1 Samuel 1. However, the adult-centered goal of his mother Hannah renders the child Samuel a passive object—ultimately a victim of what might be seen as child abandonment by his parents. But what exactly constitutes abandonment?

According to Boswell's seminal work, '"Abandonment"…refers to the voluntary relinquishing of control over their children by their natal parents or guardians, whether by leaving them somewhere, selling them, or legally consigning them to some other person or institution'.[3] I am arguing here that unless we examine the early life of Samuel and explore the assumptions of the adults who control his life, we fail to grasp the different dynamics working against each other in 1 Samuel. These dynamics are based in economics.[4] As I have argued earlier, this perspective on children stems from the ancient Israelite emphasis on the family as an economic unit, rather than one grounded in emotional/sentimental ties. As discussed in Chapter 4, the purpose of the Israelite family was to further production and to continue the kinship unit.[5] The more children, the more property a man owned. Social scientist Jack Goody labels such understandings of parent–child dynamics a

---

3. Boswell, *The Kindness of Strangers*, p. 24.
4. In American society the economic side of childhood today focuses on children as consumers of property. In pre-industrial agrarian society, children were property to be consumed by adults.
5. For an example of an application of this understanding of the sociology of the biblical family to one body of texts, see, Steinberg, *Kinship and Marriage in Genesis*.

further example of 'the hidden economy of kinship'.⁶ In the ancient Israelite family where the lineage was traced through the patriarch, both wives and children were subservient to the husband. In an effort to preserve the economics of the family, protection of family wealth took precedence over protection of wives and children. A child was chattel that could be sold or abandoned if it served the family's interests.⁷

History of Scholarship

Before going further to recover the biblical assumptions about childhood as represented in 1 Samuel, I will provide a brief overview of scholarship on the narrative of the birth of Samuel. Although 1 Samuel has already been explored from a variety of methodological perspectives, we will see that past investigations fail to provide a culture-specific investigation of childhood from the point of view of the child Samuel.

Critical scholarly research has examined 1 Samuel 1 for its composition/ source-critical history,⁸ analyzed it as an example of the literary type-scene of annunciation,⁹ studied it as an example of the barren matriarch motif,¹⁰ and argued for it as preserving evidence of the birth narrative of Saul based on the etymology of the name Saul—not Samuel.¹¹ Furthermore, from a theological perspective, the text has been used to establish that conception comes from Yahweh, at least in special circumstances as part of God's plan.

Most recently 1 Samuel 1 has come under the scrutiny of feminist methodologies.¹² 1 Samuel 1.11 has been cited as evidence that a woman's vow

---

6. Goody, *The Development of Marriage and Family in Europe*, pp. 183-93. An earlier example of 'the hidden economy of kinship' related to the costs of a girl's dowry.

7. Boswell, *The Kindness of Strangers*.

8. Marc Brettler, 'The Composition of 1 Samuel 1–2', *JBL* 116 (1997), pp. 601-12.

9. Robert Alter, *The Art of Biblical Narrative* (New York: Basic Books, 1981), pp. 82-87.

10. Mary Callaway, *Sing, O Barren One: A Study in Comparative Midrash* (SBLDS, 91; Atlanta: Scholars Press, 1986), pp. 35-57.

11. Arguments that the narrative fits the etymology of the name Samuel can be found in P. Kyle McCarter, Jr, *I Samuel* (AB, 8; Garden City, NY: Doubleday, 1980), p. 62 and James S. Ackerman, 'Who Can Stand before YHWH, This Holy God? A Reading of 1 Samuel 1–15', *Prooftexts* 11 (1991), pp. 1-25 (3-4). The evidence rests on the repeated use of the name 'Saul' *(šā'ûl)*, from the Hebrew root 'to ask' or 'to lend' in Hannah's statement that she asked for him *(šě'iltiw)* (1 Sam. 1.20; cf. 1.17) and how she lends him to Yahweh *(hiš'iltihû)* (1.28).

12. E.g., Yairah Amit, '"Am I not more devoted to you than ten Sons?" (1 Samuel 1:8): Male and Female Interpretations', pp. 68-76; Lillian R. Klein, 'Hannah: Marginalized Victim and Social Redeemer', pp. 77-92; Carol Meyers, 'Hannah and her Sacrifice: Reclaiming Female Agency', pp. 93-104, all in *A Feminist Companion to Samuel and Kings* (ed. Athalya Brenner; Sheffield: Sheffield Academic Press, 1994); Carol Meyers,

could stand without the consent of her husband, despite the law in Num. 30.6-8 stating that a wife's vows are subject to her husband's approval. The focus of feminist interpretation of 1 Samuel rests on the character of Hannah and her determination and independence in circumstances requiring that a wife bear a son to her husband. Just as feminist perspectives on the text argue that male scholarship has obscured Hannah's importance in the text, I argue that an adult-centered perspective, the insider 'emic' point of view of the Hebrew Bible, has obscured the perspective of the child in the text.

Taking Samuel's Rights Seriously:
Whose Life Is It, Anyway?

In pursuing a child-centered reading of the birth of Samuel, we should acknowledge that the story of 1 Samuel 1 has been labeled 'The Legitimacy of Samuel',[13] 'Birth and Dedication of Samuel',[14] 'Samuel's Birth Narrative',[15] 'The Child Asked of God',[16] and other titles. One perspective that is noticeably lacking in this previous research is once again the perspective of the child—Samuel as a subject in his circumstances, or the sociology of the child.

'The Hannah Narrative in Feminist Perspective', in *'Go to the land I will show you': Studies in Honor of Dwight W. Young* (ed. Joseph E. Coleson and Victor H. Matthews; Winona Lake, IN: Eisenbrauns, 1996), pp. 117-26 (123). From a feminist literary perspective, the story is an example of the type-scene of 'the hero's mother'; see Athalya Brenner, *The Israelite Woman: Social Role and Literary Type in Biblical Literature* (The Biblical Seminar, 2; Sheffield: JSOT Press, 1985), pp. 92-98. For another feminist critique of these type-scenes as supporting male perspectives, see Esther Fuchs, 'The Literary Characterization of Mothers and Sexual Politics in the Hebrew Bible', in *Feminist Perspectives on Biblical Scholarship* (ed. Adela Yarbro Collins; SBLCP, 10; Chico, CA: Scholars Press, 1985), pp. 117-36 (118-19). For an analysis of the economics of Hannah's sacrifice to God when she dedicates Samuel in 1.24, see Carol Meyers, 'An Ethnoarchaeological Analysis of Hannah's Sacrifice', in *Pomegranates and Golden Bells: Studies in Biblical, Jewish, and Near Eastern Ritual, Law, and Literature in Honor of Jacob Milgrom* (ed. D.P. Wright, D.N. Freedman and A. Hurvitz; Winona Lake, IN: Eisenbrauns, 1995), pp. 77-91.

13. Walter Brueggemann, *First and Second Samuel* (Interpretation: A Bible Commentary for Teaching and Preaching; Louisville, KY: John Knox Press, 1990), pp. 10-28. 'The Legitimacy of Samuel' includes 1 Sam. 1–3. Brueggemann argues that the opening chapters of 1 Samuel legitimize Samuel as the deliverer of Israel through the hand of God.

14. George B. Caird, *The First and Second Books of Samuel* (IB, 2; Nashville: Abingdon Press, 1953), pp. 876-82.

15. Robert P. Gordon, *I & II Samuel* (Old Testament Guides; Sheffield: JSOT Press, 1984), pp. 23-24.

16. Hertzberg, *I & II Samuel*, pp. 21-26.

Given that Samuel is too young to speak for himself about the circumstances of his life in 1 Samuel 1, how do we interpret what happens to him in this chapter? I maintain that Samuel's dedication to cultic service by his parents (Elkanah does not object to Hannah's plan; 1 Sam. 1.22-23) would today be identified as child abandonment. Hannah's vow promises to dedicate, literally 'to give' (*nātan*) the hoped-for child to cultic service according to the conditions associated with the consecrated Nazirite life,[17] while only vowing that her son will adhere to one of the three conditions.[18] The ability to barter with God for her child—and to promise to 'set him before' the Lord—dedicate, or abandon, him to God's service, depending on the point of view, results in her bearing a child and brings her the status of motherhood in the family of Elkanah. She voluntarily makes this vow in order to receive a child from God. She hopes that by offering the child to God, God will fulfill her wish for a child and remove the shame of a wife who has not borne a child to her husband, and therefore not yet achieved full adulthood status. Both before and after Hannah brings Samuel to Eli at Shiloh, she specifically states that she is giving her son to God (vv. 22-23, 27-28) and adds that it is because God has fulfilled her petition for a child (vv. 27-28).[19] Samuel moves from being the property of his parents to being the property of the cultic shrine at Shiloh, i.e., the property of Eli the priest and its patron deity Yahweh.[20]

Hannah's gift, while appearing to be religiously driven, also is economically motivated. A property paradigm of childhood is evidenced in this example: Samuel is property belonging to someone else and can be bartered away by his mother to Yahweh in exchange for the gift of fertility, followed

17. In 1 Sam. 1.22, *nazirite* is used in LXX (and in NRSV) but not in MT—a slight shift in meaning especially to the modern reader.
18. Hannah only specifically mentions that he will never cut his hair (1 Sam. 1.11), The two other conditions for the life of a Nazirite are (1) he abstains from drinking wine or other intoxicants and (2) he does not approach a dead body. See Num. 6.1-21 and Judg. 13.1-7. Hertzberg argues that Hannah's statement of only one of the three aspects of Nazirite vows suggests that the story may have its origins in the story of Samson; see Hertzberg, *I & II Samuel*, p. 25.
19. Thus, what is happening here is a gift exchange. For this model, see Marcel Mauss, *The Gift: The Form and Reason for Exchange in Archaic Societies* (trans. W.D. Halls; London: Routledge, 1990).
20. In 1 Sam. 1, Samuel is referred to both as a *bēn* and a *na'ar* but not as a *yeled*. Hannah refers to Samuel as a *na'ar* when he is weaned (1 Sam. 1.22) and when she acknowledges him as the child for whom she prayed (1 Sam. 1.27). Furthermore, when Samuel is brought to Shiloh for service under Eli, the text reports *wehanna'ar nā'ar* (v. 24). Hertzberg understands the phrase to refer to age, 'although the child was still young' (*I & II Samuel*, p. 27), while Revell translates 'the lad became a servant' (*The Designation of the Individual*, p. 31). The contrast between these two translations illustrates the scholarly discrepancy regarding definitions of the term *na'ar* discussed previously.

by her expected subsequent rise in status in the family of her husband Elkanah. Moreover, the story supports institutional interests in ancient Israel through its example of the appropriateness of dedicating one's child to a lifetime of service to God. Initially, Samuel is the property of his mother—or father?—and later he becomes the property of Eli and a permanent resident in the sanctuary at Shiloh where he basically earns his keep in the service of Yahweh. Although such behavior towards Samuel comports with the paradigm of the child as property, from the perspective of the child with rights of its own, Samuel is denied any chance to choose his fate when he is bartered away by Hannah. As chattel, he was never given such an opportunity.

In an economic sense, a child's value and identity was formed based on membership in a family, i.e., a patrilineage, and what the child owed the parent based on this family identity. The economic value of a child is seen, for example, in 2 Kgs 4.1,[21] when children are taken by a creditor to pay off a debt. Control over a child's fate resided in the hands of the child's parents when the child was viewed as property. By the same token, in the case of Samuel, his dedication to Yahweh at Shiloh required the sacrifice of his freedom of choice as his parents fulfill Hannah's vow.

The ideology surrounding the firstborn son in ancient Israel helps us understand the perspective of the child Samuel as property to be given away. Because Israel was dedicated to God, God spared them when slaughtering the firstborn of the Egyptians (Exod. 12.29). The selection of the firstborn of Israelite and Egyptian families suggests a theological and sociological ideal of the special nature of the firstborn son. A sociological approach to the dedication of the firstborn to Yahweh interprets Samuel and the food that accompanies his dedication at Shiloh (1 Sam. 1.24) as a payment to God for a gift given or a request fulfilled. Hannah's vow would appear to be a promise to fulfill God's claim on the firstborn, although the child is *her* firstborn, not the firstborn of Elkanah.[22] 1 Samuel 1.4 is clear that Peninnah, Elkanah's other wife, has already borne him both sons and daughters. Possibly this text, in conjunction with the stories of Abraham, Hagar, Sarah, and their sons Ishmael and Isaac—of whom only the latter is nearly sacrificed, in a literal sense—leads us to assume that the claim on the firstborn applied to the offspring of the primary wife and not a secondary wife. 1 Samuel 1.2 lists Hannah's name before Peninnah's as the wives of Elkanah. However, while Abraham leaves to offer Isaac to God without Sarah's knowledge in Genesis 22, Hannah vows her hoped-for child to God without Elkanah's knowledge, who evidently agrees with Hannah's plan since he could have nullified her vow but didn't (Num. 30.6-8).

21. This is also seen in Exod. 13.13; 34.20; Num. 18.15-16.
22. Both Exod. 13.12-15 and Num. 18.15-16 state that the firstborn male of every human womb is to be redeemed.

The emphasis here on the economic side of childhood underscores the axis on which much of the sociology of childhood in the biblical world turns. The topic of the worth of a child—whether it is economic or sentimental value—brings us to 1 Sam 1.8. Here Elkanah has given more portions to his wife Peninnah and her sons and daughters than he has to his barren wife Hannah. Hannah weeps because of her childlessness and Peninnah's taunting, provoking a response from Elkanah that Yairah Amit translates as, 'Am I not more devoted to you than ten sons?' whereas others simply translate, 'Am I not more to you than ten sons?' The question is, what does this statement mean? What is Elkanah trying to say? Although Amit argues that Elkanah's words express his devotion to his wife Hannah,[23] Westbrook locates the statement in the context of ancient Near Eastern adoption texts, and he remarks on the similarity between the reference to ten sons in 1 Sam. 1.8 and in the extra-biblical data.[24] He uses the ancient Near Eastern adoption documents to explain the difference between 1 Sam. 1.8 and Ruth 4.15b, with its reference to Ruth being more valuable to Naomi than seven sons. Regarding Elkanah's meaning, Westbrook writes, 'His point seems to be that a husband, like an adopted son, can more than make up for the lack of natural offspring'.[25] However, this interpretation fails to grasp the significance of motherhood for Hannah vis-à-vis Peninnah in this text, and in ancient Israelite society. In order for Hannah to be a full adult, she needs more than a husband; she needs a son to legitimize her place in Elkanah's family, even though as a result of her vow, her son will not grow up with her and Elkanah. Thus, Elkanah's love for Hannah does not make up for her childlessness prior to the birth of Samuel. Through the birth of a son whom she dedicates to the shrine of Yahweh, Hannah contributes to the future of the Israelite people. Samuel's role in the life of the Israelite community becomes crucial for its survival.

As noted above, much of how we think about children in any society—past and present—depends on an adult point of view that determines how a child is treated. Of course, a child's age and level of maturity has bearing on whether or not s/he can speak for her/himself about her/his future. Yet to discuss these issues takes us away from Samuel's perspective. Was he happy or sad about being placed with Eli? Was he well-fed in his new home? Were there other children around? Who were his teachers? Was he old enough to remember his siblings, the children of Peninnah? We will never know the answers to these questions because the cultural and social processes at work in the construction of childhood for Samuel as presented in the Hebrew

---

23. Amit, 'Am I Not More Devoted to You Than Ten Sons?', p. 75.
24. Raymond Westbrook, '1 Samuel 1:8', *JBL* 109 (1990), pp. 114-15.
25. Westbrook, '1 Samuel 1:8', p. 115.

Bible render him as property to be invested according to his parents' interests. Samuel's life was not his own. Social construction of family life in ancient Israel gives little concern for individual autonomy of any family members.

It is clear from the analysis above of 1 Samuel that the social understanding of childhood in the biblical text is linked to the economic value of the child: the text reveals a model of children as the property of their parents. The biblical example of 1 Samuel 1, in dialogue with contemporary Western discussions about the protection of children and their rights, such as the UNCRC provides, juxtaposes two documents that can both challenge and inform each other in thinking about 'the best interests of the child'. The story of the child Samuel in the Hebrew Bible reveals issues of children's vulnerability to their parents and the need for safeguards to protect the interests of children—even against their parents.

Chapter 8

EXODUS 21.22-25: IS THE FETUS A LIFE?

Thus far I have answered the central question 'What is a child in the Hebrew Bible?' through linguistic and narrative analyses. My findings to this point support the thesis that in biblical Israel, childhood was a socially constructed category shaped by factors such as the economic functions associated with social age (the work or activities done), gender, and family structure (e.g., monogamy versus polygamy). I now turn to ideas about the status of the fetus and investigate whether cultural constructions of the unborn in ancient Israel acknowledge their personhood within the categories of childhood revealed previously.

My focus in this chapter is Exod. 21.22-25, found in the Book of the Covenant (Exod. 20.21–23.33). I question whether or not a fetus was recognized as a life in a law addressing injury to a pregnant woman. In asking this question, I continue to explore where biblical Israel drew the boundaries between a life and a nonlife. Was the status of a fetus in biblical Israel determined by the biological stage of development it had reached when the circumstances of Exod. 21.22-25 occurred? Was a miscarried fetus deemed to be the termination of a nonlife? The answer to these questions determines nothing less than whether the death of a fetus in an accident was ruled a murder, which would be the only legal conclusion if the fetus was considered a life in Exod. 21.22-25.[1]

Exodus 21.22-25 reads as follows:

> (22) When men are fighting and they strike a pregnant woman and her fetus/children (*yĕlādeyhâ*) come out but there is no serious injury (*'āsôn*), he will be fined as the husband of the woman exacts from him, and he will pay as is determined by arbitration (*biplilîm*).[2] (23) But if there is a serious injury

---

1. I use the English term 'fetus' although I recognize that it carries particular emotional valence in Western culture. It is difficult to find an appropriate translation for what is being discussed in the law because the 'fetus' is referred to in Hebrew as a *yeled*, which when translated 'fetus' may or may not have the same nuances as the English word.

2. The meaning of the Hebrew *biplilîm* is uncertain. The NRSV translates, 'paying as much as the judges determine'. For the multiple interpretations of this term that are possible, see David P. Wright, *Inventing God's Law: How the Covenant Code of the*

('āsôn), you[3] will give life for life, (24) eye for eye, tooth for tooth, hand for hand, foot for foot, (25) burn for burn, wound for wound, bruised for bruise.

As we begin to analyze the legislation of Exod. 21.22-25, we must be mindful of the contemporary controversy on when life begins and whether or not the fetus is a life in order to avoid skewing an ancient text with issues contested in the modern world. On this topic, anthropologist Montgomery writes that despite Christian values concerning the life status of a fetus, currently:

> [t]he boundaries between child, fetus, and embryo are extremely blurred, often representing the distinction between person and non-person, and in some cases between life and nonlife. Ideas concerning these boundaries are problematic, culturally specific, and deeply contested: as Lynn Morgan puts it, '"the fetus" is a culturally specific conceptual entity and not a biological 'thing', and...is created in particular cultural circumstances'. Thus a child may be recognized as fully human from the moment of conception (the position of the modern Catholic Church), or it may be seen as becoming a person more gradually, and in some cases, may not be recognized as a full human being until several days or months after its birth.[4]

As we will now see, the modern investigator discovers that in the Hebrew Bible ideas about the status of the fetus, like ideas regarding childhood, are culturally constructed categories. Contemporary Western legal definitions used to mark the boundaries of the start of life either at the moment of conception or at the moment of birth, cannot be easily or automatically transferred from the present into the past.[5]

Exodus 21.22-25 and the History of Scholarship

The law of Exod. 21.22-25 breaks down into two parts: vv. 22-23 and vv. 24-25. Together these two parts address injury to a pregnant woman and the economic interests owed to her husband when she miscarries as a result of

---

Bible Used and Revised the Laws of Hammurabi (New York: Oxford University Press, 2009), p. 436 n. 119. The text appears to imply that the amount of the monetary penalty is not fixed.

3. Verse 23 is formulated as a second-person directive, as opposed to normal third-person formulations of rulings. On the potential significance of this shift, see Wright, *Inventing God's Law*, p. 183.

4. Montgomery, *An Introduction to Childhood*, p. 80. See Lynn M. Morgan, 'Imagining the Unborn in Ecuadoran Andes', *Feminist Studies* 23 (1997), pp. 323-50 (329). In this quotation the term 'non-person' means, non-human, i.e., not being considered a full human being.

5. Although this chapter is intended to continue the discussion of the social construction of childhood in ancient Israel, it cannot avoid touching on issues regarding the contemporary debate on abortion.

being struck in a fight between two men. In the first part of the law, Exod. 21.22-23, we are presented with the conditions of the case (a fight between two men/individuals) and the consequences of these conditions (one of the men accidentally strikes a pregnant woman and her unborn child). Verse 22 qualifies the consequences of the fight by noting that no serious injury (*'āsôn*) occurs. The second part of the law, v. 23, rules on what should be done in the event that the fight causes a serious injury (*'āsôn*) resulting in death: 'If there is a deadly accident, you shall give a life for a life'. In other words, the principle of *lex talionis*, equal restitution or retaliation, applies if death occurs from the fight. The principle of *lex talionis* continues in the second part of the law, where vv. 24-25 qualify the principle of substitution to the circumstances when death does not occur from the fight but there is injury to body parts.

There are many different interpretations of this law and many different issues that scholars have focused on in past research. This long history of critical study extends far beyond my interest in the socially constructed category of childhood and the status of the fetus; it is both impossible and unnecessary to summarize the history of scholarship on Exod. 21.22-25. However, a brief survey of some of the issues that are relevant to my research will provide background for the present investigation and introduce the topics that inform my study of this passage.

Past critical biblical scholarship has focused on: (1) the history of the composition of the law, (2) the revision and interpolation of the law, i.e., were vv. 24-25 originally separate from the preceding two verses; and (3) the comparative study of Exod. 21.22-25 in light of the law codes from surrounding ancient Near Eastern law codes (LH 209-210; MAL 21, 51, 52; and HL 17, 18). Issues of the legal dependency between Israelite and these ancient Near Eastern law codes have been a source of continuing scholarly deliberations. The three issues listed above come together and relate directly two issues: whether the fate of the unborn child or the mother who is injured is the primary concern of the law and whether the money paid to the husband is for injury to the fetus or to the pregnant woman or both (i.e., the payment is for the total value lost, including time). Scholars also debate whether Exod. 21.22-23 was originally followed by the *lex talionis* in vv. 24-25. They attempt to answer this question by comparing the law in the Covenant Code with LH 209-210.[6] LH 209-210 reads as follows:

---

6. For example, Bernard S. Jackson, 'The Problem of Exod, xxi 22-5: (*ius talionis*)', *VT* 23 (1973), pp. 273-304 argues that vv. 24-25 are not original to the text; hence, originally, *'āsôn* referred to the death of the unborn child. This is also the position of Eckart Otto, 'Town and Rural Countryside in Ancient Israelite Law: Reception and Reaction in Cuneiform and Israelite Law', *JSOT* 57 (1993), pp. 3-22. Houtman maintains that v. 22 refers to the death of the unborn child and that v. 23 refers to the death of the

(209) If a person (*awīlum*) strikes an *awīlum*-woman (a woman of the *awīlum* class) and causes her to miscarry her fetus, he shall weigh out ten shekels of silver for her fetus. (210) If that woman dies, they shall kill his daughter.[7]

To resolve the questions of the tradition-historical relationship between the biblical law and earlier cuneiform legal traditions such as LH 209-210, David P. Wright proposes that the CC is dependent on the LH. This theory of dependency plays a role in answering a related question about the text, i.e., whether or not Exod. 21.22-25 was originally one law or whether vv. 24-25 is a later literary insertion. Based on the connections he makes between LH and CC, Wright asserts:

> The first laws [Exod. 21:22; LH 209] in both passages consider a case where the child is born dead, and the second laws [Exod. 21:23-25; LH 210], a case where the mother also dies or, according to the talion extension in CC suffers injury. This correlation puts to bed the argument that in a supposed earlier formulation that lacked verses 24-25, CC's two laws were concerned only with the status of the child, with verse 22 treating premature birth (but not death of the child) and verse 23 dealing with miscarriage... In any case, the talion law in verses 23b-25 has to be considered part of the original text... Its presence constrains the interpretation of the miscarriage laws and forces one to understand 23a as referring to the woman's death.[8]

---

pregnant woman; see Cornelis Houtman, *Das Bundesbuch: Ein Kommentar* (Documenta et Monumenta Oritentalis Antiqui, 24; Leiden: E.J. Brill, 1997), pp. 159-60; also see his, *Exodus*, III (Historical Commentary on the Old Testament; Leuven: Peeters, 2000), pp. 160-71.Thus one sees that there are as many interpretations of the enigma of this law as there are scholars who work to interpret its difficulties. For example, Bernard S. Jackson, 'The Pregnant Woman Victim', in *Wisdom-Laws: A Study of the Mishpatim of Exodus 21:1–22:16* (New York: Oxford University Press, 2006), pp. 209-39 returns to the law again more recently and shifts the focus of his scholarly attention to the relationship between Exod. 21.22-25 and the foreign wisdom tradition. In this article he concludes, 'The best explanation of the paragraph on miscarriage may be that it is written for an audience which possessed greater familiarity with foreign wisdom, a different more theoretical and sophisticated audience from that to which the practical wisdom of the *Mishpatim* was addressed' (p. 239).

7. *ANET*, p. 175.

8. Wright, *Inventing God's Law*, p. 177. The two fate theory (v. 22 dealing with the premature birth, but not death, of the child and v. 23 addressing miscarriage, i.e., death of the child, but possibly also the woman) is found in Jackson, 'The Problem of Exod. xxi 22-5 (*ius talionis*), pp. 271-304, which was later reprinted in *Essays in Jewish and Comparative Legal History* (SJLA, 10; Leiden: E.J. Brill, 1975), pp. 75-107 and was then updated in his 'The Pregnant Woman Victim', pp. 209-39. The argument is picked up by, e.g., H. Wayne House, 'Miscarriage or Premature Birth: Additional Thoughts on Exodus 21:22-25', *WTJ* 41 (1978), pp. 108-23; for a critique, see Samuel E. Loewenstamm, 'Exodus xxi 22-25', *VT* 27 (1977), pp. 352-60.

Wright's argument for the content and structure of CC based on LH may help explain the structure of Exod. 21.22-25 in the CC, but there is still the problem of interpreting the distinct differences between the laws as stated in the Hebrew Bible and in LH. Specifically, in LH 209-210 the assumption is that the attack against the pregnant woman was deliberate and the law calls for the death of the assailant's daughter in the event that the pregnant woman dies as a result of the attack. However, while LH is clear that the object of the injury in law 209 was the fetus and the death of the pregnant woman is the concern of law 210, the wording and syntax of Exod. 21.22-25 create ambiguity and make it difficult to determine the object of the injury redressed by the biblical law.[9]

The Hebrew Phrase ויצאו ילדיה

One difficulty in deciding whether or not the fetus was a life in ancient Israel arises from the occurrence of the term *yeled* to refer to the unborn in Exod. 21.22-25. Does the use of the noun *yeled* in this law indicate that a fetus is a living child, a person?

The discussion of the noun *yeled* in this passage takes us back to the linguistic issues raised in Chapter 3 about the semantic pattern displayed in the Hebrew text through the range of occurrences and meanings assigned to the noun *yeled*, typically translated as 'child'. My reason for returning to questions of the meaning of this term is the terminological problem in Exod. 21.22-25 concerning the difficult phrase *wĕyāṣĕ'û yĕlādeyhâ*, literally, 'her children (ילדיה) come out' in v. 22 (plural instead of singular from *yeled*). To be clear, here in Exod. 21.22, the fetus is identified by the Hebrew word *yĕlādeyhâ*, a masculine plural form of the noun *yeled* with a feminine possessive suffix, 'her children'. Of course, according to Hebrew grammar the masculine form covers both male and female and should not be taken to read that the fetus in question was determined to be a male.

As far back as antiquity, the difficulties of the plural form in v. 22 were recognized, judging by the fact that in the LXX the Greek addresses the problem by translating the Hebrew *yĕlādeyhâ* with the Greek *paidion*, a singular term for a fully formed child. The LXX appears to correct what it recognized as an error in the MT by replacing the Hebrew plural term with a Greek singular noun.

---

9. The repetition of the term *'āsôn* in vv. 22-23 provides the basis for reading these two verses as a unit that addresses whether or not there was serious injury (*'āsôn*). This link allows us to sidestep the question of whether vv. 24-25 is a later literary insertion which expands on the *lex talionis* in v. 23. Although these two verses extend the *lex talionis*, the principle of compensation for a serious accident has already been stated in v. 23. Thus, the question of whether vv. 24-25 were original to the law takes us beyond my interest in whether a fetus was considered a human being in Exod. 21.22-23.

The terminological problem of the plural form for child, rather than the expected singular, remains. The argument that the plural form in the Hebrew should be taken at face value and that the law intends miscarriage of twins would appear to be a case of finding a translation to fit the text, rather than dealing with the difficulties of the Hebrew original. One must search further for an explanation for the use of the Hebrew plural *wĕyāṣĕ'û yĕlādeyhâ* in this law.[10] Blenkinsopp resolves the problem of the plural form in the MT and reads with the LXX in the singular.[11] Schwienhorst-Schönberger argues that the plural form is a way to refer to a single fetus.[12] The present scholarly consensus is that the text of the MT refers to a single fetus and that the noun *yeled* has the semantic range to include both a nonlife and a life according to the socially constructed categories of personhood in the Hebrew Bible.

We are reminded of the wide range in the usage of the term *yeled*: the plural word for the fetus in Exod. 21.22 is the exact same word describing the married sons Mahlon and Chilion in Ruth 1.5, *yĕlādeyhâ*[13] (allowing for the fact that these texts probably come from different historical time frames). The semantic range of the term *yeled* becomes a relevant question (again) when we acknowledge that the noun is applied in the biblical texts to the unborn as well as to sons old enough to be married. The term spans the time from before birth to marriage; it is not a noun that designates chronological

---

10. Jackson, *Wisdom-Laws*, pp. 215-61 reviews various scholarly perspectives on this phrase. Regarding the plural, Propp remarks, 'This must be taken as referring either to the potential for multiple pregnancies—"(all) her babies, (however many)"—or else to all the stuff of childbirth: water, blood, child(ren), afterbirth'. See William H.C. Propp, *Exodus 19–40: A New Translation with Introduction and Commentary* (AB, 2A: New York: Doubleday, 2006), p. 222. That the phrase in the plural is a way of referring to the fetus is argued by Ludger Schwienhorst-Schönbeger, *Das Bundesbuch* (BZAW, 188; Berlin: W. de Gruyter, 1990), pp. 97-98; *idem*, 'Auge um Auge, Zahn um Zahn', *BLit* 63 (1990), pp. 164-65. Joe E. Sprinkle remarks (The Interpretation of Exodus 21:22-25 [*Lex Talionis*] and Abortion', *WTJ* 55 [1993], pp. 233-53 [249]), '…if the author wanted to denote a miscarriage, he should have used the root שכל (a verb used of miscarriages, cf. Exod. 23:26) along with ילד…the author does not used the term for miscarriage because the plural form ילדיה is a plural of abstraction with the sense "the product of her womb", an apt term for an inadequately developed baby'. A few scholars, e.g., Crüsemann, argue that the plural is used because the phrase means that the woman loses her child-bearing abilities due to the accident; see Frank Crüsemann, *The Torah: Theology and Social History of Old Testament Law* (Minneapolis: Fortress Press, 1996), p. 160.

11. Private communication.

12. Schwienhorst-Schönberger, *Bundesbuch*, pp. 97-98; 'Auge um Auge', pp. 164-65.

13. However, in the LXX of Ruth 1.5 the sons are *huios* and not *paidon*. The latter is the term used in the LXX of Exod. 21.22 in place of the plural form ילדיה found in the Hebrew. As noted in the discussion of these terms in Chapter 3, *huios* is a relational word. In the context of describing the sons of Ruth, it is the word one would expect. However, in Exod. 21.22 the term used is *paidon*, a word that has neither age nor relationship associated with it.

age. The translation of *yeled* as 'child' in every instance it occurs in the biblical text fails to grasp the many phases of physiological and sociological development covered by this term and is certainly misleading if translated literally in v. 22 so that the fetus, a nonperson, is understood to be a 'child'.

The use of a plural form of *yeled* to designate a single fetus does not, however, resolve the issue of the fate of the unborn in Exod. 21.22-25. The phrase ויצאו ילדיה has been understood to indicate either that a miscarriage[14] or a premature birth[15] resulted from the pregnant woman being struck during a fight. The phrase is unique in the Hebrew Bible. In examples such as Gen. 25.5-26; 38.28-30; and Jer. 1.5; 20.18, the verbal root *yṣ'* refers to a live birth. When the verb *yāṣā'* is used in combination with some form of the root *mwt*, death, it refers to a miscarriage or a stillborn child, such as in Num. 12.12; Job 3.11. Moreover, biblical Hebrew contains a word for 'miscarriage' (to lose a child), *škl*, which appears over twenty times in the biblical text; there is also a root for an 'untimely birth', *npl,* found in Job 3.16; Ps. 58.8; and Eccl. 6.3.

Despite the availability of these other Hebrew terms to describe the outcome of this fight and its effect on the fetus, most contemporary biblical commentators understand the phrase *wĕyāṣĕ'û yĕlādeyhâ* to mean that the fight between the two men has resulted in a miscarriage for the pregnant woman. They arrive at this conclusion based on comparative study of the variations of case law that appear in earlier ancient Near Eastern legal collections referred to above where the circumstances of the law are believed to refer to miscarriage.[16]

14. E.g., Houtman, *Exodus*, III, p. 161.
15. E.g., Jackson, *Essays in Jewish and Comparative Legal History*, pp. 95, 99.
16. For a history of the interpretation of this law and a general discussion of difficulties with the text and the two traditions of interpreting it, see Stanley Isser, 'Two Traditions: The Law of Exodus 21:21-23 Revisited', *CBQ* 52 (1990), pp. 30-45. Reading the phrase as miscarriage are: Martin Noth, *Exodus* (trans. J. Bowden; Philadelphia: Westminster Press, 1962), p. 181; J.P. Hyatt, *Exodus* (NCB; London: Marshall, Morgan & Scott, 1971), p. 234; R.E. Clements, *Exodus* (Cambridge: Cambridge University Press, 1972), p. 138; Brevard Childs, *The Book of Exodus* (OTL; Philadelphia: Westminster Press, 1974), p. 443. Wright, *Inventing God's Law*, p. 177 argues that v. 22 refers to a case where the child dies due to the accident and that v. 23 has in mind that the woman either dies or suffers injury. Dozeman suggests that v. 22 can refer to either a miscarriage or a premature birth but based on LH 209 believes it refers to a miscarriage (Dozeman, *Commentary on Exodus*, pp. 534). Reading the phrase as premature birth, U. Cassuto, *Commentary on Exodus* (trans. I. Abrahams; Jerusalem: Magnes Press, 1967), p. 275. Jackson, 'The Problem of Exod. xxi 22-5 (*ius talionis*)', p. 292, argues that the law refers to a premature live birth but that due to interpolations, the meaning of the law changed over time. Eveline van Staalduine-Sulman, 'Between Legislative and Linguistic Parallels: Exodus 21:22-25 in its Context', in *The Interpretation of Exodus: Studies in Honour of Cornelius Houtman* (ed. Riemer Roukema; Leuven: Peeters, 2006), pp. 207-24 argues,

In order to further address the status of the fetus in Exod. 21.22-23 and the meaning and object of the term *'āsôn*, I turn next to the use of this term in this legal case to ask whether the law speaks of injury to the mother or to her unborn child. How the interpreter answers this question contributes further data to the discussion of whether the fetus is a life in ancient Israelite society. A fetus is not a life if it is the object of the non-deadly *'āsôn* in v. 22, i.e., if the offender (the man who caused the accident) is compensating the husband with money, because according to biblical understanding, one does not compensate for a life with money. On the other hand, the fetus is a life if the deadly *'āsôn* in v. 23 refers to the fetus and the principle of 'a life for a life' concerns the death of the fetus. Such an interpretation would mean that the law recognizes the unborn as a person. What is clear at this point in my investigation is that the law of Exod. 21.22-23 seeks to protect the paternal legal and economic interests of the husband of the pregnant woman and in doing so addresses the legal status of the unborn. I now focus on the ambiguity and the direct object of the term *'āson*, because the status of the fetus in Exod. 21.22-25 hangs on this uncertainty.

Who Was Hurt? 'āsôn

In order to arrive at an understanding of the status of the fetus in this text, we repeat (1) that scholars debate the meaning of the term *'āsôn* and (2) that the direct object of the term *'āsôn* is unclear. Does the term refer to the pregnant woman or to her fetus? The wording and syntax of the MT of Exod. 21.22-23 make it difficult to be certain whether the law speaks of injury to only the fetus, to the woman, or to both the fetus and the pregnant women.[17]

Westbrook, in a minority interpretation, concludes that the word *'āsôn* applies to the assailant, who is not identified. He translates *'āsôn*, 'Damage caused by an unknown perpetrator'.[18] Few scholars accept this reading of the text, which does not understand the noun *'āsôn* to refer to either the unborn or the pregnant woman. By contrast, Houtman joins most other scholars in maintaining that the term refers to the pregnant woman, not the fetus, and specifies a fatal injury. Thus, he translates v. 22, 'But she herself is not

---

'This stipulation is broad enough to cover all the cases of pregnant women as victims: miscarriage, harm to the newborn baby and harm to the woman, including her possible death' (p. 224).

17. The term also appears in Gen 42.4, 38; 44.29 with reference to Benjamin. For further discussion of the term, see Jackson, 'The Problem of Exod, xxi 22-5 (*ius talionis*)', pp. 273-304; Raymond Westbrook, 'Lex Talionis and Exodus 21, 22-25', *RB* 93 (1986), pp. 52-69; *idem*, *Studies in Biblical and Cuneiform Law* (Cahiers de la Revue biblique, 26; Paris: J. Gabalda, 1988), pp. 69-70, 80.

18. Westbrook, 'Lex Talionis and Exodus 21, 22-25', pp. 52-69.

fatally injured'.[19] According to his interpretation, if the injury to the pregnant woman does not result in her serious injury, or death, the punishment against the man who caused the injury is monetary compensation. In the event that the mother dies, the principle *lex talionis* applies, according to v. 23: 'If there is a serious harm [presumably this means a deadly accident], you will give life for life'.

Although not all scholars agree, the consensus is that the 'life for a life' in the case of death (v. 23) applies to the death of the mother, but in the event that she does not die, the monetary compensation called for in v. 22 applies to the unborn child as payment to the husband/father for the loss of the child in the case of miscarriage.[20] If this view is accepted, v. 22 applies to the fetus and vv. 23-25 concern the pregnant woman—both of whom are the property of the husband whose economic interests are undermined by the events of the fight between the two men.

The ambiguity of the object of the phrase *'āsôn*, 'serious harm' goes back to antiquity and was recognized in the LXX. The Greek text states in v. 22: 'if two men are fighting and strike a pregnant woman, and her unformed child departs (*mē exeikonismenon)*, he shall be fined...' However, in v. 23, the LXX goes on to stipulate: 'But if the child is formed, he shall give life for life'. The wording in the LXX of Exod. 21.23 refers to a specific fully formed child, *paidon*, and stipulates that the pregnancy has progressed to the stage that the unborn is recognized as a person, hence the principle of 'a life for a life' applies. It is clear that the LXX understands *'āsôn* to refer to injury to the unborn—not to the mother.

In the Greek text, the emphasis is shifted to the fetus and away from the pregnant woman, and stages of fetal development are conditions introduced into the law. The LXX appears to understand the fetus to be a life at only a particular (unstated) stage in its development[21] based on the use of the noun *paidion*, a word that refers to a fully formed child without specifying the age of the child. The LXX recognizes the unborn as a person with legal rights. However, the LXX reading does not resolve the difficulties of the Hebrew

---

    19. Houtman, *Exodus*, III, pp. 160, 163, 168.
    20. Dozeman, *Commentary on Exodus*, pp. 534-35.
    21. That a fetus was not a life from conception is stated by the Jewish author Philo, *Spec. Leg.* 3.108-9: 'If a man comes to blows with a pregnant woman and strikes her on the belly and she miscarries, then, if the result of the miscarriage is unshaped and undeveloped, he must be fined both for the outrage and for obstructing the artist Nature in her creative work of bringing into life the fairest of living creatures, man. But if the offspring is already shaped and all the limbs have their proper qualities and places in the system, he must die, for that which answers to this description is a human being, which he has destroyed in the laboratory of Nature who judges that the hour has not yet come for bringing it out into the light, like a statue lying in a studio requiring nothing more than to be conveyed outside and released from confinement'.

original nor does it find support in the MT. Rather, the Greek syntax is much clearer than the MT and appears to be an attempt to resolve the ambiguity surrounding the identity of the injured party in the Hebrew original.

The MT makes no provisions for stages of development in the pregnancy; unlike the LXX it does not distinguish between an unformed and a formed fetus. Thus, in the LXX the issue concerning economic compensation is the age/viability of the unborn—a distinction that is absent in the original Hebrew. Exodus 21.22 in the MT refers to injury to the fetus. The law provides economic compensation to the father of the miscarried fetus in the amount 'as the assessors determine', because a fetus is a nonperson; if it were considered a life, the principle of *lex talionis* in v. 23 would apply.[22]

We conclude from the previous discussion that life does not begin at conception in ancient Israelite society based on the socially constructed category of the fetus in Exod. 21.22-25. The fetus is a nonperson. Rather, the law addresses compensation to the husband for injury (both non-serious and deadly) to the pregnant mother. Verse 22 assumes that a miscarriage has occurred but that the woman herself is not seriously hurt; the compensation to the husband is for injury to her. The principle of *lex talionis* in v. 23 also addresses the circumstances of the mother as a result of the fight between men.

Finally, I note that if by some chance v. 22 does intend that the compensation to the father be for the lost fetus, this still affirms my conclusion that Exod. 21.22 does not understand the fetus as a life. There is no monetary compensation for human life according to the biblical perspective. This interpretation would still lead to the conclusion that the fetus is not a life but property. A fetus would have no legal rights as a nonperson but as property would have a economic value due to the father.

In summary, based on the preceding analysis, I argue that in the law under review here the fetus is not a person and that personhood does not begin at conception. I acknowledge that the MT of Exod. 21.22-23 (unlike the LXX) does not distinguish between an unformed and a formed fetus. These findings

---

22. The question of the object of the *'āsôn* for which there is monetary compensation brings up the related issues of who determines the sum of money to be paid to the husband and how much monetary compensation he receives. In Exod. 21.22, the exact amount of the fine to be paid if there is no serious injury is not specified. The amount of money involved appears to be determined at the discretion of the husband of the pregnant woman, with restrictions on the amount paid by the guilty party to be qualified by the *biplilîm*. The word *biplilîm*, like the noun *'āsôn*, presents another terminological problem. It is an infrequently used noun that also occurs in Deut. 32.31 and Job 31.11. Most commentators relate the term *biplilîm* to the root *pll*, 'to judge, to arbitrate'.

The LXX translates, *meta axiōmatos*, 'according to the judicial assessment'. In this verse, the law indicates that monetary compensation, and not the substitution of a life, is the appropriate penalty against the individual who caused the accident.

are consistent with my earlier conclusions that the socially constructed categories of childhood in the biblical text recognize a male newborn as not deemed fully human until he is circumcised eight days after birth and with cross-cultural data that suggests an Israelite girl was acknowledged as a full person only with the onset of menstruation. These findings challenge the contemporary Christian understanding of the legal rights of the fetus and the modern Western ethnocentric perspective that the moment of physical birth is the moment when an individual becomes fully human.

Conclusions

As established in Exod. 21.22-25, the preceding analysis maintains that the fetus is not a life. I have arrived at this conclusion by raising the questions of: (1) who is injured in the circumstances described in Exod. 21.22-25 and (2) to whom the penalty applies as a result of the injury inflicted when men are fighting. My discussion of these questions contributes to further understanding of the Israelite culture-bound construction of childhood. I argue that the law addresses injury to the pregnant woman. The payment of money indicates that the fetus is not a life; birth is not the boundary of life and therefore a miscarriage does not mean loss of life and can be compensated for by money. The analysis in this chapter leads to the conclusion that a fetus was a nonperson and not protected by the law of *lex talionis*. However, the father has legal rights and so for him, the fetus (and its mother) is economic property, and the father is compensated for its loss. The protection of the law focuses on the father's loss of property and not the individual of the fetus.

The matter of payment for the loss of the unborn raises again the nature of the economic aspects of childhood: the loss of future income from a miscarriage elicits financial compensation to replace the productive and reproductive resources that accrue to a family household with a live birth once it is deemed fully human. The fetus is a *yeled* but not a social person; it is property but not a legal person because it has yet to develop to the point of being able to contribute to the economics of the family. Thus, although the text does not give the reason for the payment to the father when the fetus is lost, compensation is a means of acknowledging the delayed future revenue that would accrue to the father had the fetus survived and started on the life cycle continuum towards adulthood.

Does the compensation come because the fetus had legal rights? No. Is the payment compensation for either the loss of a valuable commodity to its father or because of his investment in the fetus up until the termination of the pregnancy? Yes. Once again we see that a child was an economic investment in the future of a family household. If the mother dies, however, the principle of *lex talionis* applies because she, too, is a valuable commodity to her husband and is recognized as a person. Exodus 21.22-25 establishes that the fetus has economic value to the father as property but that the unborn has no legal rights because it is not a life from the perspective of the formulation of this law.[23]

23. The medieval French rabbi Rashi puts Exod. 21.22-25 into 'market value' terms: 'Causing the death of a fetus is not a capital offense, but the person responsible must pay damages. These damages are assessed by the court in response to a claim made by the father. Such monetary damages are computed in the following manner: The court evaluates the woman as if she were a slave with a market value. She would be worth more when she is pregnant, because a prospective buyer would receive not only her services, but also her newborn as a slave. The reduction of value as a result of the accident is the damage that the court requires the assailant to pay'; see Nosson Scherman (ed.), *The Chumash: The Stone Edition* (Brooklyn, NY: Mesorah Publications, 11th edn, 1993), p. 423.

Part 3

FROM THE HEBREW BIBLE TO TODAY:
STASIS AND CHANGE

Chapter 9

SOCIALLY CONSTRUCTED CATEGORIES OF CHILDHOOD

As explained at the start, my experiences working with children in a Guatemalan orphanage, as well as my active ongoing volunteer work in Chicago and teaching experiences at DePaul University, led me to write this book. My time with the infants in a *hogar* in a developing country made me wonder about the relationship between childhood in a lower socioeconomic group home (such as the one in Guatemala where I volunteered) and childhood in the privileged setting of a first world country like the US.[1] My questions were only compounded when I began working in the Illinois legal system as a volunteer for CASA and experienced the (mis)handling of cases of children through the foster care system. The more work I did and the more I taught about children, the more sensitive I became to the culturally constructed nature of perspectives on children and childhood. As a biblical scholar and an historian of ancient societies, I had to ask myself whether modern scholarly interpretations of the biblical data on children were anachronistic readings of the text based on modern values of the child as innocent and in need of special protection and the belief that 'God loves children'. This book explores some of these issues and attempts to answer some of my many questions concerning the perspectives on children past and present, here and there.

My question throughout has been a simple one: 'What is a child in the Hebrew Bible?' I have argued that the contemporary idealization of childhood in middle-class America and Western Europe as a period of protected physical and emotional well-being, coupled with uncritical readings of biblical tradition, combine to obscure the economic conceptualizations of childhood and instances of violence against children in biblical texts. I maintain that modern Western perspectives on what is healthy and normal in the raising of children may tell us more about ourselves than they do about what children across the globe need in order to thrive in their individual settings. I have not assumed that the needs of children can be universalized according

    1. I recognize that not every child in the US leads a privileged life, even compared to children's lives in less developed countries. All the same, there is typically a gap between the experiences of childhood in a developing country and in a first world country.

to one set of assumptions. Whereas some contemporary scholars in the West view children as 'innocent and precious', such ideas are recent narrow cultural constructions. Economic sociologist Viviana Zelizer argues that the value of a child in the US is based on the child's emotional importance to its parents and not to its economic contributions to the family, a conclusion that contrasts with what would have been the case in a pre-modern agrarian society such as ancient Israel.

In his book *Centuries of Childhood*, French historian Philippe Ariès proposes that childhood is a socially constructed phase of the human life-cycle that only began to emerge as a state separate from adulthood around the end of the fifteenth century in Western Europe. Although many scholars have challenged Ariès thesis that childhood as a distinct phase of life is a relatively recent innovation, they have accepted his conclusion that childhood is a culture-bound construction. The sociology of childhood is now based on this fundamental perspective, despite the fact that critics of Ariès correctly point out that his work is Eurocentric, is based on artistic renditions of children, and fails to take into account issues of gender and class.

Despite the limitations in Ariès's work, in the preceding chapters I have searched for evidence in the Hebrew Bible that would either support or undermine Ariès's theory that childhood as a culturally constructed, distinct phase of life emerged in the late medieval period. I have found in the biblical text evidence to argue against Ariès on the timing of the historical recognition of childhood as a distinct phase of life and to support the thesis that ancient Israel recognized childhood as a stage of life separate from adulthood and assigned culture-bound social meanings to this phase in the human life-cycle.

I build on the sociology of childhood—that childhood is a social construct—by contrasting ideas about children in biblical Israel with contemporary scenarios about childhood in American today. I have examined understandings of the meanings of childhood, both past and present, in light of issues raised in the UNCRC and its concerns for 'the best interests of the child'. I have also explored the conflicting images of the child that have resulted from the transformation from the biblical ideology of the child as a private economic asset to current Western attitudes of the child as an individual with rights of her or his own. It has become quite evident that the biblical perspective on children and childhood is distinct from modern first world ideas of childhood as a special time in life when the child is innocent and in need of special treatment.

The texts of the Hebrew Bible, rather than strict etymological analyses, have served as the ethnographic data on which this study of children and childhood was based. Linguistic analysis of the typical nouns for 'child', *na'ar* (נער) and *yeled* (ילד), has failed to shed much light on the cultural construction of childhood in ancient Israel or on the social location of the child. It may have come as a surprise to some that there is enough data in the texts of the Hebrew Bible to apply sociological methods to draw useful and important conclusions concerning the culture-bound conceptualizations of 'the child' in biblical Israel. I examined theories on the social construction of childhood to see the economic factors that contributed to the construction of childhood in ancient Israel. Models of agrarian societies, where the importance is on production and reproduction, fit the biblical evidence. In such societies, the family was an economic unit. Families tended to live in extended households in order to increase the productivity of the household economy. This model of family structure challenges modern concepts of the nuclear family as the universal ideal for raising children. In contrast to the ideology of Western societies, where many think about what a parent owes a child in her/his upbringing, in traditional village subsistence economies such as ancient Israel, the emphasis is on what a child owes a parent. Children were important in ancient Israel, not as individuals in their own rights, but because they were integral members of the patrilineal family unit whose continuation of the kinship unit depended on their births and survival into adulthood. The individual child was economic family property whose function was to carry forward the production and reproduction of the family into the next generation.

In summary, thus far I have exposed the differences in the roles of children in two very opposite, in some ways polarizing, economic systems: agrarian Israel versus capitalist and post-industrialized economies. The function of children as economic producers in the family in ancient Israel decreased with capitalism. These changing circumstances are, in some sense, where Western values originated: capitalism as an economic system reorganizing social roles compared to those in agrarian societies.

I build on this insight and argue here that understanding childhood in the Israelite family depends on the place of the child in the developmental cycle of family life. The birth order of children had significance for their experiences of childhood because it resulted in different treatment for each child within the family unit. The extended family and the need for production and reproduction not only raised issues of children's birth-order, but it also introduced the socio-economic status of both wives and children, and the realization that differing childhoods existed for the children in a family,[2] depending on whether a child was the product of a monogamous or a

---

2. Of course the same claim is true today regarding the variances of childhood experiences. Different childhoods exist in all sorts of different family arrangements and according to all kinds of different points of identification. The cultural, historical, political, and economic contexts are as relevant to the sociology of childhood in ancient Israel as they are today.

polygamous family and whether or not the child was a boy or a girl. In this investigation of the meaning and content of childhood in the Israel of the Hebrew Bible, I examined the extended family structures and concern for family preservation, from a patrilineal perspective, from one generation to the next.

The function of a child was for the survival of the family unit. Social circumstances and changing historical conditions were variables in the economic value of a child and affected the meaning of being a child. As the examples of the childhood of Ishmael and Isaac (Gen. 21) illustrated, child abandonment was a social mechanism to control family structure and limit inheritance to the primary heir to the patrilineage.

Childhood appears in the texts to be a phase of life defined not only by chronological age (circumcision eight days after birth) but by developmental categories, such as weaning, and by a child's ability to contribute to the family income, i.e., to family survival. Age-based categories of behavior must be interpreted for the meanings they held in ancient Israel with regard to when membership in the community occurred and what economic functions became associated with childhood and adulthood. It is the task of scholarly analysis to investigate the separation between childhood and adulthood and to assign significance to these boundaries if scholars aim to understand the socially constructed nature of life in ancient Israel.

We have seen that gender is an important variable in determining the conceptualization of an Israelite child and the economic value of a child. Gender is also relevant in determining the boundary between being a non-person, i.e., not being considered a full human being, and being a person. The ritual of circumcision brought a newly born male into the family at the age of eight days (Lev. 12.3). Circumcision is a *rite of passage* ritual, albeit at only eight days of age, which serves as a boundary marker transforming a male from a nonhuman into a full person on the path to adulthood and into someone who will perpetuate the production and reproduction goals of the family household. Weaning is another such ritual. The biblical text reveals that the boundaries between a fetus, a newborn, and a child do not conform to certain culturally specific notions about when life begins, particularly for those who argue that life begins at conception. According to the biblical text, personhood is not ritualized for girls when they are infants (Lev. 12.5), although the evidence suggests that a baby girl is a gendered person when she is 15 days old. Menstruation most likely served as the *rite of passage* that marked the transition towards adulthood. For a girl, the blood of menstruation may have marked the nexus between gender and personhood and signaled passage to the next phase in the life cycle when a girl's childhood began to come to an end. With the onset of menstruation, a girl entered the next stage of social age as she moved to adolescence and prepared for marriage and childbearing. I suggest that only through childbearing was a girl considered to have completely moved out of childhood and fully into adulthood; menstruation was the biological marker for girls which truly began the separation between childhood and adulthood. This was followed by the ritual of marriage, and childbearing was the ultimate stage of female adulthood. It would seem that the beginning of inclusion in the kinship community was different for boys and girls as each gender had to pass through different transitional phases and assumed more and more social responsibilities in the movement from childhood into the social world of adulthood. However, for both boys and girls, full adulthood was a status achieved by arriving at the social ages of marriage and fathering/bearing a male heir to the patrilineage.

Read against the backdrop of the UNCRC, the narratives of the Hebrew Bible such as the ones recounting the expulsion of Ishmael after the birth of Isaac and the circumstances of the birth and the dedication of Samuel to the service of Yahweh provide concrete examples of child abandonment—possibly even child abuse[3]—in biblical Israel in fulfillment of parents' needs. However, when we look carefully at the objections to the UNCRC voiced by those who uphold the sovereignty of parents over children, such as those recounted in Chapter 2, one finds that circumstances for children in many places in the world, including in the US, are not so different than they were in biblical times.

Viewed from a contemporary perspective such as the one found in the UNCRC, 1 Samuel 1 denies the child rights. In the Hebrew Bible, the child's interests in her/his own fate are of little concern to the adult authors of the texts. In biblical Israel, children were property, subject to physical discipline;[4] they could be sacrificed, and they could be abandoned. They were subject to abuse at the hands of their own parents. As the examples of the abandonment of Ishmael (by his father Abraham; Gen. 21.14-21) and of the near sacrifice of Isaac (by his father Abraham in Gen. 22) make clear, the biblical data do not reveal a child-friendly society.[5] It is only because Abraham has demonstrated a willingness to give up his sons Ishmael and Isaac that God promises in exchange to give Ishmael and Isaac a multitude of descendants (Gen. 22.16-18).

---

3. David Jobling, *1 Samuel* (Berit Olam; Collegeville, MN: Liturgical Press, 1998).
4. 'He who spares the rod hates his son, but he who loves him is diligent to discipline him' (Prov. 13.24).
5. For an analysis of these texts that comes to the same conclusions, see Terence E. Fretheim, '"God Was with the Boy" (Genesis 21:20): Children in the Book of Genesis', in Bunge (ed.), *The Child in the Bible*, pp. 3-23.

The UNCRC provides mixed messages about childhood globally[6] because the document is shaped by Western values. Moreover, it assumes that all children have the same access to economic resources and have the same continuing access to natural resources such as clean water. Where in reality do we see ecological equity for all children? Further, the UNCRC universalizes the age of adulthood at eighteen (with the exception of allowing for children to be enlisted as soldiers at age 15)—rather than defining adulthood by contextualizing it based on competence, as I believe should be done. Ultimately, the document generalizes the category of 'children' and uses age as a fixed category rather than recognizing that children across the globe may have the capacity to act as competent independent agents at different ages. In some settings, the age range for childhood may be brief and parents may not be able to economically support a child until the age of eighteen. Nonetheless, to speak of the rights of a child without relying on age generalizations shifts the emphasis from the child as object of protection to the child as an independent being who can determine her/his own rights.

There are human rights abuses of children in the US that go unnoticed and misunderstood. Although the impression persists that child prostitution is a willing act, recent laws on human trafficking specify otherwise: 'Sex trafficking involves the recruitment, harboring, transportation, provision, or obtaining of a person for the purpose of a commercial sex act in which a commercial sex act is induced by force, fraud, or coercion, or in which the person forced to perform such an act is under the age of eighteen years old'.[7] Moreover, 'Young girls make up the majority of the approximately 2 million children worldwide who are sexually exploited each year. Globally, between 50 and 60 percent of the children who are trafficked into sexual slavery are under age 16. 25 % of all child sex tourists around the world are U.S. citizens.'[8] The rights of children are being violated in our own neighborhoods, but few understand the facts on child sex trafficking, to take just one example.

Laid side by side, the Hebrew Bible and its interpreters, and the UNCRC and its critics and proponents, each in their own ways, raise questions of what are the best interests of children, who has the right to decide what these interests should be, and whether these interests are being met. When should a child be protected? When should a child be a self-determining individual? Both documents reveal competing systems of rights, i.e., adult rights versus children's rights. Furthermore, neither the Bible nor the UNCRC adequately consider how racism, poverty, and sexism have bearing on the social construction of childhood. This fault may lie with the fact that both documents

---

6. Myers, 'The Right Rights?', pp. 38-55.
7. Http://www.humantrafficking.neu.edu/background/ (accessed 30 March 2012).
8. Http://modern-injustice.com/category/sex-trafficking/ (accessed 30 March 2012).

are too narrow in their scope to address the full range of issues faced by children past and present. Neither document recognizes the social construction of the category of childhood and the diversity of childhood experiences. I suggest that one reason for this failure lies in the fact that adults are prescribing what children need rather than relying on children as informants. 'Children are and must be seen as active in the construction and determination of their own social lives, the lives of those around them and of the societies in which they live. Children are not just the passive subjects of social structures and processes'.[9]

In order to grasp notions of childhood in the Bible and to decide how and when they are relevant today to the contemporary discussion on social change for the well-being of the world's children, we must renew interest in the parent-child relationship. The 'child-centered' family in the US manifests a particular softness towards children and tends to view childhood as an overly sentimentalized time in life, a different perspective than the ones of either the UNCRC or the Hebrew Bible. As Steven Mintz states, the message children receive in the US is a 'most disturbing' contradiction. Based on the integration of children early in life into the consumerism of American society, children are pushed to grow up quickly while at the same time they are protected due to the innocence of membership in what is assumed to be a particularly vulnerable group in society.[10] If Mintz is correct, in the US we do not see children as having reached full membership in society while they are children, a viewpoint similar to the one uncovered regarding children in ancient Israel. It is hard to find evidence in the Hebrew Bible that the 'best interests of the child' guided decisions on childhood.

In order to move forward in bringing about changes for the social welfare of children worldwide, we must further explore how the appropriation of new paradigms of children, i.e., the notion of children as entitled to both protection and to personal rights, brings about for some an argument for the return to an older paradigm of children as property, the perspective of some in the US who oppose the UNCRC. Only by recognizing that competing models of childhood lie behind these arguments will it be possible to recognize the threats that proponents of each paradigm feel about the other models when they advocate for 'the best interests of the child'. Each paradigm of childhood challenges the assumptions of the other. In the end, 'the antagonists are not merely quarreling over 'facts'; they practice in "different worlds"'.[11] As we examine these different worlds, we may need to challenge the ideals of the UNCRC and accept that it is not always in the best interest

---

9. Prout and James, 'A New Paradigm for the Sociology of Childhood?', p. 8.
10. Mintz, *Huck's Raft*, pp. 381-83.
11. Lee, 'Three Paradigms of Childhood', p. 605.

of a child, for example, to dwell under the same roof as her/his parents or even in her/his country of birth.

Furthermore, other issues in the UNCRC challenge contemporary North American ideologies which generalize about the best interests of a child: (1) In many settings not all children are viewed as having the same inherent worth; (2) A child's illness is not always viewed as a problem requiring medical attention but may be seen as a result of the intervention of divine forces; (3) Arguments for a child's right to an education fail to address global contexts where literacy is not as important as it is in other settings and where building schools will not solve the economic problems faced by young people. For example, the UNCRC fails to address the fact that in Albania 'up to 90% of girls in rural areas don't go to school for fear of being abducted and sold into sexual servitude'.[12] These facts underline the diversity of experiences of childhood across the globe and contribute to our recognition that both in the ancient Israelite past and in the present children's interests were and are defined by adult concerns.

In 2007, Michael Freeman wrote an important article entitled, 'Why It Remains Important to Take Children's Rights Seriously'.[13] Freeman recognizes, as do many, that the UNCRC is not a perfect document. Among its many shortcomings, its Western biases define childhood and children's rights too narrowly. As stated in Chapter 2, critics of the UNCRC fear that to give rights to children is to diminish the authority of parents, and neglect the interests of adults, and undermine the family as an institution. According to such critics, the social construction/definition of childhood is that of someone without rights; 'children's rights are an oxymoron'.[14] These issues lead Freeman to ask: 'But how are we to get from "rhetoric" to "rights"?'[15] This is not the place to rehearse all the criticisms of children's rights today, although the examples from the Hebrew Bible warn us of the potential dangers of neglecting children's rights. If children's rights are not acknowledged, adults run the risk of abandoning children and viewing them as their parents' property.

Freeman argues against critics of children's rights that children do have human rights, 'the whole range of civil, political, social, economic and cultural rights'.[16] Rights are the basis for agency and advocacy; they can lead to

---

12. David Masci, 'Human Trafficking and Slavery', *The CQ Researcher* 14 (2004), pp. 1-22 (3).
13. *International Journal of Children's Rights* 15 (2007), pp. 5-23.
14. Freeman, 'Why It Remains Important to Take Children's Rights Seriously', p. 19. Although the quotation comes from Freeman, he is paraphrasing his critics and does not share this perspective.
15. Freeman, 'Why It Remains Important to Take Children's Rights Seriously', p. 17.
16. Freeman, 'Why It Remains Important to Take Children's Rights Seriously', p. 7.

action. The question for some is: Should children have these rights? Freeman relies on the writing of Hannah Arendt to answer this question and argues, 'The most fundamental of rights is the right to possess rights'.[17] Because the function of my work is more than simply as intellectual exploration, I quote again from Freeman on the conceptualization of children in the contemporary world (in light of what has been uncovered from the record of the Hebrew Bible). As Freeman puts it, 'Rights are important because they recognize the respect their bearers are entitled to. To accord rights is to respect dignity: to deny rights is to cast doubt on humanity and on integrity. Rights are an affirmation of the Kantian basic principle that we are ends in ourselves, and not means to the ends of others.'[18] The story of the expulsion of Ishmael and Hagar in Genesis 21 serves as an example from the Hebrew Bible of what can happen when children (and adults) are perceived as objects rather than subjects of their own lives.

What can we learn from all this? The evidence appears to be complex and contradictory at times. Western proponents of children's need for protection and individual rights must face their ethnocentrism before it will be possible to impose values from one economic setting onto others where, for example, emphasis is placed on the wisdom of the elders—not on the emotional value of the young to their parents. Culture-bound ideas of the social construction of childhood must be exposed for exactly what they are—social constructions—in order to truly speak about the best interests of the child and to incorporate those interests into a wide range of institutions and contexts.[19] Based on my experiences with social service agencies that are intended to protect children, this is a problem that still confronts children today.

17. Freeman, 'Why It Remains Important to Take Children's Rights Seriously', p. 8. See Hannah Arendt, *The Origins of Totalitarianism* (London: André Deutsch, 1986), p. 296.
18. Freeman, 'Why It Remains Important to Take Children's Rights Seriously', p. 7. Freeman is referring to Immanuel Kant, *Groundwork of the Metaphysics of Morals* (originally published 1783; Cambridge: Cambridge University Press, 1997).
19. For further, and provocative, thoughts on this topic, see the remarks of Lancy, *The Anthropology of Childhood*, pp. 373-74. He argues that, 'traditional economies are very successful at providing a comfortable standard of living and that children willingly replicate the systems that have worked in the past. There is a font of knowledge on how to adapt to a particular environment and to maintain sufficiently harmonious relations within the community so that children are cared for… Attempts to repackage the traditional culture and deliver it to students in classrooms seems perverse. They'd be better off avoiding the classroom and hanging around working adults.' It is important to note that Lancy is not arguing that in such contexts all children should go without education. The infrastructure of a culture must make provisions for the disenfranchised to receive an education but must also have jobs for them that will make it possible for them to take their place in the village economy and exercise agency in their lives. See also, Freeman, 'Why It Remains Important to Take Children's Rights Seriously'.

Understanding that childhood is a cultural construction can contribute to the mechanisms by which the best interests of the child are challenged and changed, if need be.

Future research should examine the ramifications for the social construction of childhood in the Hebrew Bible if an individual is unable to assume 'adult' responsibilities as a result of physical, cognitive, or emotional disabilities. I refer to disabilities as a broad social construct as it would apply in ancient Israel, not as the term is applied in a Western medical model. Although biblical Hebrew has no exact word equivalent to the English term 'disability', the texts describe conditions whose existence clearly affects the person who is being described. The social meaning of a disability for the classification of childhood is not the subject of many texts in the Hebrew Bible.[20]

Finally, I return to the question of 'What is a child?' Can the contrasts between the Hebrew Bible and its various interpretations, the UNCRC and its various critical readings, the reservations and comments of the signatories, and the often unexamined attitudes about children in every culture lead to a meaningful exposition of the conceptualization of childhood in these contexts past and present? My answer to this question is yes. Despite the polarizing differences between the agrarian economic system of ancient Israel and industrialism and post-industrialism in the present, in neither time nor setting are children treated as fully human. In many ways, the past and the present have more in common when it comes to attitudes towards children than we might have initially thought. Although we cannot change the past, its lessons make it evident that much work remains to be done to make the world today a better place for children everywhere.

---

20. Disability studies include: Hector Avalos, *Illness and Health Care in the Ancient Near East: The Role of the Temple in Greece, Mesopotamia, and Israel* (HSM, 54; Atlanta: Scholars Press, 1995); Hector Avalos, Sarah J. Melcher and Jeremy Schipper (eds.), *This Abled Body: Rethinking Disabilities in Biblical Studies* (Atlanta: Society of Biblical Literature, 2007); Saul M. Olyan, *Disability in the Hebrew Bible: Interpreting Mental and Physical Differences* (Cambridge: Cambridge University Press, 2008). Rebecca Raphael, *Biblical Corpora: Representations of Disability in Hebrew Bible Literature* (New York: T. & T. Clark, 2008); Jeremy Schipper, *Disability Studies and the Hebrew Bible: Figuring Mephibosheth in the David Story* (New York: T. & T. Clark, 2006) but they do not consider cognitive or physical disabilities in children. The exception is the study by Schipper, who focuses on Mephibosheth (2 Sam. 4.4; 9.1-13) who was dropped at the age of 5 by his nurse and became lame. The few details regarding him add little to our understanding of the impact of physical disability on the definition of childhood; as a grandson of Saul (he was the son of Jonathan) he had a privileged position in the events that unfolded as David came to power.

BIBLIOGRAPHY

Ackerman, James S., 'Who Can Stand before Yhwh, This Holy God? A Reading of 1 Samuel 1–15', *Prooftexts* 11 (1991), pp. 1-25.
Alter, Robert, *The Art of Biblical Narrative* (New York: Basic Books, 1981).
Amit, Yairah, '"Am I not more devoted to you than ten sons?' (1 Samuel 1:8): Male and Female Interpretations', in Brenner (ed.), *A Feminist Companion to Samuel and Kings*, pp. 68-76.
Arendt, Hannah, *The Origins of Totalitarianism* (London: Andre Deutsch, 1986).
Ariès, Philippe, *Centuries of Childhood: A Social History of Family Life* (trans. Robert Baldrick; New York: Vintage, 1962).
Arnett, Jeffrey Jensen, 'Emerging Adulthood: A Theory of the Development from the Late Teens through the Twenties', *American Psychologist* 55 (2000), pp. 469-80.
— *Emerging Adulthood: The Winding Road from the Late Teens through the Twenties* (New York: Oxford University Press, 2004).
Avalos, Hector, *Illness and Health Care in the Ancient Near East: The Role of the Temple in Greece, Mesopotamia, and Israel* (HSM, 54; Atlanta, GA: Scholars Press, 1995).
Avalos, Hector, Sarah J. Melcher and Jeremy Schipper (eds.), *This Abled Body: Rethinking Disabilities in Biblical Studies* (Atlanta, GA: Society of Biblical Literature, 2007).
Bakke, O.M., *When Children Became People: The Birth of Childhood in Early Christianity* (trans. Brian McNeil; Minneapolis: Fortress Press, 2005).
Bar-Efrat, Shimon, *Narrative Art in the Bible* (Sheffield: Sheffield Academic Press, 1997).
Barr, James, *The Semantics of Biblical Language* (Oxford: Oxford University Press, 1961).
Baxter, Jane, *The Archaeology of Childhood: Children, Gender, and Material Culture* (Gender and Archaeology; Walnut Creek, CA: AltaMira Press, 2005).
Bernat, David A., *Sign of the Covenant: Circumcision in the Priestly Tradition* (Atlanta, GA: Society of Biblical Literature, 2009).
Blenkinsopp, Joseph, 'The Family in First Temple Israel', in Perdue *et al.* (eds.), *Families in Ancient Israel*, pp. 48-103.
— *The Pentateuch: An Introduction to the First Five Books of the Bible* (New York: Doubleday, 1992).
Block, Daniel I., 'Marriage and Family in Ancient Israel', in *Marriage and Family in the Biblical World* (ed. Ken M. Campbell; Downers Grove, IL: InterVarsity Press, 2003), pp. 33-102.
Boswell, John, *The Kindness of Strangers: The Abandonment of Children in Western Europe from Late Antiquity to the Renaissance* (New York: Pantheon, 1988).

Brenner, Athalya, *The Israelite Woman: Social Role and Literary Type in Biblical Literature* (The Biblical Seminar, 2; Sheffield: Journal for the Study of the Old Testament Press, 1985).
Brenner, Athalya (ed.), *A Feminist Companion to Samuel and Kings* (Sheffield: Sheffield Academic Press, 1994).
Brettler, Marc, 'The Composition of 1 Samuel 1–2', *JBL* 116 (1997), pp. 601-12.
Brueggemann, Walter, *First and Second Samuel* (Interpretation: A Bible Commentary for Teaching and Preaching; Louisville, KY: John Knox Press, 1990).
Bunge, Marcia J. (ed.), *The Child in Christian Thought* (Grand Rapids, MI: W.B. Eerdmans, 2001).
— *The Child in the Bible* (Grand Rapids, MI: W.B. Eerdmans, 2008).
Caird, George B., *The First and Second Books of Samuel* (IB, 2; Nashville: Abingdon Press, 1953).
Callaway, Mary, *Sing, O Barren One: A Study in Comparative Midrash* (SBLDS, 91; Atlanta, GA: Scholars Press, 1986).
Cassuto, U., *Commentary on Exodus* (trans. I. Abrahams; Jerusalem: Magnes Press, 1967).
Childs, Brevard, *The Book of Exodus* (OTL; Philadelphia, PA: Westminster Press, 1974).
Chisholm, James S, 'Learning "Respect for Everything": Navajo Images of Development', in *Images of Childhood* (ed. C. Philip Hwang, Michael E. Lamb and Irving E. Sigel; Hillsdale, NJ: Lawrence Erlbaum Associates, 1996), pp. 167-83.
Clements, R.E., *Exodus* (Cambridge: Cambridge University Press, 1972).
Coats, George W., *Genesis with an Introduction to Narrative Literature* (FOTL, 1; Grand Rapids, MI: W. B. Eerdmans, 1983).
Coleman, James S., *The Adolescent Society: The Social Life of the Teenager and its Impact on Education* (Glencoe, IL: Free Press of Glencoe, 1961).
Conklin, Beth A., and Lynn M. Morgan, 'Babies, Bodies, and the Production of Personhood in North America and a Native Amazonian Society', *Ethos* 24 (1996), pp. 657-94.
Cooey, Paula M., 'Neither Seen nor Heard: The Absent Child in the Study of Religion', *Journal of Childhood and Religion* 1.1 (2010), pp.1-31 1 (http://www.childhoodandreligion.com/JCR/Volume_1_(2010)_files/CooeyMarch2010.pdf).
Coontz, Stephanie. *The Way We Never Were: American Families and the Nostalgia Trap* (New York: Basic Books, 1992).
Crouch, Carly L., 'Funerary Rites for Infants and Children in the Hebrew Bible in Light of Ancient Near Eastern Practices', in *Feasts and Festivals* (ed. C.M. Tuckett; Leuven: Peeters, 2009), pp. 15-26.
Crüsemann, Frank, *The Torah: Theology and Social History of Old Testament Law* (Minneapolis: Fortress Press, 1996).
Cutler, B., and MacDonald, John, 'Identification of the Na'ar in the Ugaritic Texts', *UF* 8 (1976), pp. 27-35.
Day, Peggy L., 'From the Child Is Born the Woman: The Story of Jephthah's Daughter', in her *Gender and Difference in Ancient Israel* (Minneapolis: Fortress Press, 1989), pp. 58-74.
Donaldson, Mara E., 'Kinship Theory in the Patriarchal Narratives: The Case of the Barren Wife', *JAAR* 49 (1981), pp. 77-87.
Dozeman, Thomas B., *Commentary on Exodus* (Grand Rapids, MI: W.B. Eerdmans, 2009).

— 'The Wilderness and Salvation History in the Hagar Story', *JBL* 117 (1998), pp. 23-43.
Eilberg-Schwartz, Howard, *The Savage in Judaism: An Anthropology of Israelite Religion and Ancient Judaism* (Bloomington: Indiana University Press, 1990).
Eng, Milton, *The Days of our Years: A Lexical Semantic Study of the Life Cycle in Biblical Israel* (New York: T. & T. Clark, 2011).
Erikson, Erik H., *Childhood and Society* (New York: W.W. Norton, 1950).
Evans, Geoffrey, 'Rehoboam's Advisers at Shechem, and Political Institutions in Israel and Sumer', *JNES* 25 (1966), pp. 273-79.
Fewell, Danna Nolan, *The Children of Israel: Reading the Bible for the Sake of our Children* (Nashville, TN: Abingdon Press, 2003).
Fleishman, Joseph, *Father–Daughter Relations in Biblical Law* (Bethesda, MD: Capital Decisions, 2011).
Fontaine, Carole R., '"Here comes this dreamer": Reading Joseph the Slave in Multicultural and Interfaith Contexts', in *Genesis* (ed. Athalya Brenner, Archie Chi-Chung Lee and Gale A. Yee; Texts @ Contexts; Minneapolis: Fortress Press, 2012), pp. 131-45.
Freeman, Michael, 'Why It Remains Important to Take Children's Rights Seriously', *International Journal of Children's Rights* 15 (2007), pp. 5-23.
French, Valerie, 'Children in Antiquity', in *Children in Historical and Comparative Perspective: An International Handbook and Research Guide* (ed. Joseph M. Hawes and N. Ray Hiner; Westport, CT: Greenwood Press, 1991), pp. 13-29.
Fretheim, Terence E., '"God was with the boy" (Genesis 21:20): Children in the Book of Genesis', in Bunge (ed.), *The Child in the Bible*, pp. 3-23.
Fuchs, Esther, 'The Literary Characterization of Mothers and Sexual Politics in the Hebrew Bible', in *Feminist Perspectives on Biblical Scholarship* (ed. Adela Yarbro Collins; SBLCP; Chico, CA: Scholars Press, 1985), pp. 117-36.
Garroway, Kristine Sue Henriksen, 'The Construction of the "Child" in the Ancient Near East: Towards an Understanding of the Legal and Social Status of Children in Biblical Israel and Surrounding Cultures' (PhD diss, Hebrew Union College, 2009).
Gennep, Arnold van, *The Rites of Passage* (Chicago: University of Chicago Press, 1960).
Goldschmidt, Walter, *Culture and Behavior of the Sebei* (Berkeley, CA: University of California Press, 1976).
Goody, Esther, *Parenthood and Social Reproduction: Fostering and Occupational Roles in West Africa* (Cambridge: Cambridge University Press, 1982).
Goody, Jack, *The Development of the Family and Marriage in Europe* (Cambridge: Cambridge University Press, 1983).
Gordon, Robert P., *I and II Samuel* (Old Testament Guides; Sheffield: JSOT Press, 1984).
Gray, John, *I and II Kings: A Commentary* (OTL; Philadelphia: Westminster Press, 1963).
Gruber, Mayer I., 'Breast-Feeding Practices in Biblical Israel and in Babylonian Mesopotamia', *Journal of Ancient Near Eastern Studies* 19 (1989), pp. 61-83.
— 'Review of Carolyn S. Leeb, *Away from the Father's House: The Social Location of the* Naʻar *and* Naʻarah *in Ancient Israel*', *JQR* 43 (2003), p. 615.
Hamilton, Victor P., *The Book of Genesis: Chapters 18–50* (NICOT; Grand Rapids, MI: W. B. Eerdmans, 1995).
Harkness, Sara, and Charles M. Super, 'The Cultural Construction of Child Development: A Framework for the Socialization of Affect', *Ethnos* 11 (1983), pp. 221-31.
— 'Why African Children Are So Hard to Test', in *Cross-Cultural Research at Issue* (ed. L.L. Adler; New York: Academic Press, 1982), pp. 145-52.

Headland, Thomas N., Kenneth L. Pike, and Marvin Harris, *Emics and Etics: The Insider/Outsider Debate* (Frontiers in Anthropology. Newbury Park, CO: Sage Publications, 1990).

Hertzberg, Hans Wilhelm, *I and II Samuel* (trans. J.S. Bowden; Philadelphia: Westminster Press, 1974).

Herzog, Kristen, *Children and our Global Future: Theological and Social Challenges* (Cleveland, OH: Pilgrim Press, 2005).

House, H. Wayne, 'Miscarriage or Premature Birth: Additional Thoughts on Exodus 21:22-25', *WTJ* 41 (1978), pp. 108-23.

Houtman, Cornelis, *Exodus*, III (Historical Commentary on the Old Testament; Leuven: Peeters, 2000).

— *Das Bundesbuch: Ein Kommentar* (Documenta et monumenta orientalis antiqui, 24, Leiden: Brill, 1997).

Hyatt, J.P., *Exodus* (NCB; London: Marshall, Morgan & Scott, 1971).

Ilan, David, 'Mortuary Practices at Tel Dan in the Middle Bronze Age: A Reflection of Canaanite Society and Ideology', in *Archaeology of Death in the Ancient Near East* (ed. Stuart Campbell and Anthony Green; Oxford: Oxbow, 1995), pp. 117-37.

Isser, Stanley, 'Two Traditions: The Law of Exodus 21:21-23 Revisited', *CBQ* 52 (1990), pp. 30-45.

Jackson, Bernard S., *Essays in Jewish and Comparative Legal History* (SJLA; Leiden: Brill, 1975).

— 'The Pregnant Woman Victim', in *Wisdom-Laws: A Study of the Mishpatim of Exodus 21:1–22:16* (New York: Oxford University Press, 2006), pp. 209-39.

— 'The Problem of Exod. xxi 22-5 (*ius talionis*)', *VT* 23 (1973), pp. 273-304.

James, Alan, and Allison Prout (eds.), *Constructing and Reconstructing Childhood: Contemporary Issues in the Sociological Study of Childhood* (London: Falmer Press, 1995).

Jay, Nancy, *Throughout your Generations Forever: Sacrifice, Religion, and Paternity* (Chicago: University of Chicago Press, 1992).

Jenks, Chris, *Childhood* (London: Routledge, 1996).

Jensen, David H., *Graced Vulnerability: A Theology of Childhood* (Cleveland, OH: Pilgrim Press, 2005).

Jobling, David., *1 Samuel* (Berit Olam; Collegeville, MN: Liturgical Press, 1998).

Kamp, Kathryn A. (eds.), *Children in Prehistoric Puebloan Southwest* (Salt Lake City: University of Utah Press, 2002).

Kamp, Kathryn A., and John C. Whittaker, 'Prehistoric Puebloan Children in Archaeology and Art', in Kamp (ed.), *Children in Prehistoric Puebloan Southwest*, pp. 14-40.

Kant, Immanuel, *Groundwork of the Metaphysics of Morals* (Cambridge: Cambridge University Press, 1997).

King, Philip J., and Lawrence E. Stager, *Life in Biblical Israel* (Louisville, KY: Westminster/John Knox Press, 2001).

Klein, Lillian R., 'Hannah: Marginalized Victim and Social Redeemer', in Brenner (ed.), *A Feminist Companion to Samuel and Kings*, pp. 77-92.

Knight, Douglas A., *Law, Power, and Justice in Ancient Israel* (Library of Ancient Israel; Louisville, KY: Westminster/John Knox Press, 2011).

Koepf, Laurel, '"Give me children or I shall die": Children and Communal Survival in Biblical Literature' (PhD diss., Union Theological Seminary, 2012).

Koskenniemi, Erkki, *The Exposure of Infants among Jews and Christian in Antiquity* (The Social World of Biblical Antiquity, 2/4; Sheffield: Sheffield Phoenix Press, 2009).

Kraemer, David, *Reading the Rabbis: The Talmud as Literature* (New York: Oxford University Press, 1996).

Kuper, Adam, *The Reinvention of Primitive Society: Transformation of a Myth* (Florence, KY: Taylor & Francis, 2005).

Lancy, David F., *The Anthropology of Childhood: Cherubs, Chattel, Changelings* (Cambridge: Cambridge University Press, 2008).

Larsson, Mikael, 'In Search of Children's Agency: Reading Exodus from Sweden', in *Exodus and Deuteronomy* (ed. Athalya Brenner and Gale A. Yee; Texts @ Contexts; Minneapolis: Fortress Press, 2012), pp. 79-94.

Laslett, Peter, 'Introduction: The History of the Family', in *Household and Family Life in Past Time* (ed. Peter Laslett and R. Wall; Cambridge: Cambridge University Press, 1972), pp. 1-90.

Lauterbach, Jacob Z. (ed.), *Mekhilta de-Rabbi Yishmael*, I–III (Philadelphia: Jewish Publication Society of America, 1949).

Lee, John Alan, 'Three Paradigms of Childhood', *Canadian Review of Sociology and Anthropology* 19 (1982), pp. 591-608.

Leeb, Carolyn S., *Away from the Father's House: The Social Location of the* Na'ar *and* Na'arah *in Ancient Israel* (JSOTSup, 301; Sheffield: Sheffield Academic Press, 2000).

Lemche, Niels P., *Early Israel: Anthropological and Historical Studies on the Israelite Society before the Monarchy* (VTSup, 37; Leiden: E.J. Brill, 1985).

LeVine, Robert A., 'Ethnographic Studies of Childhood: A Historical Overview', *American Anthropologist* 109 (2007), pp. 247-60.

Linton, Ralph, 'Age and Sex Categories', *American Sociological Review* 7 (1942), pp. 599-603.

Loewenstamm, Samuel E., 'Exodus xxi 22-25', *VT* 27 (1977), pp. 352-60.

MacDonald, John, 'The Status and Role of the *Na'ar* in Israelite Society', *JNES* 35 (1976), pp. 147-70.

Malamat, Abraham, 'Kingship and Council in Israel and Sumer: A Parallel', *JNES* 22 (1963), pp. 247-53.

Masci, David, 'Human Trafficking and Slavery', *The CQ Researcher* 14 (2004), pp. 1-22.

Matthews, Sarah H., 'A Window on the "New" Sociology of Childhood', *Sociology Compass* 1 (2007), pp. 322-34.

Mauss, Marcel, *The Gift: The Form and Reason for Exchange in Archaic Societies* (trans. W.D. Halls; London: Routledge, 1990).

McCarter, P. Kyle, Jr, *I Samuel* (Anchor Yale Bible Commentaries, 8; Garden City, NY: Doubleday, 1980).

Mead, Margaret, *Coming of Age in Samoa* (New York: New American Library, 1928/1961).

Mercer, Joyce Ann, *Welcoming Children: A Practical Theology of Childhood* (St Louis: Chalice Press, 2005).

Meyers, Carol, 'An Ethnoarchaeological Analysis of Hannah's Sacrifice', in *Pomegranates and Golden Bells: Studies in Biblical, Jewish, and Near Eastern Ritual, Law, and Literature in Honor of Jacob Milgrom* (ed. David Noel Freedman, A. Hurvitz and David P. Wright; Winona Lake, IN: Eisenbrauns, 1995), pp. 77-91.

— 'Hannah and her Sacrifice: Reclaiming Female Agency', in Brenner (ed.), *A Feminist Companion to Samuel and Kings*, pp. 93-104.
— 'The Hannah Narrative in Feminist Perspective', in *'Go to the land I will show you': Studies in Honor of Dwight W. Young* (ed. Joseph E. Coleson and Victor H. Matthew; Winona Lake, IN: Eisenbrauns, 1996), pp. 117-26.
— 'Material Remains and Social Relations: Women's Culture in Agrarian Households of the Iron Age', in *Symbiosis, Symbolism, and the Power of the Past: Canaan, Ancient Israel, and their Neighbors from the Late Bronze Age through Roman Palaestina* (ed. William G. Dever and Seymour Gitin; Winona Lake, IN: Eisenbrauns, 2003), pp. 425-44.
— 'Procreation, Production, and Protection: Male–Female Balance in Early Israel', *JAAR* 51 (1983), pp. 582-86.
Miller-McLemore, Bonnie J., *Let the Children Come: Reimagining Childhood from a Christian Perspective* (San Francisco, CA: Jossey–Bass, 2003).
Mintz, Steven, *Huck's Raft: A History of American Childhood* (Cambridge, MA: Harvard University Press, 2004).
Montgomery, Heather, *An Introduction to Childhood: Anthropological Perspectives on Children's Lives* (Oxford: Wiley–Blackwell, 2008).
Morgan, Lynn M., 'Imagining the Unborn in Ecuadoran Andes', *Feminist Studies* 23 (1997), pp. 323-50.
Murray, J.A.H. (ed.), *The Compact Edition of the Oxford English Dictionary* (New York: Oxford University Press, 1971).
Myers, William E., 'The Right Rights? Child Labor in a Globalizing World', *The Annals of the American Academy of Political and Social Science* 575 (2001), pp. 38-55.
Nakhai, Beth Alpert, 'Female Infanticide in Iron II Israel and Judah', in *Sacred History, Sacred Literature. Essays on Ancient Israel, the Bible, and Religion in Honor of R.E. Friedman on his Sixtieth Birthday* (ed. Shawna Dolansky; Winona Lake, IN: Eisenbrauns, 2008), pp. 257-72.
Noth, Martin, *Exodus* (trans. J. Bowden; Philadelphia, PA: Westminster, 1962).
Oden, Robert A., 'Jacob as Father, Husband, and Nephew: Kinship Studies and the Patriarchal Narratives', *JBL* 102 (1983), pp. 189-205.
— 'The Patriarchal Narratives as Myth: The Case of Jacob', in *The Bible without Theology: The Theological Tradition and Alternatives to It* (San Francisco: Harper & Row, 1987), pp. 106-30.
Olyan, Saul M., *Disability in the Hebrew Bible: Interpreting Mental and Physical Differences* (Cambridge: Cambridge University Press, 2008).
Otto, Eckart, 'Town and Rural Countryside in Ancient Israelite Law: Reception and Reaction in Cuneiform and Israelite Law', *JSOT* 57 (1993), pp. 3-22.
Palladino, Grace, *Teenagers: An American History* (New York: Basic Books, 1996).
Parker, Julie Faith, 'Suffer the Little Children: A Child-Centered Exploration of the Elisha Cycle' (PhD diss., Yale University, 2009).
Parsons, Talbott, 'Age and Sex in the Social Structure of the United States', *American Sociological Review* 7 (1942), pp. 604-16.
Perdue, Leo G., Joseph Blenkinsopp, John J. Collins and Carol Meyers (eds.), *Families in Ancient Israel* (The Family, Religion, and Culture; Louisville, KY: Westminster/ John Knox Press, 1997).
Pollack, Linda, *Forgotten Children: Parent–Child Relations from 1500 to 1900* (New York: Cambridge University Press, 1983).

Polzin, Robert, *Samuel and the Deuteronomist: A Literary Study of the Deuteronomic History*. II. *1 Samuel* (Bloomington: Indiana University Press, 1993).
Postman, Neil, *The Disappearance of Childhood* (New York: Vintage Books, 1982).
Prewitt, Terry J., 'Kinship Structures and the Genesis Genealogies', *JNES* 40 (1981), pp. 87-98.
Propp, William H.C., *Exodus 19–40: A New Translation with Introduction and Commentary* (AB, 2A; New York: Doubleday, 2006).
Prout, Alan, and Allison James, 'A New Paradigm for the Sociology of Childhood? Provenance, Promise and Problems', in James and Prout (eds.), *Constructing and Reconstructing Childhood*, pp. 7-33.
Quortrup, Jens, 'Sociology of Childhood: Conceptual Liberation of Children', in *Childhood and Children's Culture* (ed. Flemming Mouritsen and Jens Quortrup; Odense: University Press of Southern Denmark, 2002), pp. 43-78.
Rad, Gerhard von, *Genesis: A Commentary* (trans. John H. Marks; Philadelphia, PA: Westminster, rev. edn, 1972).
Raphael, Rebecca, *Biblical Corpora: Representations of Disability in Hebrew Biblical Literature* (New York: T. & T. Clark International, 2008).
Revell, E.J., *The Designation of the Individual: Expressive Usage in Biblical Narrative* (Kampen: Kok, 1996).
Ridgely, Susan B., *The Study of Children in Religion: A Methods Handbook* (New York: New York University Press, 2011).
Roth, Martha, 'Age at Marriage and the Household: A Study of Neo-Babylonian and Neo-Assyrian Forms', *Comparative Studies in Society and History* 29 (1987), pp. 715-47.
Rothschild, Nan A., 'Introduction', in Kamp (ed.), *Children in Prehistoric Puebloan Southwest*, pp. 1-13.
Rousseau, Jean Jacques, *Emile* (trans. B. Foxley; New York: Dent, 1957).
Said, Edward W., *Orientalism* (New York: Pantheon Books, 1978).
Sapir, Edward, *Selected Writings in Language, Culture, and Personality* (ed. David G. Mandelbaum; Berkeley, CA: University of California Press, 1985).
Scherman, Nosson (ed.), *The Chumash: The Stone Edition* (Brooklyn, NY: Mesorah Publications, 11th edn, 1993).
Schipper, Jeremy, *Disability Studies and the Hebrew Bible: Figuring Mephibosheth in the David Story* (New York: T. & T. Clark, 2006).
Schloen, J. David, *The House of the Father as Fact Symbol: Patrimonialism in Ugarit and the Ancient Near East* (Studies in the Archeology and History of the Levant; Winona Lake, IN: Eisenbrauns, 2004).
Schofer, Jonathan, 'The Different Life Stages: From Childhood to Old Age', in *The Oxford Handbook of Jewish Daily Life in Roman Palestine* (ed. Catherine Hezser; Oxford: Oxford University Press, 2010), pp. 327-43.
Schwartz, Theodore, 'The Acquisition of Culture', *Ethos* 9 (1981), pp. 10-16.
Schwienhorst-Schönberger, Ludger, 'Auge um Auge, Zahn um Zahn', *BLit* 63 (1990), pp. 163-75.
— *Das Bundesbuch* (BZAW, 188; Berlin: W. de Gruyter, 1990).
Shanahan, Suzanne, 'Lost and Found: The Sociological Ambivalence toward Childhood', *The Annual Review of Sociology* 33 (2007), pp. 407-28.
Skinner, John, *A Critical Commentary and Exegetical Commentary on Genesis* (ICC; New York: Charles Scribner's Sons, 1910).

Smith, Christian, Kari Christoffersen, Hilary Davidson and Patricia Snell Herzog, *Lost in Transition: The Dark Side of Emerging Adulthood* (New York: Oxford University Press, 2011).

Smith, Daniel L., *The Religion of the Landless: The Social Context of the Babylonian Exile* (Bloomington, IN: Meyer–Stone Books, 1989).

Sofaer Derevenski, Joanna, 'Engendering Children, Engendering Archaeology', in *Invisible People and Processes: Writing Gender and Childhood into European Archaeology* (ed. J. Moore and E. Scott; London: Leicester University Press, 1997), pp. 192-202.

— 'Where Are the Children? Accessing Children in the Past', *Archaeological Review from Cambridge* 13 (1994), pp. 7-20.

Solberg, Ann, 'Negotiating Childhood: Changing Constructions of Age for Norwegian Children', in James and Prout (eds.), *Constructing and Reconstructing Childhood*, pp. 123-40.

Speiser, E.A., *Genesis* (AB, 1; Garden City, NY: Doubleday, 1964).

Sprinkle, Joe E., 'The Interpretation of Exodus 21:22-25 [Lex Talionis] and Abortion', *WTJ* 55 (1993), pp. 233-53.

Staalduine-Sulman, Eveline van, 'Between Legislative and Linguistic Parallels: Exodus 21:22-25 in its Context', in *The Interpretation of Exodus: Studies in Honour of Cornelius Houtman* (ed. Riemer Roukema; Leuven: Peeters, 2006). pp. 207-24.

Stager, Lawrence E., 'The Archeology of the Family in Ancient Israel', *BASOR* 260 (1985), pp. 1-35.

Stähli, Hans-Peter, *Knabe–Jüngling–Knecht: Untersuchungen zum Begriff Na'ar im Alten Testament* (Beiträge zur biblischen Exegese und Theologie, 7; Frankfurt: Peter Lang, 1978).

Steinberg, Naomi, '1 Samuel 1, the United Nations Convention on the Rights of Children, and "the Best Interests of the Child"', *Journal of Childhood and Religion* 1 (2010), pp. 1-23, http://www.childhoodandreligion.com/JCR/Volume_1_(2010)_files/SteinbergApril2010.pdf.

— 'Alliance or Descent? The Function of Marriage in Genesis', *JSOT* 51 (1991), pp. 44-55.

— 'The Deuteronomic Law Code and the Politics of State Centralization', in *The Bible and the Politics of Exegesis* (ed. David Jobling, Peggy L. Day and Gerald T. Sheppard; Cleveland, OH: The Pilgrim Press, 1991), pp. 161-70.

— *Kinship and Marriage in Genesis: A Household Economics Perspective* (Minneapolis: Fortress Press, 1993).

— 'The Problem of Human Sacrifice in War: An Analysis of Judges 11', in *On the Way to Nineveh: Studies in Honor of George M. Landes* (ed. Stephen L. Cook and S.C. Winter; Atlanta, GA: Scholars Press, 1999), pp.114-35.

— 'Sociological Approaches: Toward a Sociology of Childhood in the Hebrew Bible', in *Essays on the Interpretation of the Hebrew Bible in Honor of David L. Petersen* (ed. Joel M. LeMon and Kent Harold Richards; Atlanta, GA: Society of Biblical Literature, 2009), pp. 251-69.

— 'Zilpah: Bible', http://jwa.org/encyclopedia/article/zilpah-bible.

Strawn, Brent A., 'Jeremiah's In/effective Plea: Another Look at נער in Jeremiah I 6', *VT* 55 (2005), pp. 366-77.

Toorn, Karel van der, *From her Cradle to her Grave: The Role of Religion in the Life of the Israelite and the Babylonian Woman* (trans. Sara J. Denning-Bolle; Sheffield: Sheffield Academic Press, 1994).

Trible, Phyllis, 'The Daughter of Jephthah: An Inhuman Sacrifice', in her *Texts of Terror: Literary-Feminist Readings of Biblical Narratives* (Overtures to Biblical Theology; Philadelphia: Fortress Press, 1984), pp. 93-116.

Turner, Victor, 'Liminality and Communitas', in *A Reader in the Anthropology of Religion* (ed. M. Lambeck; Oxford: Blackwell, 2002), pp. 358-74.

Vann, Richard T., 'The Youth of Centuries of Childhood', *History and Theory* 21 (May 1982), pp. 279-97.

Vaux, Roland de, *Ancient Israel: Its Life and Institutions* (trans. J. McHugh; New York: McGraw–Hill, 1965).

Volk, Anthony, 'The Evolution of Childhood', *Journal of the History of Childhood and Youth* 4 (2011), pp. 470-94.

Wall, John, 'Human Rights in Light of Childhood', *International Journal of Children's Rights* 16 (2008), pp. 523-43.

Weinberg, Joel, *Citizen–Temple Community* (trans. Daniel L.S. Christopher; JSOTSup, 151; Sheffield: Sheffield Academic Press, 1992).

Wenham, Gordon, *Genesis 16–50* (World Biblical Commentary, 2; Waco, TX: Word, 1994).

Westbrook, Raymond, '1 Samuel 1:8', *JBL* 109 (1990), pp. 114-15.

— 'Lex Talionis', in *Studies in Biblical and Cuneiform Law* (Cahiers de la RB, 26; Paris: Gabalda, 1988), pp. 69-70, 80.

— 'Lex Talionis and Exodus 21, 22-25', *RB* 93 (1986), pp. 52-69.

— *Studies in Biblical and Cuneiform Law* (Cahiers de la RB, 26; Paris: J. Gabalda, 1988).

Westermann, Claus, *Genesis 12–36: A Commentary* (trans. John J. Scullion; Minneapolis: Augsburg Publishing House, 1985).

Wolde, Ellen van, *Reframing Biblical Studies: When Language and Text Meet Cultural, Cognition, and Context* (Winona Lake, IN: Eisenbrauns, 2009).

Wolff, Hans Walter, *Anthropology of the Old Testament* (trans. Margaret Kohl; Philadelphia: Fortress Press, 1974).

Wright, David P., 'Homicide, Injury, Miscarriage, and Talion (Exodus 21:12-24, 18-27)', in his *Inventing God's Law*, pp. 154-91.

— *Inventing God's Law: How the Covenant Code of the Bible Used and Revised the Laws of Hammurabi* (New York: Oxford University Press, 2009).

— '"She shall not go free as male slaves do": Developing Views about Slavery and Gender in the Laws of the Hebrew Bible', in *Beyond Slavery: Overcoming its Religious and Sexual Legacies* (ed. Bernadette J. Brooten and Jacqueline L. Hazelton; New York: Palgrave & Macmillan, 2012), pp. 125-42.

Yee, Gale A., '"Take this child and suckle it for me": Wet Nurses and Resistance in Ancient Israel', *BTB* 39 (2009), pp. 180-89.

Zelizer, Viviana, *Pricing the Priceless Child: The Changing Social Value of Children* (Princeton, NJ: Princeton University Press, 1985).

Websites

'20 Things You Need to Know About the UN Convention on the Rights of the Child.' http://www.parentalrights.org/index.asp?Type=B_BASIC&SEC={B56D7393-E583-4658-85E6-C1974B1A57F8}

'Article 29.' http://www2.ohchr.org/english/law/crc.htm#art29.

'Casa of Cook County.' http://www.volunteermatch.org/search/org19953.jsp.

'Chapter Iv Human Rights.' http://treaties.un.org/pages/ViewDetails.aspx?src=TREATY&mtdsg_no=IV-11&chapter=4&lang=en

'Convention on the Rights of the Child.' http://www2.ohchr.org/english/law/crc.htm.

'Crossculturalsolutions.' http://www.crossculturalsolutions.org/

'Florida Guardian Ad Litem Program.' http://guardianadlitem.org/

'Human Trafficking.' http://www.humantrafficking.neu.edu/background/

'Modern Injustices.' http://modern-injustice.com/category/sex-trafficking/.

'Roper V. Simmons.' United States Supreme Court http://oyez.org/cases/2000-2009/2004/2004_03_633/.

'The Sociology and Anthropology of Childhood.' http://www.faqs.org/childhood/So-Th/Sociology-and-Anthropology-of-Childhood.html

Other

Dylan, Bob, 'Forever Young', in *Planet Waves* (Asylum Records, 1974).

INDEXES

INDEX OF REFERENCES

HEBREW BIBLE/ OLD TESTAMENT		17.26	88	21.20	87-89
		18.9-15	53	21.80	66
Genesis		18.10	83	22	96, 97, 103, 125
1.28	xviii	18.30-38	54		
2.24-25	53	19.8	59	22.1-19	96
2.24	53	20.12	84	22.2-3	96
4.23	35	21	xxv, 40, 47, 53, 75, 83-87, 89, 90, 92-97, 124, 129	22.2	96
6.18	54			22.5	97
11.27	96			22.6	86
11.30	84, 95, 98			22.7	97
12.1-3	51			22.8	14
12.4-9	47	21.1-21	83, 85, 93	22.12	97
12.4-6	61	21.1-7	95	22.16-18	125
15.2-4	47, 51	21.1-5	93	22.20-24	97
15.2	91	21.1-3	53, 83	24	58, 76, 96, 97
15.3	91	21.2	95		
15.5	91	21.4	16, 73, 83	24.11	81
16	47, 52, 83, 84, 86, 92, 93	21.5	92	24.24	97
		21.8-12	92	25.1-6	53, 54, 94, 95
		21.8	33, 36, 38, 73, 83, 87, 95	25.5-26	112
16.1-16	92			25.9-10	94
16.2	84			25.12-18	90, 94
16.12	90, 94	21.9	87, 88	25.12-17	94
16.15	88	21.10	87, 88	25.20–28.5	47
17	70, 90, 92, 93	21.11	55, 88	25.21	53
		21.12	87-90, 96	27	95
17.10-14	66	21.13	88, 90	27.5-14	75
17.11-12	68	21.14-21	125	28.21	48
17.12	16, 66	21.14-15	89	29–30	47
17.15-22	83	21.14	15, 61, 87-94	29.9	81
17.15	91			30.22	53
17.17	81	21.15-16	94	32.23	33
17.18	91	21.15	61, 87-90, 93	34	31, 59
17.20	91, 94			34.1	37
17.23	70, 88	21.16	87, 89, 90	34.3-4	37
17.24	92	21.17-19	94	34.3	37
17.25-26	91	21.17	87-89	34.4	33, 34, 37
17.25	16, 88, 92, 93	21.18	87-89	34.5-7	59
		21.19	93		

Genesis (cont.)		21.23	107-10,	Joshua	
34.5	37		112-15	2	62
34.7	37	21.24-25	107-10	6	62
34.13	37	22.16-17	59	11.1	61
34.14	37	22.21-22	61		
34.17	37	23.26	111	Judges	
34.25	37	34.20	103	11	59, 71
34.27	37			11.31	15
34.31	37	Leviticus		11.37	71
37.2	31	12	70	13.1-7	102
37.27-28	3	12.3	16, 66, 68,	13.5-12	31
38.12-30	54		69, 124	13.5	31
38.28-30	112	12.5	70, 124	13.7	31
42.4	113	18.20	60	13.8	31
42.38	113	19.29	62	13.12	31
44.20	35	20.9	60	19.24	59
44.29	113	21.16-24	58		
50.8	48	27.1-8	76, 77	Ruth	
		27.1-7	xxiv	1.5	34, 35, 39,
Exodus		27.5	77		40, 111
1.17	33			1.8-18	15
1.18	33	Numbers		2–3	15
1.22	61	6.1-21	102	4.15	104
2.6	31, 37	11.12	66		
2.9	73	12.12	112	1 Samuel	
2.16	58, 81	18.15-16	103	1–3	101
12.29	103	27.1-11	53, 56, 60	1	xxv, 85,
13.13	103	30.6-8	101, 103		92, 98-
20.14	60	31.35	58		102, 125
20.21–23.33	106	36.1-12	53, 56, 60	1.2	98, 103
21.4	33			1.4	103
21.7-11	62	Deuteronomy		1.5	98
21.7	58	5.16	60	1.8	104
21.12	60	5.18	60	1.11	100, 102
21.15	60	10.18	xxi	1.17	100
21.17	60	14.28-29	61	1.20	100
2.16-17	59	21.13-21	58	1.21-22	66
21.22-25	xxv, 68,	21.15-17	85	1.22-23	102
	106, 107,	21.18-21	49, 58	1.22	102
	109, 110,	21.18-20	60	1.23-28	66
	112, 113,	21.18	16	1.23-24	74
	115-17	21.20	58	1.24	36, 38,
21.22-23	107, 108,	22.13-21	49, 58, 59		101-103
	110, 113,	22.28-29	59	1.27-28	102
	115	24.19-21	61	1.27	102
21.22	31, 33, 40,	27.16	60	1.28	100
	108-15	32.25	79	2	98
21.23-25	109, 114	32.31	115	2.1-10	98

15.3	74	2	58	*Ezekiel*	
16.11	75	*Job*		9.6	74, 79
17.12-18	75	3.11	112	16.5	61
17.14	76	3.16	112		
17.17-18	75	31.11	115	*Daniel*	
17.56	75	38.41	35	1.4	34
20.22	75	39.3	35	1.10	34
22.19	74			1.15	34
		Psalms		1.17	34
2 Samuel		2.7	35		
4.4	130	8.2	74	*Joel*	
6.23	35	8.3 ET	74	1.16	75
9.1-13	130	58.8	112	4.3	33, 37
13.8	81	110.3	33		
13.21	15	148.12	79	*Zechariah*	
				8.4-5	37, 38
1 Kings		*Proverbs*		8.5	33
3.4-15	31	5.15-20	61		
3.7	36	13.24	125	APOCRYPHA	
3.16-28	36	31	60	*2 Maccabees*	
3.25	36			7.27	66
3.26	36	*Ecclesiastes*			
3.27	36	3.1-8	78	BABYLONIAN TALMUD	
11.20	92	4.13	35	*Yebamot*	
11.42	32	6.3	112	70a-72a	69
12.8	34	11.9-10	33, 65		
12.10	34			PHILO	
12.14	34	*Isaiah*		*De specialibus legibus*	
14.21	32	9.5	35	3.108-9	114
17.17-24	35	11.7	35		
		11.8	74	NEAR EASTERN	
2 Kings		22.4	89	INSCRIPTIONS	
4.1	52, 103	23.10	89	*Hittite Laws*	
		28.9	66	17	108
2 Chronicles				18	108
1.1-15	32	*Jeremiah*			
9.30	32	1.5	112	*Laws of Hammurabi*	
10.8	34	6.11	xxiv	209-210	108-10
10.10	34	20.18	112	209	109, 110, 112
10.14	34	31.20	35		
12.13	32	44.7	74	210	109, 110
31.16	66	51.22	xxiv, 78		
				Middle Assyrian Laws	
Nehemiah		*Lamentations*		21	108
5.1-6	62	2.11	74	51	108
14.23	37	4.3-4	66	52	108
		4.4	75		
Esther					

INDEX OF AUTHORS

Ackerman, J.S. 100
Alter, R. 100
Amit, Y. 100, 104
Arendt, H. 129
Ariès, P. 4, 5
Arnett, J.J. 12
Avalos, H. 130

Bakke, O.M. 16
Bar-Efrat, S. 90
Barr, J. 27
Baxter, J. 5
Bernat, D.A. 66
Blenkinsopp, J. 46, 65, 66, 74, 76
Block, D.I. 77, 79
Boswell, J. 3, 99, 100
Brenner, A. 101
Brettler, M. 100
Brueggemann, W. 101
Bunge, M.J. xxiii

Caird, G.B. 101
Callaway, M. 100
Cassuto, U. 112
Childs, B.S. 112
Chisholm, J.S. 18
Christoffersen, K. 12
Clements, R.E. 112
Coats, G.W. 93
Coleman, J.S. 4
Collins, J.J. 46
Conklin, B.A. 68
Cooey, P.M. 15
Coontz, S. 17
Crouch, C.L. 59, 60
Crüsemann, F. 111
Cutler, B. 28

Davidson, H. 12
Day, P.L. 67
Donaldson, M.E. 51
Dozeman, T.B. 84, 92, 114

Eilberg-Schwartz, H. 69
Eng, M. 31, 36, 76, 80, 90
Erikson, E.H. 72
Evans, G. 34

Fewell, D.N. xxiii
Fleishman, J. 62
Fontaine, C.R. 3
Freeman, M. 23, 95, 128, 129
French, V. 4, 5, 57
Fretheim, T.E. 125
Fuchs, E. 101

Garroway, K.S.H. 15, 20, 26, 45
Gennep, A. van 20, 66
Goldschmidt, W. 45
Goody, E. 24
Goody, J. 59, 62, 100
Gordon, R.P. 101
Gray, J. 32
Gruber, M.I. 30, 66

Hamilton, V.P. 89, 92
Harkness, S. 64, 66, 72, 74
Harris, M. xxiii, 19
Headland, T.N. xxiii, 19
Hertzberg, H.W. 98, 101, 102
Herzog, K. xxiii
Herzog, P.S. 12
House, H.W. 109
Houtman, C. 109, 112, 114
Hyatt, J.P. 112

Ilan, D. 5
Isser, S. 112

Jackson, B.S. 108, 109, 111-13
James, A. 6, 8, 19, 97, 127
Jay, N. 68
Jenks, C. xxiii
Jensen, D.H. xxiii
Jobling, D. 125

Index of Authors

Kamp, K.A. xix
Kant, I. 129
King, P.J. 65, 81
Klein, L.R. 100
Knight, D.A. 50
Koepf, L. 15
Koskenniemi, E. 59
Kraemer, D. 69
Kuper, A. xvi

Lancy, D.F. 17, 129
Larsson, M. xxiii
Laslett, P. 47
Lauterbach, J.Z. 40
LeVine, R.A. 6
Lee, J.A. 9, 127
Leeb, C.S. 28, 30, 40, 88, 89
Lemche, N.P. 48, 49
Linton, R. 66, 80
Loewenstamm, S.E. 109

MacDonald, J. 28, 29
Malamat, A. 34
Masci, D. 128
Matthews, S.H. 3, 6
Mauss, M. 102
McCarter, P.K., Jr 100
Mead, M. 4
Melcher, S.J. 130
Mercer, J.A. xxiii
Meyers, C. 46, 77, 78, 100, 101
Miller-McLemore, B.J. xxiii
Mintz, S. 14, 55, 127
Montgomery, H. 11, 19, 24, 67, 71, 73, 85, 94, 107
Morgan, L.M. 68, 107
Murray, J.A.H. 11
Myers, W.E. 13, 126

Nakhai, B.A. 59
Noth, M. 112

Oden, R.A. 51
Olyan, S.M. 130
Otto, E. 108

Palladino, G. 73
Parker, J.F. 15
Parsons, T. 4

Perdue, L.G. 46
Pike, K.L. xxiii, 19
Pollack, L. 5
Polzin, R. 98
Postman, N. 13
Prewitt, T.J. 51
Propp, W.H.C. 111
Prout, A. 6, 8, 19, 97, 127

Quortrup, J. 3

Rad, G. von 93
Raphael, R. 130
Revell, E.J. 34, 38, 89
Ridgely, S.B. 7
Roth, M. 80, 81
Rothschild, N.A. 19, 20
Rousseau, J.J. 18

Said, E.W. xvi
Sapir, E. 26
Scherman, N. 117
Schipper, J. 130
Schloen, J.D. 46
Schofer, J. 40
Schwartz, T. 6
Schwienhorst-Schönberger, L. 111
Shanahan, S. 6, 7, 23
Skinner, J. 93
Smith, C. 12
Smith, D.L. 48
Sofaer Derevenski, J. 5, 20
Solberg, A. 17
Speiser, E.A. 93
Sprinkle, J.E. 111
Staalduine-Sulman, E. van 112
Stager, L.E. 29, 30, 46, 57, 62, 65, 81
Stähli, H.-P. 29
Steinberg, N. 6, 8, 47, 49-52, 54, 71, 99
Strawn, B.A. 31
Super, C.M. 64, 66, 72, 74

Toorn, K. van der 66, 71, 79
Trible, P. 67
Turner, V. 66

Vann, R.T. 5
Vaux, R. de xxiii, 64
Volk, A. 6

Wall, J. 23
Weinberg, J. 48
Wenham, G. 93
Westbrook, R. 104, 113
Westermann, C. 92, 93, 96
Whittaker, J.C. xix
Wolde, E. van 32, 35-38
Wolff, H.W. 66, 77, 79
Wright, D.P. 62, 106, 107, 109, 112

Yee, G.A. 66

Zelizer, V. 13, 52

www.ingramcontent.com/pod-product-compliance
Lightning Source LLC
Chambersburg PA
CBHW072137160426
43197CB00012B/2150